STRATEGIC HUMAN RESOURCE PLANNING APPLICATIONS

STRATEGIC HUMAN RESOURCE PLANNING APPLICATIONS

Edited by

Richard J. Niehaus

Assistant for Human Resources Analysis
Office of the Chief of Naval Operations
Washington, D.C.

PLENUM PRESS • NEW YORK AND LONDON

Library of Congress Cataloging in Publication Data

Symposium on Strategic Human Resource Planning Applications   (1985:
University of Pennsylvania, Philadelphia, Pa.)
     Strategic human resource planning applications.

     "Proceedings of the Symposium on Strategic Human Resource Planning
Applications sponsored by the Human Resource Planning Society, held
December 4–6, 1985, at the University of Pennsylvania, Philadelphia,
Pennsylvania" – T.p. verso.
     Includes bibliographies and index.
     1. Manpower planning – Congresses. I. Niehaus, Richard J. II. Title.
HF5549.5.M3S95   1985   331.11   87-11141
ISBN 0-306-42561-0

Proceedings of the Symposium on Strategic Human Resource Planning
Applications sponsored by the Human Resource Planning Society,
held December 4–6, 1985, at the University of Pennsylvania,
Philadelphia, Pennsylvania

© 1987 Plenum Press, New York
A Division of Plenum Publishing Corporation
233 Spring Street, New York, N.Y. 10013

Printed in the United States of America

PREFACE

This volume is the proceedings of a symposium entitled, "Strategic Human Resource Planning Applications" which was held at the University of Pennsylvania in Philadelphia on December 4-6, 1985. The meeting was sponsored by the Research Committee of the Human Resource Planning Society.

In developing the symposium, the Research Committee built upon a study which resulted in a broad research agenda for the Society. The thrust of that research agenda was emphasis on linking the state-of- practice with the state-of-the-art. In the case of the symposium emphasis was on the presentation of forward looking applications which could help member organizations link current practice with the research frontier.

The meeting had sessions on (1) Description of Issues, (2) Human Resource Costs and Strategy, (3) Case Studies of Strategic Planning, (4) Computer Technology and Office Automation, (4) Large Scale Forecasting and Compensation Issues, (5) Models for Policy Analysis, (6) Work Force Optimization, (7) Implementation of Information Processing Activities, (8) Productivity Analysis, and (9) Relationship of Strategy to Practice. Thirty papers were presented with discussion sessions at appropriate points in the meeting. This volume contains 18 of these papers along with an introductory paper. A short summary is also provided at the beginning of each major subdivision into which the papers are arraigned.

Thanks are in order for all who contributed to the success of the meeting. First acknowledgement should be given to the current and former members of the Research Committee who provided assistance in preparing the agenda and reviewing and refereeing the papers which appear in this volume. These current and former research committee members include: William Chew, Lee Dyer, Normand Green, Walter Griggs, Michael Hawkins, Richard Niehaus, J. Jennings Partin, Karl Price, Carol Schreiber, James Sheridan, and Jo Ann Verdin. Credit should also be given to the former Human Resource Planning Society Executive Director, Kathryn Cason, and the current Executive Director, Joy Ann Buss, as well as their able assistant, Dona La Scala.

Particular thanks should be given to the Chairman of the Research Committee, Jay Partin, who guided the success of the meeting through its many wickets. A special debt is also owed to John Eldred and Ross Weber The Wharton School at the University of Pennsylvania who not only provided on-site assistance but also made important contributions to the meeting program. Important secretarial assistance was provided by Patricia Bryson of the Office of the Chief of Naval Operations. Finally, thanks are due my wife, Mary Regina, who has given me encouragement in all phases of this endeavor.

Richard J. Niehaus

CONTENTS

SECTION 1:

INTRODUCTION

IMPLEMENTATION OF STRATEGIC HUMAN RESOURCE PLANNING APPLICATIONS

Richard J. Niehaus

Assistant for Human Resources Analysis
Office of the Chief of Naval Operations (OP-16H)
Navy Department
Washington, DC 20370

INTRODUCTION

On December 4-6, 1985 the Human Research Planning Society research committee sponsored a symposium held at the University of Pennsylvania in Philadelphia. This symposium on "Strategic Human Resource Planning Applications" consisted of 30 papers with discussion sessions at appropriate points in the meeting. This paper provides an overview of the symposium and an introduction to individual papers included in this book.

Perhaps the overriding idea which came out of the meeting was the fact that practical implementable methods are emerging which allow managers to learn more about the basic issues of strategic human resource planning. Methods were presented on ways to view human resources strategies as they relate to global organizational structures. A number of systems based in the main on microcomputer applications were presented. They allow human resource managers to have more control over the preparation of analyses and to participate more directly in larger issues involving the viability of the organization. The issues of turnover and career life cycles were topics of a number of papers. Practical real life applications of flow models to strength planning were presented.

The final papers concentrated on ways to relate planning strategies to organizational practice. Particular emphasis was on employee responses to organizational strategies including new ways to measure the motivation of professionals from an adult human development perspective. It became clear that traditional personnel research methods can now be supplemented and in fact for many applications replaced by the more powerful tools emerging on the scene.

As the title implies, this introductory paper follows the theme of the symposium which emphasizes research applications which are near or in implementation. The book is organized to flow from the general to the specific. It also is designed to run from a general overview to specific management and technical issues. Overall, there are many case studies which should be of interest to those concerned with strategic human resource planning. The next sections will follow the subdivisions under which the individual papers are organized in this volume. There was some reorganization of the flow of presentation from the order they were given at the symposium so that the more management oriented papers would precede the

more technically oriented papers. The short summaries of the papers given
below for the most part were taken from abstracts provided by the authors.
The final summary section emphasizes the opportunities for implementation of
the technology in the next few years.

GENERAL ISSUES OF STRATEGIC HUMAN RESOURCE PLANNING

This first section discusses the issues of human resource planning from
the standpoint of general strategic business planning. There were a number
of papers which provided studies to illustrate different theories of
strategic human resource planning. The usefulness of these papers is that
they are based on actual comparative studies which were matched against a
particular theoretical approach. Since the theoretical underpinnings of
strategic human resource planning are still in the formative stage, the
papers provide a baseline for developing an organized body of knowledge in
this area.

As is indicated in the initial paper by Chakravarthy entitled "Human
Resource Management and Strategic Change: Challenges In Two Deregulated
Industries", human resource issues should be considered during strategy
formulation. He indicates that human resource management is typically
relegated to human resource specialists in an organization. This is due to
the perception that human resource issues need attention only after a firm's
strategies have been formulated. However, such activities like infusing a
firm with new skills, transforming its culture, and modifying its management
style often need longer lead times than that required to reconfigure a
firm's product-market strategy. His paper discussed the consequences of
failing to integrate human resource management with strategy formulation
using examples from the recently deregulated telecommunications and
financial services industries. These examples are discussed using eight
major firms in these industries which have had to reformulate their
strategies due to deregulation.

In a deregulated environment, Chakravarthy indicates that there are
substantial payoffs for both technological and marketing innovations. He
indicates that a firm can respond to this challenge in three ways: domain
defense, domain offense, and domain creation. The longer run strategies of
most of the firms studied was oriented to become a full line domain creative
organization. The keys to this goal appears to be motivating employees
towards a new mission, developing requisite skills, and nurturing an
appropriate climate. The bottleneck in or opportunity for achieving these
goals is the mind set of the current or acquired management staff. In
summary, he indicates that there are at least three areas in which human
resources can facilitate strategic change. These include: (1) nurturing
skills to promote strategic flexibility, (2) encouraging managers to
discover versatility in their management styles, and (3) integrating team
building with contractual incentives.

In the next paper by Dyer and Shafer entitled "Formulating Human
Resource Strategies in a Professional Service Firm: A Systematic Approach",
another concept is discussed. This paper documents the efforts being made
by Touche Ross, a "Big Eight" public accounting firm, to adopt a more
strategic approach to the management of human resources. It begins with
brief descriptions of the firm, the extant concept of strategic human
resource management (SHRM) and the role of human resource planning (HRP) in
fostering SHRM. Three types of planning processes are identified: plan
based, project based, and population based. Dyer and Shafer indicate that
collectively these three planning processes constitutive a comprehensive
approach to HRP discussing the design and implementation of each.

As with the initial paper, Dyer and Shafer indicate that a strategic

approach to the management of human resources means the development of a
culture in which human resources are an integral component of the business
equation. In a comprehensive approach, plan based or formal HRP is used at
the corporate level to promulgate firm-wide philosophies and priorities
concerning human resources. At the lower business levels the HRP plan is
used to identify major human resource issues and develop action plans for
dealing with these issues. Project based HRP takes place in the context of
the relatively informal deliberations undertaken by task forces and project
teams that are from time to time constituted to examine strategic business
issues and make appropriate recommendations. This is in recognition of the
fact that in most organizations strategic business planning usually lags
strategic business thinking. The role of population based HRP is to focus
on a particular group of presumably critical employees to assure that they
and their potential replacements receive the care and feeding necessary to
assure an ongoing supply and to meet evolving needs. The main body of the
paper discusses each of these planning processes in relationship to the
management of Touche Ross concluding with a delineation of the key factors
being considered in the introduction of such a system of managing human
resources in the firm.

In the study discussed by Broderick in the paper "Pay Policy,
Organization Strategy and Structure: A Question of "Fit", Broderick
investigated policy decisions on middle management pay and their
relationship to business strategy. Compensation directors at 208
manufacturing firms answered questions on pay structure, level, mix,
incentives and administration, and firm business strategy. This study
examines the notion that the better the "fit" between pay policy and
organization characteristics such as business strategy, the higher the
organization performance. There were two theoretical reasons offered for
the higher organization performance attributable to "fit" relationships
between pay policy and other organizational characteristics. First, if pay
policy is contingent on an organization's business strategy then appropriate
employee behaviors are more likely to be defined and rewarded. Second, the
notion of "fit" includes congruency between pay policy and the
organization's design and administrative style.

The results of the Broderick study suggested that pay decisions
reflect seven broader dimensions of policy including the issues of:
participation, authorization, formalization, standardization, external
competitiveness, membership vs. performance, efficiency vs. growth. The
questionnaire results were also able to be fitted into a behavioral model
identifying three types of organization: Defenders, Prospectors and
Analysers. The Defender has a narrowly defined, stable product market
strategy. The Prospector emphasizes an innovative, dynamic approach to
product market definition. The Analyzer is characterized by a mixed product
market strategy in which some of its product markets are stable and narrowly
defined, but others are more dynamic and innovative. Using these
definitions, the results supported that pay policy varies systematically
with business strategy. For example, firms with a strategy of maintaining
market share emphasized centralized pay administration and cost performance
criteria. The results of the Broderick study represent a first step in
examining the more fundamental question of "Does pay policy that "fits"
business strategy improve organization performance?".

An important theoretical and practical issue of relating strategic
human resource planning is how one's organization is doing in relationship
to the competition. An empirical study relating strategies of staffing
control to practice is given in the paper by Kay and Lesher entitled "Human
Resource Costs and Business Strategy: Striving for Competitive Advantage in
the Pharmaceutical Industry". They approach their study from the point of
view that control over staffing levels and costs is a critical component in

the competitive positioning and resultant profitability of many industries.
Staff levels are a function of many variables, including the strategic
thrust of the organization. Kay and Lesher feel that simply reviewing
current business plans to determine optimal staffing levels is not
sufficient. It is also important to track historical data that reflect the
effects of different strategies and economic situations on staff size, or
make comparisons with competitor staffing levels against their strategies.

The Kay and Lesher methodology used what they call the Human Resource
Cost Strategy (HURCOS) model. This is a three-step consulting process which
uses data from a variety of human resource areas. The first phase consists
of a series of on-site interviews and tailored questionnaires. In the
second phase, HURCOS draws comparisons between each company and its
strategic competitors. The final phase links business strategy to the human
resource cost structure. A variety of data and charts are used to show how
this HURCOS model was applied in studying the pharmaceutical industry. The
authors conclude that there are direct relationships of human resource costs
to general business strategies. From the study one could conclude that as
general rule, a formal analysis of the internal staffing in relationship to
the competition should be done at the appropriate point in developing and
conducting strategic human resource planning activities.

EMPLOYEE RESPONSES TO ORGANIZATIONAL STRATEGIES

The papers in the book deal in one way or another with relating
strategy to practice. The previous section took a top down view where
theoretical concepts were provided and then compared with specific cases or
plans from the point of view of the firm or organization. This section
looks at the other side of the equation from the point of view of employees
and their responses to organizational plans, strategies and change. This
reality testing provides a perspective from the employee approaches to their
lives and careers. These papers were placed at this point in the book so
that parts of all the issues affecting strategic human resource planning
could be brought together near the beginning. After these papers from the
employee perspective, the remaining papers in the book will concentrate on
specific management and technical issues.

In their paper "What Motivates Technical Professionals to Contribute
Their Best Effort and Maintain Their Commitment to their Organization?",
Griggs and Manring take a novel human development approach to flesh out the
issues. Ten major technically driven organizations collaborated in a study
aimed at determining the key factors related to motivation and retention of
engineers and scientists. The results of the study demonstrate that the
nature of the work itself, organizational processes, which determine how
work is allocated and evaluated, and the sense of having a career, are
regarded as more important than traditional monetary and non-monetary reward
and recognition practices. The power of the study derives from its
identification of differences, based on age of the respondents and
organizational culture, which provide clear guidelines for a more focused
approach to human resource management.

The Griggs and Manring study combines a very pragmatic approach with
the use of very powerful evaluation tools based on the use a specialized
goal programming methodology using linear programming. This study has
provided a wealth of data which can be used in two essential ways: (1) the
data provide a well-grounded analysis of many areas of organizational
concern relating to increasing the contribution and retention of technical
professionals, (2) the data provide a base line against which organizations
can measure the effectiveness of planned interventions. With the
participation of ten organizations and over 900 technical professionals,
this study demonstrates that innovation and organizational effectiveness are

best served not just by rewarding them following their achievements but by fostering the conditions which enable and inspire them to contribute their creative efforts.

Portwood and Price in their paper "Employee Responses to Organizational Strategies: The Forgotten Variable in Human Resource Forecasting" focus on the impact of proposed changes on existing human resources. Human resource forecasts deal most often with positions, rather than people. Individual reactions are discounted, or are assumed to be random, and therefore inconsequential. Rarely do forecasts include a systematic survey of employee perceptions, expectations, and aspirations as part of a comprehensive analysis of current inventory. Managers planning strictly on the basis of these position-based forecasts have thus, at times, had to cope with unanticipated employee responses, including productivity, resistance to suggested shifts in location and/or career paths, and even sharply increased rates of retirement and turnover.

The purpose of the Portwood and Price paper was to demonstrate, using a representative case study, the importance of employee attitudes and career preferences on the outcome of organizational planning and change efforts. The case also provides several examples of constructive organizational responses which may be used when data on such attitudes and aspirations are available. The primary focus is on the reasons why, and areas where, employee perceptions may have a significant impact on the accuracy and reliability of projections generated by traditional human resource forecasting and planning systems.

The paper by Gaertner discusses "Executive Career Patterns and Organizational Adaption to Change". Interview and documentary data from three organizations are used to analyze the way in which organizational careers in general and the career experiences of executives in particular are related to an organization's ability to adapt to change. Each organization went through a period of significant change and each pursued change differently. In no case, were existing career patterns used to help the organization adapt to changing business conditions. In all three organizations existing career paths were either ignored or disrupted, and in all three "new blood" was brought in to help cope with change.

Gaertner identified several ways in which career patterns potentially can facilitate adaption to change. These included: variety in career experience among top executives (no cloning), career patterns that provide the opportunity for future executives to manage a whole but small part of the business early in their careers, exposure to many different management styles and functional areas, and structural changes that allow risk and uncertainty to be managed in specialized organizational units. While these results are tentative and based on only three cases, they give insights into the ways in which organizations adapt to increased uncertainty in their environments and the role that career patterns can play in the process of adapting to such change.

STRATEGIES FOR PRODUCTIVITY MANAGEMENT

In this section of the book, the emphasis is shifted back to a management perspective in terms of strategies and methodologies which can be employed for productivity management of human resources. There has been much written around the issue. On the other hand there has been a lot less written concerning strategies and methods which have some promise of leading to productivity improvement. The three papers in this section home in on ways that may have some promise.

The theme of the paper "Strategies for Managing Productivity

Improvement" by Mactaggart is that improvements in productivity can be
brought about by developing a planning framework which focuses on critical
aspects of human resource management. The paper presents strategies for
allocating, deploying and using the organization's human resource as part of
its fundamental process of managing change. Human resource planning is
seen as the linking pin to the better allocation and more efficient use of
personnel, so leading to better control over payroll costs. The paper is
set in the context of Canada's federal public service. The contention is
that the strategies which are discussed would have as much application in
major divisions of a large corporation as in the discrete and largely
autonomous structures within the Canadian governmental bureaucracy for which
they were designed.

Mactaggart discusses a number of strategies which he feels are not
mutually exclusive, and can be combined in 'mix and match' fashion to suit
an organization's particular situation. Numerical examples are coupled with
the discussion of methods of strategy development. The examples are
developed in the context of a work force drawdown where the parallel
objective is to see if a significant cutback can be made without seriously
harming the public or employee's interests. Finally, references are made
throughout the paper to the responsibilities of functional specialists,
outlining what sort of support management should expect to receive from
them.

The next two papers in this section are by Bolda discussing
productivity issues relating to strategies for making training and sourcing
decisions based on productivity considerations. The first paper entitled
"Forecasting the Cost-Benefits of Job Training" reviews procedures used by
personnel researchers at General Motors. This recent pilot study was aimed
at forecasting cost-benefits associated with proposals for job training and
retraining of factory workers, both skilled and unskilled. The study used
manager-judges to help set the basic parameters and then checked the results
using theoretical methods refined from the personnel research literature.
The task team consisted of training researchers, operating managers, experts
in manufacturing technology, and staff personnel. Among the task team's
efforts were to provide input into: definition of factory job classification
clusters, identification of training needs, development of proposed training
contents, cost estimation, and administration of a plant-level
questionnaire.

The output of the training study reported by Bolda included using
manager-judges to measure the impact of the proposed job training
experiences on employee productivity. An estimate was made of the "dollar
value of performance" by comparing judgments of the current value of
employee performance with judgments of job performance values after exposure
to each of the two training packages developed in the study. With this
judgment method a total net gain to the firm from using the training
packages for the study group would be $12,450,000 with the benefits of that
training expected to accrue over two and one half years. As a rough check on
the judgement method, a theoretical method was used with the results
indicating a total net gain of $12,720,000. Bolda feels that the small
margins of difference between corresponding estimates, particularly in the
skilled area, suggests that the judges performed their tasks thoughtfully.

The second study by Bolda is titled "Individual Productivity: A
Sourcing Analysis". In this study involving maintenance and tool room jobs,
attention is turned to which source of job entrants will be the most
productive. In this case the sources include: from the internal work force
through completion of a formal selection-training process, from the internal
work force through completion of an informal selection-training process, or
from direct hire from the external work force. As in the first study

manager-judges were used providing input on (1) the "dollar value of performance" of the current incumbents, and (2) paired comparison judgements relating to the productivity of "average-performing employees" in seven source-categories.

The specific conclusions from the data presenting in the Bolda job sourcing study indicate that there are sharp differences in job performance/productivity of employees who entered maintenance and toolroom jobs from different selection-training backgrounds. Also that the more carefully conceived and structured selection-training backgrounds appear to produce significantly greater productivity, both upon program completion and thereafter. Further, the performance worth of formal training graduates does not appear to diminish with several years' experience. In a more general way, the Bolda study indicates the worth of using subjective manager-judge approaches particularly if the results are "sense-checked" with a large group of manager-experts.

FORECASTING AND TURNOVER CONTROL

The remainder of the papers of the book focus on the implementation of computer-assisted approaches to and support for strategic human resource planning. This section includes papers describing applications in the fundamental areas of forecasting and turnover control. Of particular interest is the fact that the forecasting methods are beginning to appear either as microcomputer models or mainframe-microcomputer systems. This section concentrates on applications involving practical ways to obtain manpower forecasts or to project the internal work force. The section which follows this one will broaden the topic to include the more complex issues which arise when the external work force and compensation planning are included.

The paper by Bulla and Scott titled "Manpower Requirements Forecasting: A Case Example" describes an application in the Houston Lighting and Power Company. This system was developed to help the company manage its work force in light of changing needs for energy coupled with more assertive regulations concerning cost control. The system described by Bulla and Scott contains the elements needed for effective manpower requirements forecasting. The output of this system is a forecast of gross staffing requirements by primary personnel skill groupings. This forecast is used to control the development of the firm's training and development plan.

A microcomputer approach was used by Bulla and Scott in the data manipulation relying on such tools as the LOTUS 1-2-3 spreadsheet. The Houston Lighting and Power manpower requirement forecasting outputs have been used for the following types of studies: (1) Span of Control identifying the projected ratio of employees per management level or combination of levels, (2) Customers per Employee Ratios for better productivity measurements, (3) Needs/Surplus Assessments to permit identification of position classifications exhibiting substantial year-to-year variability, and (4) Skill Group Studies defining how the work force is changing with respect to the projected number of bargaining unit, non-exempt, professional, and management employees reflected in the forecast. The forecasting system is being extended to replace the firm's bottom-up labor-budget process with one that uses a top-down approach. This will include a review on ways to optimize the system and integrate it with other management systems.

The next paper by Bres, Niehaus, Sharkey, and Weber is entitled "Use of Personnel Flow Models for Analysis of Large Scale Work Force Changes". This study documents the use of flow models to assist managers in the U.S. Naval Sea Systems Command in responding to a requirement to significantly reduce

the number of shipyard employees in a relatively short period of time. In
this case reductions of over 12,000 employees were mandated to occur spread
over eight shipyards with up to a 34% reduction in one case. In order to
plan for the required reductions, it was necessary to be able to project the
number of employees who can be expected to leave voluntarily. It is also
useful to know the number expected to transfer from one occupation to
another within each shipyard period by period.

Several models were developed using personnel movement or transition
data developed on a mainframe computer and downloaded to a microcomputer.
Two models were incorporated into a LOTUS 1-2-3 spreadsheet program with the
first model designed to allow the work force to "run down" by normal
attrition. The second model included manpower requirements goals for each
period such that the number of employees needed to be hired or reduced for
each job category in order to meet the goals was provided in the output. A
more comprehensive "flexible" flow model was also developed to balance work
force flows across time periods as well as between job categories. This
latter mainframe based model was developed for one of the shipyards to
permit comparative analysis with the spreadsheet results. These models are
being integrated into the strategic and operational planning accomplished in
the management of the naval shipyards.

The paper by Hawkins "New Technology for Controlling Turnover" combines
into one model a number of techniques for controlling personnel turnover.
This model is built around classical statistical quality control methods.
The idea is to try to develop standards for turnover and then determine if
the current level of turnover is "too high" or "too low". A review is
provided of different definitions of turnover and then related to the issue
of accomplishing the analysis in practice.

Much of the Hawkins paper is instructional in the ways to develop
turnover statistics with examples of what has worked in the past. The value
of this work is that it provides a method to graphically develop individual
turnover charts along with the relationship between turnover and length-
of-service or age. In this way one can combine the effects of short term
changes in turnover with the longer term cumulative length-of-service
factors underlying employee tenure.

WORK FORCE DYNAMICS AND COMPENSATION POLICY

In this section the technologies for forecasting and turnover control
are extended to include models for human resource supply-demand as
comprehensive systems. All the efforts have strong computer-assisted
components using or planning to use microcomputers were appropriate. The
models were aimed at compensation and retention issues in terms of the
effects of broad strategic policy issues affecting the staffing and
retention of the organizations involved.   Quigley and Henshaw in their
paper "A Model to Simulate the Effects of Work Force Dynamics on
Compensation Policy" describe work underway at Lockheed Missiles and Space
Company. Their work force movement model provides compensation planners
with a precise, yet flexible system for determining the actual costs of
merit fund (or any salary action) distributions over time. The micro
computer based model provides corporate decision makers with an effective
guide for planning annual salary actions. It accounts for the interaction of
terminations, hiring, promotions and merit fund decisions in one LOTUS 1-2-3
spreadsheet. Sensitivity analyses can be performed to simulate any number
of factors affecting work force dynamics.

The model development by Quigley and Henshaw relied on mainframe
analytical tools such as the SAS (Statistical Analysis System) to derive the
necessary empirical distributions and to determine the starting state of the

work force. These data were then entered into a microcomputer spreadsheet
model using a single hierarchy Markov type process that transitions the work
force from a starting state to a point one year later. The paper provides a
number of sensitivity studies showing the results to be extremely accurate.
This paper illustrates that through careful work using readily available
microcomputer software, one can considerably improve the value of policy
planning information at a low cost.

A comprehensive supply-demand model system is described by Atwater,
Bres, Cecil, Nelson, Niehaus, and Rosasco in their paper "Decision
Information Support for a Comprehensive Retirement System Conversion". The
authors discuss the development and use of large scale modeling systems to
evaluate the impacts of proposed legislative changes of the Federal
retirement system on the Department of the Navy. The probable impacts are
of high level concern since the Navy employs over 325,000 civil servants
many of whom are in high technology jobs. The graphical displays in the
paper show the impacts of three highly complex (two Senate and one House)
proposals as they relate to the current Civil Service Retirement System.

The key issue discussed in the Atwater, et. al. paper is the impact of
the proposed new retirement systems on the retention of Navy civilian
employees. The influences of uncertain and cyclical labor markets, various
retirement options in other employment sectors, and the tastes and
preferences of the Navy work force are key factors in this analysis.
Another issue is the linkage of micro and mainframe computers in the overall
decision modeling process to make the most expeditious use of the latest
available computer technology. Finally, there is a review of the
relationship of these retention studies to the planned development of more
comprehensive human resource supply-demand planning systems to provide
continuing long term information support.

Lacy in the paper entitled "Analyzing the Link between Compensation and
the Quit Decisions of Civil Service Employees" describes another
comprehensive compensation based modeling effort. This work encompasses the
over one million civil service employees of the Department of Defense. The
paper begins with a descriptive account of the demographics and of the
recent historical retention statistics of the DoD work force. Lacy points
out as the nation's largest employer, DoD policy makers have a stake in the
compensation decisions affecting that work force. The issue of erosion of
Federal pay and how that might affect retention is the overriding concern of
the models that were developed and tested.

The Annual Cost of Leaving II (ACOL II) model described by Lacy is an
extension of complex econometric models originally developed to study
military compensation issues. This ACOL II model determines the probability
that a person will quit in the next year by comparing the future life time
income the civil servant could expect if he remained at least one more year
with what he could expect if he quit for a non-Federal job or for not
working immediately. A wide variety of variables are used to develop the
model results. The statistical findings upholds the hypothesis that DoD
civilians are more likely to quit Federal service as the potential value of
lifetime compensation in the government falls relative to private sector
earnings. At a more detailed level, the results indicated the areas of
strength and were the model prototype might be improved. Lacy concludes the
paper with a discussion of the applicability of the models to the private
sector and how this work will be extended in the future.

IMPACT OF INFORMATION PROCESSING ON HUMAN RESOURCE PLANNING

This section provides a final paper which discusses a survey of
the state of information processing support on human resource planning as of

the end of 1985. The availability of computational support particularly as
an activity in the human resources and planning departments has changed the
level of acceptance of analytical efforts. The final summary section of this
introductory paper will include a discussion of information support as
reflected in all of the papers in this volume. This summary will be done in
context with the 1985 survey as well as with historical and future trends as
observed by the volume editor.

In the paper "Current Trends in the Use of Computer Technology by Human
Resource Managers" by Verdin and Pagano provide the results of a phone
survey of 81 members of the Midwest Human Resource Planners Group. The
organizations represented were generally large, with average total sales of
$4.8 billion and over 15,000 employees. Thirty-seven percent of the sample
were manufacturing firms, 24 percent were in financial services, and the
remaining 39 percent in a variety of types of retailing and service firms.
The thrust of the study was on who uses human resource information support
and how its use might affect productivity and quality of output.

The results of the Verdin and Pagano study indicate that human resource
managers and professionals in large firms are using computer technology
themselves. This trend was found for all managerial levels including over 40
percent of top managers. The larger percentage of applications were
automation of the traditional concerns such as applicant tracking and
training administration. About one third of the respondents reported using
the systems for forecasting, career or succession planning activities. There
were many applications which used mainframe/ minicomputers in combination
with microcomputers. The majority of users cited special projects as a
beneficial way to use computer technology. Ninety percent of the respondents
felt department productivity and quality of output was higher since
automation. Verdin and Pagano feel that the trends will continue in the
future with computer-assisted information support becoming just another tool
for use in managing many different human resource functions.

The final paper by Wilson discusses the "Deployment of a Microcomputer
based Human Resource Management System (HRMS) as a Distributed Information
System: Human Resource Policy Management Implications and Impact". This is
a case study of the use of multiple microcomputers in various geographic
locations for supporting the human resource management function. This
paper is timely as it confirms the conclusion of the Verdin and Pagano study
with a comprehensive case example.

The study by Wilson documents the use of distributed information system
and the subsequent changes in operations of the human resource function.
The study covers the system components, objectives and design with a focus
on changes in the ability to analyze and report information for decision
making. A particular dichotomy is between the "real system" and the
"conceptual system orientation. As human resources develops more skills
with conceptual information system information management, there is an
increasing impact on the planning, strategy development, and policy making
dimension of human resources management.

SUMMARY

The papers in this volume indicate that strategic human resource
planning applications are spreading among major employers. The theoretical
basis for such planning is also becoming solidified with more emphasis on
integration with the business plans of the enterprise as a whole. While the
papers indicate there is still much testing remaining to validate such
concepts, the basic idea to accomplish such integrated approaches has been
affirmed. The emphasis is on using the needed management techniques and
supporting technology in whatever form possible as long as effectiveness and

productivity can be enhanced. The issue of management commitment appears to
have been overcome in many organizations.

The recent operational applications are for the most part based on
analytical techniques which have a fairly long history of development. This
fact is in line with experience in other management areas. In the late
1960's and early 1970's there was a strong emphasis on the use of management
science, operations research and behavioral science techniques. In this era
many of the basic ideas were first upgraded to be able to use larger scale
analytical models. When brought to the level of practical applications,
these models were found to be wanting either in terms of being too data
intensive or too costly to operate. Currently, many of these problems
including the availability of end user computer support and of necessary
data bases are being solved. The papers in this volume represent the
practical expression of this reemergence of formal decision oriented
analysis.

The use of microcomputers by managers and in this case human resource
planning professionals represents a revolution rather than an evolution in
the use of analytical techniques. The important point is the hands-on
access to the computer-assisted tools with computational resources greater
in many cases than the mainframes available in the 1970's. In many
organizations the microcomputer is being coupled with data sets downloaded
from mainframes. In the past in order to accomplish a study, the human
resource manager had to go to a small group of professionals or even more
distantly to the data processing group

and in many cases was not in control. Now, the end user has a better chance
to control his/her own destiny being able to make substantive impacts on
corporate policy. The studies in this volume show how simple as well as
elegant applications are emerging with this shift of technology to the
functional departments.

The development of strategic human resource planning applications can
be expected to accelerate over the next few years. The better applications
will be improved to the point that standard packages will be available for
the end user who wants menu driven software. Many of the analytical
techniques will reemerge not only in the simpler versions which are reported
in this volume but in the more comprehensive forms which are tucked away in
the literature. This will put pressure on the need for new research to
improve the techniques themselves to take advantage of the extensive
computational resources already available or on the horizon.

In summary, the applications in this volume were for the most part
written for consumption by managers to learn the state of practice of
strategic human resource planning. Trends are also provided as to the
direction of the state of the art. As such, these papers from the Human
Resource Planning Society Philadelphia research symposium form an important
part of the baseline for the future.

SECTION 2:

GENERAL ISSUES OF STRATEGIC HUMAN RESOURCE PLANNING

This section discusses the issues of human resource planning from the standpoint of general strategic business planning. The papers in this section are based on actual comparative studies which were matched against a particular theoretical approach. Since the theoretical underpinnings of strategic human resource planning are still in the formative stage, the papers provide a baseline for developing an organized body of knowledge in this area.

Chakravarthy indicates that human resource management is typically relegated to human resource specialists in an organization. This is due to the perception that human resource issues need attention only after a firm's strategies have been formulated. However, such activities like infusing a firm with new skills, transforming its culture, and modifying its management style often need longer lead times than that required to reconfigure a firm's product-market strategy.

The paper by Dyer and Shafer documents the efforts being made by Touche Ross, a "Big Eight" public accounting firm, to adopt a more strategic approach to the management of human resources. It begins with brief descriptions of the firm, the extant concept of strategic human resource management (SHRM) and the role of human resource planning (HRP) in fostering SHRM. Three types of planning processes are identified: plan based, project based, and population based.

The study by Broderick investigated policy decisions on middle management pay and their relationship to business strategy. This study using data from 208 manufacturing firms examines the notion that the better the "fit" between pay policy and organization characteristics such as business strategy, the higher the organization performance.

An important theoretical and practical issue of relating strategic human resource planning is how one's organization is doing in relationship to the competition. An empirical study relating strategies of staffing control to practice in the pharmaceutical industry is given in the paper by Kay and Lesher. They approach their study from the point of view that control over staffing levels and costs is a critical component in the competitive positioning and resultant profitability of many industries.

HUMAN RESOURCE MANAGEMENT AND STRATEGIC CHANGE:

CHALLENGES IN TWO DEREGULATED INDUSTRIES

Balaji S. Chakravarthy

School of Management
University of Minnesota
271 19th Avenue, South
Minneapolis, MN 55455

INTRODUCTION

The importance of human resource management to strategic adaptation has been widely discussed by both scholars (Fombrun, Tichy, and Devanna, 1984) and popular writers (Peters and Waterman, 1983) alike. A well adapted firm must not only formulate an effective strategy, but it must also align its various administrative systems to its chosen strategy (Pascala and Athos, 1981). Its 7-Ss, i.e. its Strategy, Structure, Systems, Style, Shared values, Staff, and Skill must be aligned for it to be well adapted (Waterman, 1979). Human resource management is concerned with several of these Ss. It focuses on the recruitment, training, and development of personnel; design of reward systems; nurturing of management styles; and institutionalization of values that are in keeping with the firm's strategy.

Given the long lead times required for developing personnel, altering management style, or transforming company culture, human resource management should really be an integral part of strategy formulation. However, only a few firms like IBM, General Electric, and Intel follow such a practice (Tichy, Fombrun, and Devanna, 1984). Human resource management is often unfortunately viewed as an aspect of strategy implementation. This paper describes some of the difficulties in effecting strategic change when human resource management is not integrated with strategy formulation.

The examples cited in this paper are all drawn from two recently deregulated industries; telecommunications and financial services. Deregulation has forced firms in these two industries to reformulate their strategies. They offer, therefore, a rich setting in which to observe how firms manage strategic change. Eight firms in the selected industries were studied using published information and field interviews.

The paper is divided into three sections. The first section describes briefly the current strategic posturing of the eight selected firms in their respective industries. The second section discusses some of the major bottlenecks that the sample firms face in successfully implementing their chosen strategies. The concluding section explores how human resources can be managed more proactively to diffuse some of these bottlenecks.

STRATEGIC POSTURING IN THE TWO DEREGULATED INDUSTRIES

Economic deregulation dramatically alters the competitive dynamics of
an industry, by facilitating the entry of new competitors, and expanding the
strategic choices available to existing firms (Bowman and McWilliams, 1985).
A firm can posture itself in this new environment by following any one of
three generic product-market strategies: full line, specialization, or
focus (Waite, 1982). A full-line strategy requires the offering of a broad
range of services nationally. A specialization strategy is comparatively
limited in its range of services. A focus strategy is further limited in
its geographic coverage.

Deregulation has also heightened the importance of innovation to
competitive success. In the 1970s, the telecommunications and financial
services industries exhibited signs of maturity, i.e. no major changes in
the products and services offered, and in the productive systems used to
provide them (Abernathy, Kantrow, and Clark, 9183). Innovation was not
rewarded. In a deregulated environment, however, there are substantial
payoffs for both technological and marketing innovations. A firm can
respond to this challenge with one of three domain management strategies:
Defense, Reaction, and Pro-action (Chakravarthy, 1986). Defense refers to a
strategy where the firm tries to mobilize regulatory support, in conjunction
with other similar firms, so as to protect its product-market niche.
Reaction refers to a strategy where the firm tries to imitate innovations
introduced by competitors. Proaction is a strategy where the firm tries to
innovate new niches.

The product-market and domain management strategies pursued by a firm
define its strategic group (Chakravarthy, 1986). Figure 1 describes four
strategic groups that appear to be viable in the two industries studied
(Chakravarthy, 1985a). Each has an unique product-market and domain
management strategy. Moreover, each group is also associated with an unique
set of tangible and intangible resources. Tangible resources include the
firm's finances and physical capacities. They are the critical determinants
of a firm's product-market strategy. Intangible resources refer to the
firm's technological strengths, and reputation. They are the key
determinants of the type of domain management strategy that a firm can
pursue. The eight firms in our sample represent each of the four viable

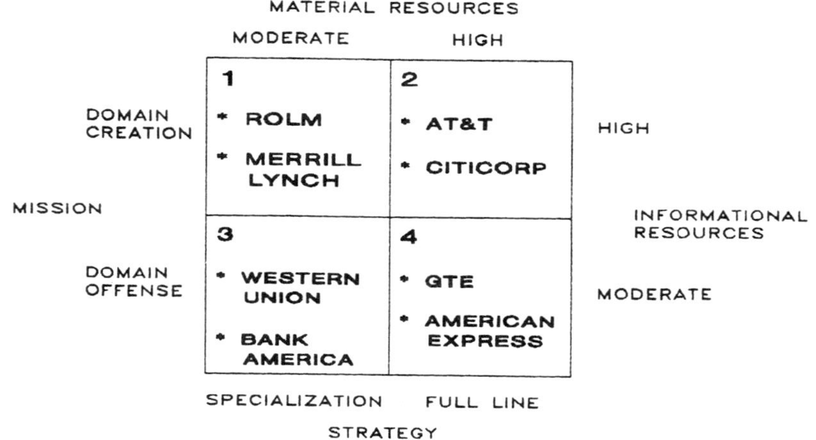

Figure 1: Viable Strategic Groups

strategic groups (Figure 1). Their current strategic postures are briefly
described below:

   Cell 1 (specialization and proaction). Many of the firms in this group
were responsible for the early assaults on regulation. The group presently
contains, for example, Rolm in the telecommunications industry, and Merrill
Lynch in the financial services industry. Rolm is primarily a competitor in
medium size Private Automatic Branch Exchanges. Merrill Lynch seeks to
offer innovative financial products to upscale retail and institutional
customers. They are both firms that focus on product innovation. The major
challenge for them is to protect their proprietary know how, reputation and
innovative ability.

   Both Rolm and Merrill Lynch, however, are also planning a transition to
cell 2. Rolm has acquired a powerful parent, IBM, and has thus been able to
improve its product offering through joint development with IBM. Merrill
Lynch, on the other hand, seeks to expand its product offering, both through
internal development and acquisitions.

   Cell 2 (full line and proaction). AT&T and Citicorp are two examples
of firms that are closest to being in this strategic group.

   AT&T offers a full range of telecommunications products including
customer premise equipment, PBX equipment, central office switches, and
long-distance services for business and residential customers. Given its
long history of technological innovations, the company's mission is to
differentiate itself in each of its businesses and to create new businesses.
   Citicorp either offers or has plans to offer the following financial
services: Individual Banking, Institutional Banking, Investment Banking,
Insurance, and Information Services. The five Is, as they are called at
Citicorp, represent one of the widest offerings in the financial services
industry. The sixth I in Citicorp jargon is Innovation. Citicorp's mission
is to be the most aggressive and entrepreneurial firm in its industry. It
has been aggressive in searching for legal loopholes to diversify its
services.

   This is a very difficult strategic group to belong to. The
environmental turbulence that firms in this group must manage is the
highest, because of both the diversity in their portfolio as well as their
proactive stance in all of their markets.

   Cell 3 (specialization and reaction). This strategic group is similar
to cell 1 in that it seeks a distinctive niche. However, unlike firms in
that cell, firms in cell 3 do not seek product innovations but rather
specialize on some aspect of manufacturing, distribution, or marketing.
They are seldom the innovators of a new business, but are often good
imitators, deriving their competitive advantage from lower costs, and better
service.

   In the telecommunications industry, for example, Western Union wants to
be the best electronic mail company, though it was not a pioneer in that
business. In the financial services industry, many smaller money center
banks like Bankers Trust and troubled giants like BankAmerica seek an unique
operational competence to successfully differentiate themselves from their
competitors.

   Cell 4 (full line and reaction). Firms like GTE in the telecommunications industry, and American Express in the financial services
industry, belong to this group. This is often the preferred strategic group
for a diversified firm (Lawrence & Dyer, 1983). Firms in this group are not
necessarily reactive in all of their businesses. However, reaction is the
predominant predisposition of such a firm.

GTE has one of the widest range of product offerings in the
telecommunications industry, second only to AT&T. While its technology
strengths are impressive, it does not seek risky entry into untried
businesses. Its current strategy is not to innovate new riches, but rather
to react quickly to changes made by competitors.

American Express has diversified through recent acquisitions into
insurance, retail brokerage, and institutional banking. Its earlier
aspirations were to exploit the synergisms between these diverse businesses
through new product offerings. However, its current strategy is more
modest. I seeks to assimilate the various acquisitions that it has already
made, before attempting to exploit the synergisms between them.

STRATEGIC PREDISPOSITION AS A BOTTLENECK TO CHANGE

Even though all eight rirms in our sample have espoused viable
strategies that are consistent with their resource endowment, they (with the
possible exception of Citicorp) have been unable to implement them
successfully. The primary bottleneck to strategic change seems to be the
firm's earlier strategic predisposition.

Strategic predisposition reflects how an organization tends to behave
over time and across different situations (Miles, 1982). In a relatively
stable environment, such as under regulation, each firm learns to align its
administrative systems to its strategy through a trail and error process.
The resulting fit, while well suited to that environment, can entrench the
firm in behaviors that are unsuited to its changed strategy. One way to
understand the strategic predisposition of the sample firms is then to
examine their strategies prior to deregulation.

In the regulated era, no firm in the telecommunications or financial
services industries was allowed to pursue a full-line strategy, with the
sole exception of AT&T. The predominant strategy, therefore, was
specialization (Figure 2). Similarly, most firms in the two industries were
reactive. There were few rewards for being innovative, and several legal
restrictions for entering new domains. However, some enterprising firms in
both industries did challenge these regulatory barriers through their
technological and marketing ingenuity. Merrill Lynch's attempts to enter
individual banking through the Cash Management Account, Citicorp's attempts
to get into interstate banking, MCI's entry into long distance voice
communication, and Rolm's invasion of the interconnect market are
illustrative of these challenges (Figure 2).

The implementation difficulties faced by a firm can be expected to vary
directly with the degree of transformation that it seeks in its product-
market and domain management strategies. Figure 2 sketches the various
transitions that are being attempted.

Even for firms that are not attempting to change their strategic group
at the present time, deregulation has brought some new challenges to their
human resource management function. Increased competition has made
operating efficiency a key factor for success. In addition, the new
emphasis on innovations has also caused firms to reevaluate the relevance of
their organization structures and control systems.

Firms like BankAmerica and Western Union seem so distracted by their
current financial problems, they do not seek major shifts in their strategic
postures at the present time. Their focus is primarily on improving their
operating efficiency, through down sizing and restructuring of their

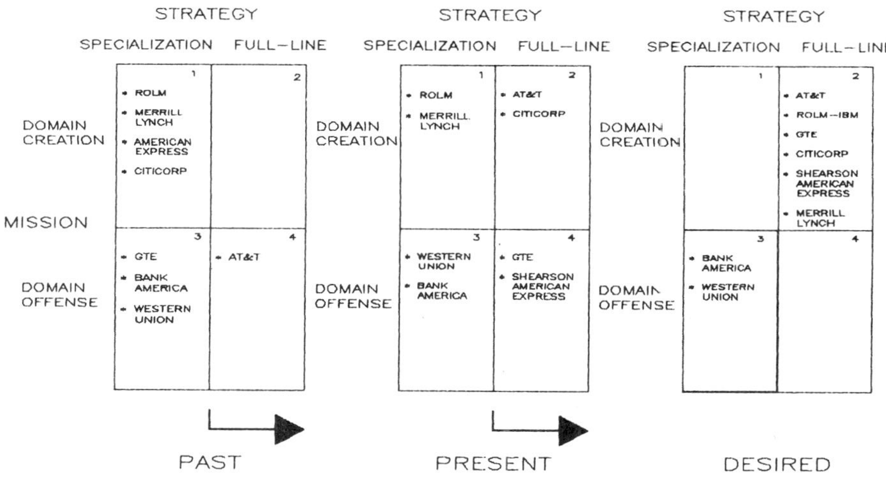

Figure 2: Predispositon as a Hurdle for Strategic Change

organizations. The major human resource management challenge for these two
firms is to meet this goal without major loss of employee morale.
BankAmerica has sweetened its early retirement benefits, and stepped up its
retraining activities in an effort to make the organizational changes more
palatable to its employees.

In contrast with the above firms, AT&T, Rolm, Merrill Lynch, GTE,
Citicorp, and Shearson-American Express have all planned on ambitious
transitions. Of these, AT&T and Citicorp are perhaps closest to meeting
their objectives, having planned their diversification strategies around
internal development. Rolm had to merge with IBM to broaden its product
scope and customer base. Similarly, GTE, Merrill Lynch, and American
Express have resorted to acquisitions to diversify their product portfolio.
The three most troublesome areas that have hindered strategy implementation
in this group: motivating employees to support the new strategies,
developing requisite personnel, and modifying the company's culture.

<u>Motivating Employees To Support New Strategies</u>

Merrill Lynch faces this challenge. It is attempting a transition to a
proactive, full-line strategy. The major bottleneck in this endeavor has
been its freewheeling sales culture. Products managers have not been able
to get the attention of the company's brokers, especially on new products
that are targeted at the low end of the market. The company has, therefore,
recently organized itself by client categories, using salaried service
representatives and specialists for nontraditional products and low ticket
purchases (Business Week, 1984a).

The new structure, however, has had its own share of difficulties.
Brokers are already loaded with a diverse range of products from bonds to
tax shelters. The restructuring will add even more to that diversity,
making it difficult for any account executive to explain all of these
intelligently to the customer. Moreover, the incentive systems of the
company induce its brokers to pay disproportionate attention to proven
products and established customers. The challenge for Merrill Lynch is to
modify its incentive systems, as a first step in transforming its sales
culture.

GTE faces a similar challenge. It is a company that has been administered meticulously from the top. Corporate staff is very powerful at GTE and only recently have line managers gained control over even largely operational programs, like productivity improvement and quality control (Wysocki, 1984). The company relies a lot of formal systems, studies and meetings. Mr. Theodore Brophy, the Chairman and Chief Executive of the company, is known as a proper and meticulous executive. While this "bureaucratic" administrative arrangement was excellently suited to the company under regulation, GTE may inadvertently stifle even the limited creativity that it requires to compete in cell 4 unless the company changes its administrative orientation. A more bottom-up planning process will be better suited to the company's change context.

Developing Requisite Skills

This has been one of AT&T's major challenges. The company needs to strengthen its marketing team in order to carry its technological innovations to commercial success. Its difficulties in this area are due primarily to a domineering engineering culture (Langley, 1984a).

The marketing department at AT&T was established only in 1959 "to respond to and not anticipate" customer needs. Preacting to a customer need was considered an "artificial" sale, and was therefore frowned upon (Schlesinger, Dyer, and Clough, forthcoming). It was only with Archie McGill's arrival from IBM in the 1970s that a marketing function started taking root in the company. Unfortunately, however, Mr. McGill resigned in 1983 before he could build creditability and respect for the marketing function (Langley, 1984b). Some of his marketing managers have since left the company. The challenge for AT&T is not only to find suitable replacements for these managers, but to retain the new hires or transferees and empower their roles by modifying the company's existing engineering culture.

Nurturing an Appropriate Culture

This seems to have been a problem faced by all of the firms studied, especially those that have sought acquisitions or mergers as the way to implement their strategies. The problems faced by American Express and Rolm best illustrate the difficulties in consummating mergers and acquisitions.

When American Express first launched its aggressive acquisition strategy, American Express' dream was to create "One Enterprise" that would integrate all of its financial service offerings. However, its inability to mesh the radically different cultures of the acquired companies has seriously detracted from that dream. For example, the aggressive Wall Street style of Shearson, the more conservative "square-headed Minnesota" culture of IDS, the old low-key, long on trust values of Fireman's Fund, and the schizophrenic trader cum investment banker orientation of Lehman Bros., all form part of the American Express cultural mosaic.

Individually each acquisition has the potential of making American Express the "One Enterprise" that it wants to be. However, its toughest challenge is in successfully integrating these companies. As Walt Wriston, the former Chief executive of Citicorp observed:

"Their (American Express) management team has been assembled mostly by purchase... I don't think there's any question that if a team has played together for 10 years, you have a better chance on a Saturday afternoon, than the all-star team that was assembled that morning" (Business Week, 1984, p. 118-122).

Top management does not seem to have been specially sensitive to this
cultural diversity, resulting at times in loss of employee morale and even
resignations. Sanford Weill, until recently the president of American
Express, caused resentment at Fireman's Fund by his aggressive Wall Street
style of layoffs, and frequent executive conferences. Peter Cohen, the
current chairman of Shearson, has angered some Lehman employees by refusing
to negotiate with them on annual bonuses and medical benefits (both of which
were very attractive at Lehman). Coming from a paternalistic environment,
some of these employees were absolutely outraged when they were subjected by
Shearson to lie detector tests on their gambling habits. (Hilder and Metz,
1984). While many of these policies may have justification, the speed at
which they are being implemented may seriously undermine the key resource in
a service business, i.e., skilled and motivated employees.

More ominously, the "Shearsonifying" of American Express that Weill and
his lieutenants attempted has already had a serious backlash not only from
employees in the new acquisition but also from its stalwarts in the old
travel-related service business -- a comparatively genteel bureaucracy. It
is pertinent to note that Mr. Weill's replacement as president comes from
the travel-related service business.

Rolm faces a similar challenge. Its organization structure differs
from that of other telecommunications companies in that its communications
division reverted to a functional structure from a product-centered
structure just before its acquisition by IBM. While this allowed for
several operating synergisms, it also detracted from a market orientation.
As an independent, Rolm could compensate for this deficiency through the
enterpreneurship of its employees, and its control and incentive system
which was informally tailored to each manager.

However, as an integral part of IBM the company faces severe challenges
in retaining elements of its personnel policies that encourage
entrepreneurship, while introducing others that are more appropriate for
melding its operations with that of IBM. Describing the gap between the two
cultures, M. Kenneth Oshman, a founder and chief executive officer of Rolm,
observed::

"We're used to kicking off an important development on the basis of
three engineers looking at the problem on a half-time basis for three or
four weeks. We fly from intuition. IBM, on the other hand, flies from
business cases. They'll assign 15, 20 maybe 200 people to examine every
issue. We are always optimistic, they are cautious. It's not as risky, but
it takes longer to get off the dime" (Sanger, 1985).

While IBM has been very sensitive not to overtly tamper with Rolm
autonomy so far, analysts speculate that several moves are afoot to
integrate the two sales and development teams (Levine, 1985). Their
cultural diversity may spark some resentment at that time.

STRATEGIC HUMAN RESOURCE MANAGEMENT

The strategic planning system used by a firm helps communicate its
mission to business unit managers and provides a forum for negotiating
strategies to accomplish that mission. The authority to implement these
strategies is defined by the firm's organization structure. However,
structure is meaningless without a complementary planning, control, and
incentive system. Systems can take five or more years to take firm root
(Lorange, 1980). Staffing the organization with the right skills is another
long lead time activity. Finally, transforming the culture of a firm and
infusing it with a new leadership style can take anywhere from six to twenty
years (Kotter, 1982; Uttal, 1983). Unless all of these elements (Figure 3)

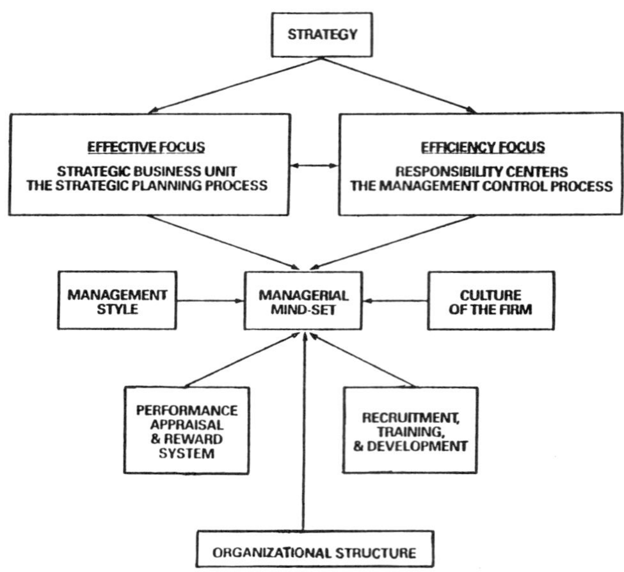

Figure 3: Achieving Goal Congruence

are managed proactively and in concert, the implementation bottlenecks
mentioned in the previous section will continue to persist.

Anticipating environment change should not normally be a problem. For
example, deregulation of the two industries studied has been gradual,
stretching over a period of a decade in the case of financial services and
over two decades in the case of telecommunications (Chakravarthy, 1985b).
It was brought about incrementally in both industries, partly in response to
technological change, and in part due to competitive moves that exploited
legal loopholes. Such changes should be routinely monitored by a firm's
strategic planning system. This concluding section explores ways in which
human resource management can respond to these early warning signals.

Based on the case histories described in this paper, there are at least
three major areas in which human resources can be preactively managed to
facilitate strategic change:

1. nurturing skills to promote strategic flexibility,

2. encouraging managers to discover versatility in their
    management styles, and

3. integrating team building with contractual incentives.

<u>Strategic Flexibility</u>

The recruitment, training, and development activities of a firm are
typically governed by its current mission and strategy. However, human
resource planning must ensure that critical skills (like marketing at AT&T)
are developed in anticipation of environmental change. Conversely, the firm
must also phase out in a planned manner skills that are likely to become
obsolete. BankAmerica, for example, could have anticipated the push towards
increased efficiency in a deregulated environment, and begun its
restructuring activities earlier. A continuous audit of the firm's skill
portfolio can help top management identify retraining needs in time and thus
avoid massive retrenchment and/or recruitment.

Forecasting the skills that would be in short supply (or in excess)
requires a careful assessment of the shifts in a company's business
portfolio and the technologies it uses to support its businesses. This
calls for close cooperation between human resource managers and strategic
planners. It also calls for a careful evaluation by human resource managers
of the demand and supply for the needed skills in external factor markets.

Logical as the above proposal may sound, developing new skills ahead of
their requirement (either through new hires or retraining) is a rarity.
Human resource budgets are typically tied to a business plan, and
consequently are forced to lag strategic decisions. However, just as a
central R&D budget to fund projects that no business unit will sponsor, so
too must a central human resource budget be provided to nurture critical
human resource skills not linked to a specific business plan. Individual
business unit managers can be apportioned a portion of this central human
resource budget, either through direct subsidies for the "super numeraries"
on their payroll and for sponsoring special training and development
programs, or by "forgiving" some laxity in their profit performance. The
prime mover for this plan should naturally be the human resource specialist
in an organization. However, top management support is crucial to its
implementation.

<u>Versatility</u> <u>of</u> <u>Styles</u>

Most large diversified corporations use some variant of portfolio
planning for making strategic decisions (Haspeslaugh, 1982). One of the
attendant ills with this approach is the type casting of managers with a
narrow managerial style (Chakravarthy, 1984). Building versatility, like
building flexibility, is not in the short term interests of a company. It
is far more prudent from an efficiency standpoint to hone a manager's skills
in accomplishing a single mission than to train him to be versatile.

While it is possible that not all managers can be versatile in their
management styles (Hersey and Blanchard, 1977), it is important that the
company has the opportunity to discover the ones that are. Human resource
planning must allow every manager job rotation through a variety of business
missions. Here again strong commitment is required from top management to
ensure that the necessary job rotation is provided. It is only through this
process that the company can identify potential general managers, and help
in their development. A versatile manager would be better able to handle
cultural diversity, and would not impose a singular style on all businesses
-- as was the case at American Express. Moreover, such managers are less
likely to resist change. They are more self-assured.

<u>Integrating</u> <u>Team</u> <u>Building</u> <u>with</u> <u>Contractual</u> <u>Incentives</u>

The design of a control and incentive system assumes that an
enforceable performance contract can be drawn up between the principal (CEO)
and the agent (business unit manager). This condition obtains only when
there is information symmetry between top management and the business unit
manger (Chakravarthy and Zajac, 1984). This is a rarity in most large
diversified corporations.

Under conditions of information asymmetry, however, the only real
control that a CEO can exercise is through the choice of a trustworthy
business manager. Well managed companies like General Electric and Texan
Instruments have, therefore, integrated their strategic planning and
manpower review systems. In General Electric, Session C -- a manpower
review has been synchronized with the review of business plans (Browne,
1982); and in Texan Instruments the KPA (Key Personnel Analysis) has been
tied to the company's strategic planning system (Lorange and Vancil, 1977).

A manager's skills, attitudes, style, and loyalty are some of the
factors that determine his selection. The human resource specialist in an
organization must help in identifying and developing such managers.

REFERENCES

Abernathy, W.J., A.M. Kantrow, and K.B. Clark. **Industrial Renaissance,** (New
    York: Basic Books, 1983).

Bowman, E.H. and B.G. McWilliams, "The Same Fruit From Different Trees:
    Common Effects of Deregulation in Three Separate Industries, "**The Wharton
    Annual,** 1985, pp. 63-71.

Browne, Paul, "General Electric Company: Background Note on Management
    Systems, 1981" In R. Vancil, **Implementing Strategy: The Role of Top
    Management,** (Boston: Harvard Business School, 1982, pp. 77-85)

Business Week, "Merrill Lynch's Big Dilemma," January 16, 1984a,
    pp. 60-67.

Chakravarthy, Balaji, S., "Strategic Self-Renewal: A Planning Framework for
    Today," **Academy of Management Review,** Vol. 9,
    No. 3 (July, 1984) pp. 536-547.

Chakravarthy, Balaji, S. "Competing in a Deregulated Environment: The
    Strategic Options," Working Paper UP 85-03, Reginald Jones Center, The
    Wharton School, 1985a.

Chakravarthy, Balaji, S. "Deregulation as Environment Change," Working Paper
    WP 85-02, Reginald Jones Center, The Wharton School, 1985b.

Chakravarthy, Balaji, S. "Strategic Adaptation to Disruptive Change: The
    Case of Deregulation," Working Paper WP 84-07, (REV), Reginald Jones
    Center, The Wharton School, 1986.

Chakavarthy, Balaji, S. and E. Zajac, "Tailoring Incentive Systems to a
    Strategic Context," **Planning Review,** Vol. 12, No. 6 (November, 1984) pp.
    30-35.

Fombrun, Charles, J, Noel M. Tichy, Mary A. Devanna, **Strategic Human
    Resource Management,** (New York, John Wiley & Sons, 1984).

Haspeslagh, P., "Portfolio Planning: Uses and Limits," **Harvard Business
    Review,** Vol. 60, No. 1, 1982, pp. 58-73.

Hersey, Paul and K.H. Blanchard. **Management of Organizational Behavior:
    Utilizing Human Resources,** (Englewood Cliffs, N.J.: Prentice-Hall, Inc.,
    1977).

Hilder, David, B. and Tim Metz, "A Spate of Acquisitions Puts American
    Express in a Management Bind," Wall Street Journal, August 15,1984, p.1.

Kotter, John P. **The General Managers,** (New York: Free Press, 1982).

Langley, M., "AT&T Marketing Men Find Their Star Fails to Ascend as
    Expected," Wall Street Journal, February, 1984a.

Langley, M., "AT&T Manager Finds His Effort to Galvanize Sales Meets
    Resistance," Wall Street Journal, February 13, 1984b.

Lawrence, P. and D. Dyer. Renewing American Industry, (New York: The Free Press, 1983).

Levine, Jonathan B., "How IBM is Getting the Most Out of Rolm," Business Week, November 18, 1985, pp. 110-111.

Lorange, Peter, Corporate Planning: An Executive Viewpoint, (Englewood Cliffs, N.J.: Prentice-Hall, Inc., 1980).

Lorange, Peter, "Organization Structure and Process," In William D.Guth, editor, Handbook of Business Strategy, (Boston, Mass: Warren, Gorham and Lamont, 1985, pp. 23.1-31).

Lorange, Peter, and Declan C. Murphy, "Strategy and Human Resources: Concepts and Practice," Human Resource Management, Vol. 22, Nos.1/2, 1983, pp. 111-133.

Lorange, Peter, and Richard F. Vancil, Strategic Planning Systems, (Englewood Cliffs, NJ: Prentice-Hall, 1977).

Miles, Robert, H., Coffin Nails and Corporate Strategies, (Englewood Cliffs, NJ: Prentice-Hall, 1982).

Pascale, R.T. and A.G. Athos. The Art of Japanese Management, (New York: Warner Books, 1981).

Peters, T.J. and R.H. Waterman. In Search of Excellence: Lessons from America's Best Run Companies, (New York: Harper & Row, 1982).

Sanger, D.E., "The Changing Image of IBM," The New York Times Magazine, July 7, 1985, p.42.

Schelsinger, L.A., Dyer, D. and Clough, T.N. Recasting Bell: From Monopoly to Competition at AT&T, forthcoming.

Tichy, N.M., C.J. Fombrun and M.A. Devanna, "The Organizational Context of Strategic Human Resource Management," in Fombrun, Tichy, and Devanna, op. cit., 1984, pp.19-32.

Utal, B., "The Corporate Culture Vultures," Fortune, October 17, 1983, pp. 66-72.

Waite, D.C. II, "Deregulation and the Banking Industry." Bankers Magazine, January-February, 1982, pp. 26-35.

Waterman, R.H., "Structure is not Organization." McKinsey Staff Paper, June, 1979.

Wysocki, Jr., B., "The Chief's Personality Can Have a Big Impact - For Better or Worse," Wall Street Journal, September 11, 1984, p.1.

FORMULATING HUMAN RESOURCE

STRATEGIES IN A PROFESSIONAL SERVICE FIRM: A SYSTEMIC APPROACH

Lee Dyer* and Richard A. Shafer**

* 393 Ives Hall-Nyssilr
  Cornell University
  Ithaca, NY 14853

* Touche Ross & Co.
  1633 Broadway
  New York, NY 10019

INTRODUCTION

Today's organizations are continually being challenged to become more strategic in their management of human resources. But, what does this mean? How is it done?

This paper documents our efforts to answer these questions at Touche Ross. We begin by describing briefly the firm, our concept of strategic human resource management (SHRM), and the role of human resource planning (HRP) in fostering SHRM. We then go on to describe the theoretical underpinnings of our particular approach to HRP, the three major planning processes we are attempting to deploy, and the change strategy that is being used to weave these processes into the fabric of the firm.

Since we have come less far than we have to go, what is presented here is a road map and a progress report. It will be a while before "the rest of the story" is known.

THE FIRM

Touche Ross (TR) is one of a group of major international public accounting firms often referred to as the "Big Eight." Its U.S. revenues exceed $500 million a year. It has over 800 partners and more than 8000 professional and clerical employees working in 80 offices across the country. The firm has been in a period of rapid growth for several years despite the increasingly competitive nature of the public accounting industry (_The Wall Street Journal_, 1985).

Organizationally, TR is what Mintzberg (1979; see also Mintzberg and McHugh, 1985) calls an adhocracy. It operates in a dynamic and complex environment, each of its activities (audits, consulting engagements, etc.) is somewhat unique, it employs large numbers of professionals who often work in teams, much of the work is performed autonomously, and rules in the day-to-day operations of the firm. To a large extent coordination and control are achieved through informal means -- committees, task forces, adherence to professional standards, and the like.

The firm operates with a matrix structure. Below the top management
team (which is elected by the partners) are two cross-cutting lines of
authority. One consists of Associate Managing Partners, who are in charge
of various groups of offices, the Partners in Charge of these offices, and
the Directors of Operations who manage the major departments in the offices,
typically Accounting and Auditing, Tax, and Management Consulting. Under
the auspices of the firm's strategic and profits plans, the offices are
responsible for preparing their own business and profit plans, meeting the
financial and other goals laid out in these plans, and conducting the day-
to-day business of the enterprise.

The second main line of authority works through the National Functional
Directors who help set the firm's direction by playing an active role in
strategic and profit planning, and who also are responsible for promulgating
professional standards in their areas -- primarily those noted above:
Accounting and Auditing, Tax, and Management Consulting -- and for assuring
that these standards are internalized and adhered to in the field.

In addition to these two "line" organizations, the firm also has seven
major "staff" functions. One of these is Human Resources.

STRATEGIC HUMAN RESOURCE MANAGEMENT

In today's highly competitive environment (Stevens, 1985) much depends
on the firm's ability to adopt a more strategic approach to the management
of human resources. To us this means the development of a culture in which
(Dyer, 1983):

- Human resources are in integral component of the business
  equation.

- Full and timely consideration is given to the human resource
  implications of all strategic business decisions.

- Human resource decisions are driven primarily by business needs and
  only secondarily by other factors.

- Human resource activities (staffing, training, compensation, and the
  like are focused and mutually reinforcing rather than diffuse and
  relatively independent.

Can this organization nirvana be achieved? Perhaps not in its entirety.
But it is our goal, and HRP is one of the major ways it is being pursued.

HUMAN RESOURCE PLANNING

Research show that organizational approaches to HRP fall along a
continuum from focused to comprehensive (Dyer, 1985a). We are persuaded
that an all-out effort toward SHRM requires the adoption of a relatively
comprehensive approach to HRP involving three types of planning processes:
plan based, project based and population based.

Plan Based HRP

Plan based HRP, as the name suggests, occurs as an integral (or closely
related) part of formal business planning and, thus, recurs on a regular
schedule in keeping with a predetermined planning cycle.

As suggested earlier, TR annually engages in a formal planning process
which has both a business (three-year, strategy-oriented) and a profit (one-
year, action-oriented) component. The process is diagrammed in Figure 1.

Human resources enter in two ways. First, early in the process
representatives of both sides of the organizational matrix -- specifically,
Associate Managing Partners and National Functional Directors -- work with
the Human Resource function to identify human resource issues thought to be
critical to the firm. These are derived from analyses of the strategic
business directions established by the firm and functions, the strategic
plan prepared by the National Director of Human Resources, and nagging human
resource problems. The initial list of issues is distilled and refined
through discussion and eventually communicated to the offices in the form of
challenges to be addressed in their planning processes. Last year's
challenges emphasized such issues as management and leadership development
recruitment, and retention.

The second way human resources enter the planning process is through
the required documentation each office submits to the firm. Each plan must
address four topic areas in a general narrative and in more detailed
quantitative and qualitative analyses. Human resources is one of the four

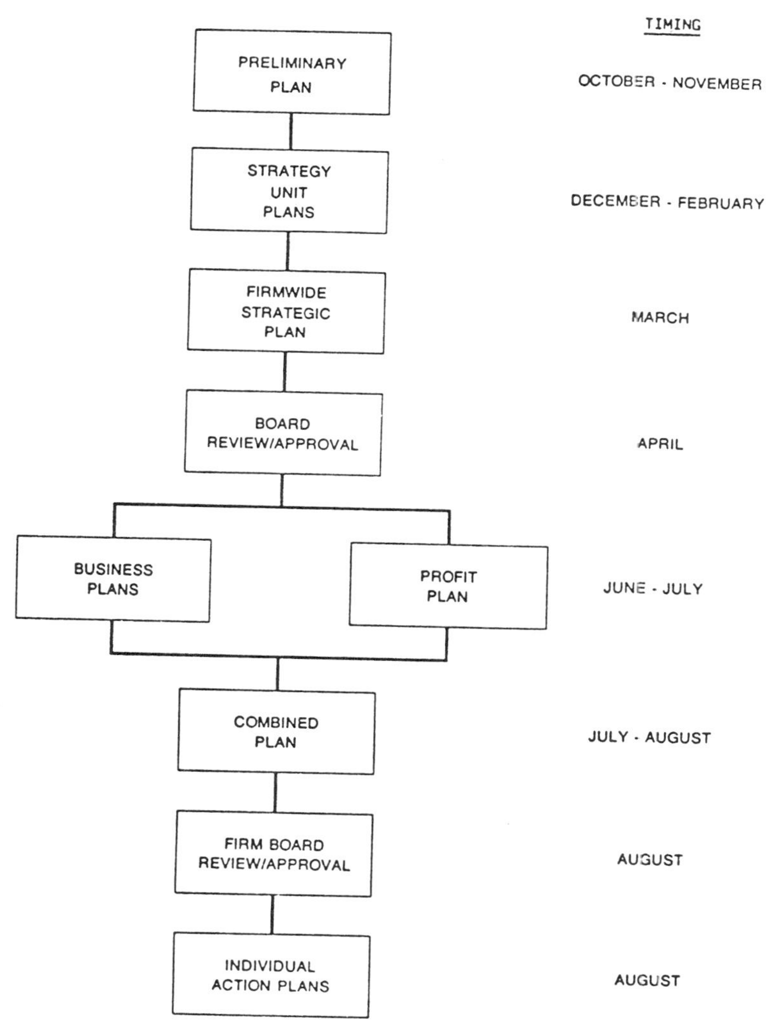

Figure 1: The 1985 Firmwide Planning Process

topic areas. The quantitative piece consists of head count and flow
projections with particular emphasis on staffing levels and turnover. The
qualitative piece details the specific action plans the office proposes to
pursue to address the challenges it received and to support its business
plans.

This approach to planning has been in place at TR for many years. A
recent review, however, revealed frequent inconsistencies among the
strategic business directions established by the firm and the offices, the
strategies promulgated by the firm's Human Resource function, the business
plans of the offices, and the quantitative and qualitative pieces of the
offices' human resource plans. Consequently, one of our goals is to tighten
these linkages.

Research suggests that there are four major ways to do this (working
from the human resource side): insertion, integration, inspection, and
interpretation (Dyer, 1984, 1985a). We are working on three of the four.

- _Insertion_ involves the introduction of releva.t human resource considerations early in the planning process. At TR this is accomplished
  through challenges, and so we have attempted to strengthen this process in three ways. First, by involving more "line" managers in the
  identification stage. Second, by having the challenges emanate from
  the National Functional Directors rather than the Human Resource
  function. Third, by substantially reducing the number of challenges.

- _Integration_ refers to the inclusion of human resource issues directly
  in the business planning process through documentation and other
  means. Two improvements were made in this area. First, the
  documentation was simplified; two complex forms were replaced by one
  simple one. As shown in Figure 2, the new form emphasizes the link
  between business plans and human resource issues by requiring the
  office planners first to list (in the left hand column) the four or
  five most important business strategies and then to indicate (in the
  remaining columns) their human resource implications and relevant
  action plans. The second improvement was to provide training for the
  human resource professionals in the offices to sharpen both their
  planning and consulting skills and to encourage them to take a more
  active role in the business and profit planning processes.

- _Inspection_ occurs when offices' business and profit plans are reviewed
  at the firm level before coming final. Ideally this review should
  focus on human resource as well as other matters. This is not yet the
  case at TR, and it is an area that is being left for future action.

- _Interpretation_ refers to the process of analyzing approved plans for
  their human resource implications and developing action plans. We
  have injected this year for the first time a firm-level analysis by
  the Human Resource function that helps in two ways. First, it
  identifies offices that have failed to plan adequately so that
  assistance can be offered where the potential problems are severe
  enough. Second, it helps to identify systemic issues that may require
  firm-wide action to address.

A review of this year's business plans show some, but somewhat less than
dramatic, improvement on the human resource side. We conclude that our
efforts to improve the up-front process through which human resource
challenges are identified and to re-do the documentation have had some
positive effect. Still, much remains to be done in these areas. WE also
need to introduce an inspection process with some teeth and to make more
systematic use of the information gleaned from the interpretation step.

32

BUSINESS STRATEGIES AND RELATED
HUMAN RESOURCE ISSUES AND ACTION PROGRAMS

OFFICE: _______________________   DATE

BUSINESS UNIT: _____A&A_____   PREPARED BY [   ] [   ]

RELEVANT BUSINESS PLAN STRATEGIES OR PROGRAMS	NATURE OF MOST CRITICAL HUMAN RESOURCE ISSUE(S) RELATED TO THOSE STRATEGIES OR PROGRAMS	HUMAN RESOURCE ACTION PROGRAMS	PERSON RESPONSIBLE	YEARS √(1)		
				86	87	88

(1) (√) FOR YEARS PROGRAM IS EFFECTIVE

Figure 2:   Form to Link Business Plans and Human Resources

Our efforts to improve the formal planning process represent only one way we are attempting to move toward the more strategic management of human resources through better HRP. Equally as important are our efforts with respect to project based planning.

Project Based HRP

Project based HRP takes place in the context of the relatively informal deliberations undertaken by task forces and project teams that are from time to time constituted to look into strategic issues (Dyer, 1985b; Quinn, 1980). It is important because in most organizations strategic thinking is often well out in front of strategic planning and where this is true it is not enough to be linked only to the latter.

Certainly at TR several strategic studies and pilot projects are often going on at the firm level and in the offices at any given time. Typically, these proceed quite far before showing up in the formal business plans. Yet, many could benefit from a human resource input early on. Thus, prudence dictates that we find ways to assure that this happens.

We have found two ways to far. Best it to make certain that "line" managers are sensitized to consider human resource issues as a matter of course. Next best, and not mutually exclusive, is to see to it that capable human resource professionals are involved at critical points. Many of TR's partners are extremely alert and capable with respect to human resource issues. But, alas, not all are. And even the best of them have been known to slight human resource issues when under pressure, or to subordinate these issues to other, more immediate concerns.

Thus, we are attempting to foster the practice of including human

resource professionals in the more important strategic decision-making
forums. The ultimate goal is to create a climate in which it would be
unthinkable not to do this. In the short run, however, we are satisfied to
pick and choose the relevant situations and attempt to earn our spurs.

This we can do by:

- Constantly working to project to key partners an air of professionalism and a sense of having something to bring to the party.
- Having tentacles out in all parts of the firm to know when and where
  strategic issues are being addressed.

- Choosing carefully the opportunities on which to work favoring those
  that offer a fighting chance of success and visible results.

- Not waiting for invitations in those situations where
  conditions are right.

- Doing a good job once involved.

Initially, a relatively small number of TR's human resource
professional have become involved in strategic projects. Their number has
been supplemented by the judicious use of consultants having expertise in
particular areas. The intent is to expand the internal resources over time,
however, through training and the development of processes and documentation
to help structure strategic interventions. (Eventually we hope to make
these aids available to "line" managers as well since the responsibility is
really theirs and at any rate the number of human resource professionals
will never be adequate to do all that needs to be done.)
At the moment, we are working on a handful of strategic projects as the
computerization of the audit planning process and the reorganization of the
firm's small business practice. Our largest project so far, however,
involves a rethinking of the nature of the firm's Accounting and Auditing
practice.

Several recent changes in the external environment have led to a
similar reexamination in several "Big Eight" (Stevens, 1985; <u>The Wall Street
Journal</u>, 1985). The search is for a new strategy to return growth and
profitability to this aspect of the business while continuing to deliver
high-quality service. At TR a number of clarifying the nature of the
practice now and three to five years out, identifying critical human
resource issues that are likely to arise during this time, and formulating
human resource models and strategies that will help the firm create a viable
practice for the future. A second task is to test and refine this process
and its supporting documentation at selected sites around the firm with the
twin goals of dissemination and learning.

On the one hand, we are conducting interviews in the leading edge
Accounting and Auditing Departments in various offices to ascertain the
steps they have taken toward the future, the human resource problems they
have run into, and the successes and failures they have had in dealing with
these problems. This is based on the premise that there is much to learn
from those who have seen the future or, at least, some significant part of
it. Figure 3 describes the basic approach and the nature of the questions
being asked.

We are also anticipating working with a small number of Accounting and
Auditing Departments that are, or soon will be, moving forward on one or
more strategic dimensions. To this end, we developed the six-stage process
described in Figure 4. It provides a way to clarify current and anticipated
states of a practice, anticipating and prioritizing major human resource

PROCESS FOR IDENTIFYING STRATEGIC DEVELOPMENTS

IN AUDITING AND ASSESSING THEIR HUMAN RESOURCE IMPLICATIONS

1. Identify accounting and auditing (A&A) practice units known to be on the leading edge with respect to:

   a. Business strategy

   b. The management of human resources

2. Among the practice leaders (group 1a), conduct interviews with Partners in Charge (PICs), Director of Accounting Operators (DAOs), and other partners and staff, as appropriate, to ascertain:

   a. The nature of their key strategies or innovations (e.g., new ways to "face off against the market," industry practices, new approaches to delivering services, use of technology). Specifically, how has the nature of the practice been altered? What is being altered? What is being done differently compared with that used to be done or with what is done in more "typical" A&A practice units?

   b. They types of human resource issues or problems that have been created or exacerbated as a result of the new approaches. To what extent have they caused difficulties or rethinking with respect to: organization structure, the number of partners and staff required, the types of skills needed, staffing ratios, partner and staff motivation or morale, etc.?

   c. The human resource actions that have been taken to deal with the aforementioned issues or problems. For example: organization restructuring, new hiring practices, training programs, procedures for assigning work, supervisory practices, reward or recognition programs, procedures for assigning work, supervisory practices, reward or recognition programs, communications or counseling.

3. Among the practice innovators in human resource management (group 1b), conduct interviews with PICs, DAOs, and other partners and staff, as appropriate, to ascertain:

   a. The nature of the innovations being tried. For   example, new approaches to attract and retain   experience hires, use paraprofessionals, reduce turnover in the 4th and 5th years, career management, etc.

   b. The factors that led up to the adoption of the new approaches.

   c. The difficulties encountered during implementation of these new approaches. The ways these were or are being overcome.

   d. The results obtained.

4. Obtain nominations of other A&A practice units that are also innovators in business strategies or human resource management practices.

Figure 3: Process for Identifying Strategic Developments

PROCESS FOR CLARIFYING BUSINESS PLANS AND

DEVELOPING SUPPORTIVE HUMAN RESOURCE STRATEGIES

STAGE	PURPOSE	ACTION STEPS
1	To develop a clear understanding of the current state of the practice, factors shaping the practice, and current human resource problems.	Data gathering: Interviews with, or discussions among key players. Collection of head count and flow statistics.
2	To formulate a vision of the practice 3 years out and for the intervening years.	Data gathering: Interviews with, or discussions among, key players. Formulation of "prototype" staffing models.
3	To anticipate the major human resource issues facing the practice during the next year or two.	Analysis: Comparisons of "should be" with "is now" (or "will be" unless changes are made). "What if" modelling.
4	To prioritize the major human resources issues and convert them to objectives.	Decision Making: Discuss and develop consensus among key players.
5	To develop action plans.	Decision Making: Discuss and develop consensus among key players.
6	To implement action plans.	Follow-up: Implement, track results, evaluate and feed back.

Figure 4: Six-Stage Process

issues, and formulating and implementing action steps. It is this process, along with the accompanying documentation (work-sheets) that we hope eventually to formalize and institution-alize firm-wide.

Our efforts to become involved in strategic decision-making in systematic way have only recently begun, and it is pre-mature to attempt an assessment of the results. One indicator of success will be the number, importance, and visibility of the projects with which we become involved. Another will be the perceptions of how helpful we are able to be. Still another will be the number of advocates we are able to create, and the extent of their firm-wide influence. The ultimate tests, however, will lie in the proportion of strategic decisions that are made only after full consideration has been given to their human resource implications and in the quality of the human resource strategies that emerge.

Population Based HRP

A strategic human resource issue that recurs in virtually all organizations is a shortfall of fully qualified people to fill critical jobs, often at high levels of management (Drucker, 1985). With their focus on specific business issues, plan and project based HRP often do a good job

of picking up particular shortages of key personnel, but fail to integrate
these into a systemic view. The role of population-based HRP (of which

succession planning is the most familiar variety) is to reinforce the
critical nature of certain employee groups and to assure that they and their
potential replacements receive the care and feeding necessary to assure an
ongoing supply to meet evolving needs.

PARTNER RESOURCE TRAINING

At TR the partners constitute a critical resource. It is, therefore,
surprising to find that the firm (not unlike its counterparts (Maister,
1982) has, heretofore, failed to develop systematic means of managing
partner development, placements, and careers. The challenge is to create
and nurture the view of partners as a highly valuable group that can and
should be managed. To this end, we have developed a concept called partner
resource planning which consists of two components: managing the partner
pool and succession planning.

Managing the Partner Pool

Here there are two objectives. One is to assure that the firm has the
right number of partners to meet its growth goals but not more than is
consistent with its profit plans. The other is to maintain promotional
opportunities for top-quality staff. Responsibility for meeting these
objectives is shared by both sides of the matrix -- the Associate Managing
Partners and Partners in Charge of the offices on the one hand and the
National Functional Directors on the other.

Currently, policy direction and control are provided by the top
management of the firm in the form of the so-called Asset Management
Committee. This Committee establishes and monitors firm-wide:

- Desired levels of partner head counts.

- Appropriate levels of inflows and outflows to meet the
  desired levels of partner head counts.

- Quality standards for the partner pool as a whole.

Each spring the National Functional Directors prepare three-year
projections of head counts and flow (promotion, recruitment, retirement,
quit, and termination) rates. Once agreed to by the Asset Management
Committee these projections become the standards against which future
developments are monitored.

Each month actual head counts and flow rates are tracked against the
plans and reported to the Committee (using the format shown in Figure 5).
Ensuing discussions can result in either an adjustment of the head count
targets (in light of unanticipated business developments) or revised action
steps to bring flow rates, and thus head counts, more in line with desired
levels. As of this writing only two months of monitoring have been
completed, so it is too early to tell exactly what the Asset Management
Committee will do. It appears, however, that it may have to assume a more
active role in the management of partner resources beginning early in 1986
if the firm is to meet its volume and profit objectives.

Succession Planning

As the Asset Management Committee -- and top management generally --
begins to take a stronger role in managing the partner pool, the need has

PARTNER HEADCOUNT AND FLOW RECORD

AS OF _______________

CATEGORY	AUDIT/ENTERPRISE		TAX		MC		ABC		ADMINISTRATION		OTHER		TOTAL FIRM	
	MRM* YTD	PROJ BAL**	MRM* YTD	PROJ BAL**	MRM* YTD	PROJ BAL**	MRM* YTD	PROJ BAL**	MRM* YTD	PROJ BAL**	MRM* YTD	PROJ BAL**	MRM* YTD	PROJ BAL**
Beginning Headcount														
Gains														
Promotions														
Senior Hires														
Mergers														
Transfers In														
Readmissions														
Other														
Total														
Losses														
Retirements														
Quits														
Terminations														
Transfers Out														
Other														
Total														
Ending Headcount														

*Most recent month.
**Variance between activity YTD and activity projected for the year.

Figure 5: Spreadsheet for Tracking of Headcounts and Flow Rates

arisen for better data concerning individual partners (for example, data on
performance, potential, special skill, and career interests). An interest is
also beginning to develop in anticipating specific openings particularly in
such critical positions as Partner in Charge and Director of Operations in
the offices and in discussing potential candidates to fill these openings.

In anticipation of these developments, we began to design a succession
planning process patterned after those used at Corning Glass Works (Dyer,
Shafer, and Regan, 1985) and IBM (Dyer and Heyer, 1985). The proposal calls
for Associate Managing Partners and Partners in Charge (of the larger
offices) to report periodically to the Asset Management Committee on the
state of their organizations and key partners in their offices, and on the
effects of their action plans to develop partners for future assignments.

It is our intent to ease into succession planning gradually. This year
the National Director of Human Resources is working informally with selected
Associate Managing Partners and Partners in Charge to develop data on anticipated openings in key positions, leaving the latter to concentrate their
reporting and, especially the preparation of individual partner development
plans. This focuses attention on partner (that is, management and leadership) development, perhaps the single most critical strategic human resource
issue facing the firm in the next few years.

TIMING

A critical issue of timing faces any organization contemplating a
comprehensive approach to HRP. Should the three types of planning be introduced
sequentially or simultaneously?

Conventional wisdom appears to favor sequencing. A common approach is
to begin with population based HRP (usually succession planning at the top)
and to move in turn to plan and project based processes as conditions permit
(Dyer, 1985a). Pattern and speed are determined by such factors as: (1) access
and credibility of those responsible for HRP, (2) experience base of the
relevant line managers, (3) availability of resources (people, time and money).

Conventional wisdom notwithstanding, at TR we have decided to tackle
all three HRP processes simultaneously. While resources are tight, other
factors favor this approach.

- First, rudiments of all three processes were already in place when we
  started. These included a human resource component in the business
  and profit plans, a core of "line" managers that were used to thinking strategically about human resources, and the Asset Management
  Committee.

- Second, the organization is very fluid, making it unclear which
  aspect of planning is most likely to take hold. Our response is to
  attack on all fronts and see what happens.

- Third, there is the matter of balance. We believe that, inasmuch as
  possible, organizations should maintain their various human resource
  activities at approximately the same level of sophistication (Baird
  and Meshoulam, undated).

- Fourth, a recent change of leadership at the top has opened a window
  of opportunity for change.

- Fifth, the need is great, and we are fully cognizant of the fact that
  once introduced, an HRP process typically takes from three to five
  years to become fully operational.

MANAGING CHANGE

The road toward SHRM and a more comprehensive approach to HRP is
neither easy nor smooth. At TR it involves the adoption of a new view of
human resources and the internalization of several new processes in an
environment that historically has eschewed such things. Success requires a
well thought out and carefully managed approach to organizational change.

Without pretending to have all the answers, we have found the following
to be useful general principles on which to build a change strategy (Dyer,
et al., 1985);

- Build on dissatisfaction (the "big D"); find it and nurture it at
  every opportunity.

- Have a clear concept of where to go, of what it means to
  manage to human resources strategically and the way HRP can
  be used.

- Build on what exists.

- Keep each process as simple as possible, consistent with the task to
  be done. Eschew sophistication for sophistication's sake.

- Focus on action; make sure every planning process ends with an
  action plan for which someone in authority is responsible.

- Be aggressive. Don't wait for invitations that may never come.
  Take advantage of every opportunity to move things along.

- Talk data not concepts. Involve managers in processes whenever
  possible waiting to sell them on concepts once the experiences
  begin to take hold.

- Assure that responsibility for SHRM and HRP stays with the
  "line"; they do, we help.

This, then, is our road map and progress report. In a nutshell we are
attempting to adapt a variety of research results and experience gleaned in
other organizations to the peculiarities of a professional service firm.
While we are learning on the move, we are firmly convinced that our efforts
are helping position the firm for continued growth and long-term
profitability.

REFERENCES

Baird, L. and Meshoulam, I., "Implementing Human Resource Strategic Manage-
    ment," unpublished manuscript, Human Resource Policy Institute, School of
    Management, Boston University (undated; circa 1983).

Drucker, P., Innovation and Entrepreneurship: Practices and Principles (New
    York: Harper & Row, 1985).

Dyer, L., "Bringing Human Resources Into the Strategy Formulation Process,"
    Human Resource Management, Vol. 22, No. 3 (Fall   1983) pp. 257-271.

Dyer, L., "Linking Human Resource and Business Strategies," Human Resource
    Planning, Vol. 7, No. 2 (Spring 1984) pp. 79-84.

Dyer, L., "A New View of Human Resource Planning" in Dyer, L. (ed), Human Resource Planning: A Case Study Reference Guide to the Tested Practices of Five Major U.S. and Canadian Companies (New York: Random House, 1985a).

Dyer, L., "Strategic Human Resource Management and Planning" in Rowland, K., and Ferris, G. (eds), Research in Personnel and Human Resource Management, Vol. 3 (Greenwich, CT: JAI Press, 1985b).

Dyer, L., "Studying Strategy in Human Resource Management: An Approach and an Agenda," Industrial Relations, Vol. 23, No. 2 (Spring, 1984), pp. 156-169.

Dyer, L. and Heyer, N., "IBM" in Dyer, L. (ed), Human Resource Planning: A Case Study Reference Guide to the Tested Practices of Five Major U.S. and Canadian Companies (New York: Random House, 1985).

Dyer, L., Shafer, R., and Regan, P. Jr., "Corning Glass Works" in Dyer, L. (ed), Human Resource Planning: A Case Study Reference Guide to the Tested Practices of Five Major U.S. and Canadian Companies (New York: Random House, 1985).

Maister, D., "Balancing the Professional Service Firm," Sloan Management Review, Vol. 24, No. 1 (Fall, 1982), pp.1-11.

Mintzberg, H., The Structuring of Organizations: A Synthesis of Research (Englewood Cliffs, NJ: Prentice-Hall, 1979).

Mintzberg, H., and McHugh, A. "Strategy Formulation in an Adhocracy," Administrative Science Quarterly, Vol. 30, No. 2 (June, 1985), pp. 160-197.

Quinn, J., Strategies for Change: Logical Incrementalism (Homewood, IL: Irwin, 1980).

Stevens, M., The Accounting Wars (New York: Macmillan, 1985).

The Wall Street Journal, "Total War: CPA Firms Diversify, Cut Fees, Steal Clients in Battle for Business," September 10, 1985, p.1.

PAY POLICY, ORGANIZATION STRATEGY AND STRUCTURE:

A QUESTION OF "FIT"

Renae F. Broderick

Assistant Professor of Human Resources
Graduate School of Management
University of California at Los Angeles
Los Angeles, California 90024

PAY POLICY AND BUSINESS STRATEGY

The notion that pay policy should be related to or vary with an organization's business strategy is grounded in the research and professional literature on pay. It implies that the better the "fit" between pay policy and organization characteristics such as business strategy, the higher the organization performance. The model in Figure 1 shows that the "fit" between policy on the design and administration of pay and overall organization strategy, design and administration influence organization performance.

There are two theoretical reasons offered for the higher organization performance attributable to "fit" relationships between pay policy and these organization characteristics. First, if pay policy is contingent on an organization's business strategy -- that is, if it is designed and administered to support business strategies -- then appropriate employee behaviors are more likely to be defined and rewarded. By rewarding the appropriate employee behaviors, the organization is sending a clear signal about what is expected. This increases the probability of the desired performance (see Lawler, 1981; Ellig, 1982; Milkovich and Newman, 1984). Second, the notion of "fit" includes congruency between pay policy and the organization's design and administrative style. Such consistency is believed to increase employee perceptions of pay policy equity. Equity perceptions can, in turn, increase employee motivation to perform (see Lawler, 1971; Salter, 1973; Lorsch and Morse, 1974; Dyer and Theriault, 1976).

Figure 1: A Model of Pay Policy, Organization and Performance

By increasing the chances of desired employee performance in these ways, pay policy appropriately related to organization strategy, design and administration could increase organization performance. If these performance relationships are true, then knowing how to develop pay policy that "fits" a particular organization could be advantageous in the management of human resources.

Unfortunately, these performance assumptions have not been tested. In part, this is due to the fact that a number of pieces needed to test the pay policy model are missing. At minimum, measures of pay policies and some definition of "fit" are needed. Measures of employee and organization performance must also be specified.

DEVELOPING MEASURES OF PAY POLICY AND "FIT"

This study focuses on the development of pay policy measures and the relationship between these measures and organization strategy. It is organized around two questions: (1) Can be important set of organization pay policies be identified and measured?; and (2) Do pay policies vary systematically across organizations with different business strategies? In order to investigate each question a search of the pay administration, human resource management and organization behavior literatures is couples with an empirical examination of pay decisions in organizations.

REVIEW OF THE LITERATURE

Identification of Pay Decisions

The study's first question involved the identification and measurement of pay policies. In the literature, decisions on pay structure and level, mix, incentives and pay administration were consistently identified as important to the overall design and administration of an organization's pay system. These decisions are listed in Figure 2 (right hand column) and described below. Pay policy decisions are distinguished from more technical pay decisions such as those on methods of job evaluation or choice of the wage survey to be used in determining pay level (Lawler, 1981; Milkovich and Newman, 1984).

Pay Structure and Level. Pay structure is defined as the distribution of money rates paid to different jobs in an organization. Pay level is defined as the average of the total distribution of these rates (see Mahoney, 1979). The actual pay structure and level for a group of jobs or employees are determined by a number of pay decisions.

For example, in developing a pay structure for a group of jobs, the organization must determine the going rate for the jobs in the external labor market. At the same time, it must decide the emphasis to place on internal norma relative to these external prices (see Livernash, 1957; Belcher, 1974; Lawler, 1981; Milkovich and Newman, 1984). Other decisions are listed under the pay structure and level heading in Figure 2.

Pay Mix. Pay mix refers to the emphasis on a particular form of pay in the total compensation package offered for a specific group of employees. Typical forms of pay include base salary, benefits and incentives (pay increases related to performance). Organization that wish to reward employee loyalty and seniority often emphasize base salary and benefits in pay mix decisions. Organizations wishing to reward employee performance -- particularly very high performance levels -- often emphasize incentives (Belcher, 1974).

Pay Incentives. The pay decisions associated with incentives require that

Pay Policies   Pay System Decisions

Design

Pay Structure & Level

1. Internal versus external equity emphasis
   - Job valuation criteria
   - Skill acquisition
   - Skill types needed
   - Pay level meets, lags leads the market

Pay Mix

2. Membership versus performance emphasis
   - % of pay in base wages
   - % of pay in benefits
   - % of pay in incentives

Pay Incentives

3. Efficiency versus growth performance emphasis
   - Timing-long/short term
   - Performance criteria
   - Amount
   - Performance criteria

Administration

Pay Communication

4. Restrictive versus open communication
   - Range of information
   - # of formal channels

Pay Centralization

5., 6. High versus low participation; authorization
   - Type of pay decision
   - Level of employee

Pay Formalization

7. High versus low formalization
   - Written regulation;
   - supervision of pay

Pay Standardization

8. High versus low standardization
   - Pay policy uniformity
   - across organization

Figure 2: Pay System Design and Administration Decisions
and Related Pay Policies

organizations determine how to best communicate to employees the broad
outlines of the performance desired. As Figure 2 indicates, there are at
least three decisions considered. The first involves the time orientation
the organization wishes to communicate and reward. By emphasizing long term
incentives (that is, pay contingent on performance over a three to five year
period) long term objectives are shown to have high priority. Alternatively,
an emphasis on short term incentives (pay contingent on a one to two year
period of performance) is a signal of the importance of short term
objectives (Ellig, 1982). The second reflects the performance emphasis
desired. Typically the literature described choices between entrepreneurial
and production (including cost control) performance criteria (for example
see March and Olsen, 1958; Galbraith, 1977). The third decision reflects
the degree of risk involved in employee attempts to perform as desired.

Pay Administration Decisions. The decisions listed under administration in
Figure 2 influence the style in which a pay system's design is developed and
maintained, day to day. The characteristics of an organization's
administration were described in the organization behavior literature as:
communication, centralization, formalization and standardization (Zey-

Ferrell, 1979). The definitions of these characteristics are extended to pay
system administration.

Communication decisions can range from an emphasis on open communication
of all types of pay information (including facts on individual salaries) to
relative restriction of information. Pay centralization decisions determine
the level at which employees participate in, and authorize, different types
of pay decisions.

Closely related to centralization are decisions that establish the
degree to which the implementation of pay system design is governed by
standard operating procedures, work rules and supervision. Examples of
formalization in a pay context might include the degree to which job
analysis, evaluation and wage surveys are governed by structured
questionnaires, evaluation manuals and established wage survey procedures.
Finally, the pay standardization decisions involve the degree to which pay is
either tailored to a specific organization unit or standardized across all
units. For example, in some firms the same performance criteria can be used
for incentives in all units. In other firms, differences in objectives may
justify establishing unique performance criteria (Salter, 1973).

Identification of Pay Policies

The literature review also suggested that the pay decisions listed in
Figure 2 might be differentially related to more aggregate pay policies.
These policies are listed in the left hand column of Figure 2, opposite the
pay decisions thought to be most directly related to each policy.

By emphasizing certain choices on the related pay decisions an
organization could communicate a specific policy intent to its employees.
For example, pay structure and level decisions emphasizing internal job
values, job specific skills, internal promotions and lagging pay levels would
tend to focus employee pay comparisons within the organization. An emphasis
on market pricing of jobs, general skills, open hiring and leading pay levels
would tend to focus employee pay comparisons outside the workplace. Choices
on pay mix decisions might be related to an emphasis on membership (base
salary and benefits) versus performance (incentives). Likewise, incentive
decisions could emphasize entrepreneurial over less risk taking production
oriented behaviors (see descriptions in Livernash, 1957; March and Simon,
1958; Belcher, 1974; Milkovich and Newman, 1984).

The many decisions making up pay administration policy could also represent distinct (albeit related) dimensions. The work of Lorsch and Allen
(1973) and Kerr (1984) suggested that policy on pay formalization might vary
with the employee level in the organization and the pay decision involved.

Pay Policy Related to Business Strategy

The second question this study investigated was, "Does pay policy vary
systematically across organizations with different business strategies?".
The literature review covered research on both strategic types and variance
in pay policy.

Strategic Types. While a wide variety of business strategies are feasible,
three distinct forms of strategy were consistently identified in the research
literature. Each type of business strategy was also associated with a
particular type of organization design and administrative style (see Burns
and Stalker, 1961; Chandler, 1962; Lawrence and Lorsch, 1967; Miles and Snow,
1978). Figure 3 depicts the three combinations of strategy, design and
administration as described by Miles and Snow (1978).

	Defender	Prospector	Analyzer
Product Market Definition	Narrow, stable product market; concerned with continued market pentration and customer service.	Changing product market emphasis; continuous search for new markets, promote reputation for innovation.	Characterized by mixed strategy; has some stable narrowly defined product markets but also some relatively innovative market definitions; tends to follow Prospectors in industry.
Technology	Single core technology with investment in improvements.	Multiple, prototype technologies; invest more in people than machines.	Some single core technologies and some investment in people and protypical technologies.
Managerial	Tends to be dominated by production, finance types, but is stable.	Tends to change often, but dominated by marketing; R&D types.	Dominated by marketing and applied research; relatively stable.
Design/ Administration	Functional division of labor, highly formalized, promotion from within, centralized.	Divisional or product centered division of labor; few formal work rules or standards, internal labor market relatively open, decentralized.	Divisionalized or matrix structure; combination of decentralized unstructured work and centralized formalized work activity.
Performance Criteria	Performance standards established and compared to past performance. Standards based on cost savings.	Performance measured on market outcomes compared against key competitors.	Performance measured on a combination of cost efficiency standards and markets outcome comparisons.
Organization	American Brands Lincoln Electric	Phillip Morris, USA Hewlett Packard	R.J. Reynolds Texas Instruments

Figure 3. Strategic Business Unit Types (Miles & Snow, 1978)

These three strategic types of organization are: Defenders, Prospectors and Analyzers. The Defender has a narrowly defined, stable products market strategy; its structural design is functional; and its administrative style tends to be centralized, formal and standardized. The Prospector, on the other hand, emphasizes an innovative, dynamic approach to product market definition; it's structural design tends to be divisional or product-based; and its administrative style, decentralized, informal and nonstandardized. The Analyzer is characterized by a mixed product market strategy in which some of its product markets are stable and narrowly defined, but other are more dynamic and innovative. Analyzers often have matrix or divisional type structural designs with administrative styles representing some combination of those typical of Defenders and Prospectors.

<u>Variance in Pay Policy Dimensions</u>. Figure 4 summarizes proposals about how pay policy dimensions might be expected to vary with strategic type. Each of the eight pay policies presented earlier (Figure 2, left hand column) are listed. The pattern of pay policies associated with the strategic types reflects the Miles and Snow (1983) descriptions of the human resource policies typical of each.

For example, they indicate that the human resource policies of Defenders emphasize job specific skills, retention, promotion from within and production or cost based performance criteria. Pay design compatible with these policies might emphasize internal equity, membership rewards and

<u>Strategy Organization Types</u>

<u>Policy Dimensions</u>	<u>Defender</u>	<u>Prospector</u>	<u>Analyzer</u>
<u>Pay Design</u>			
1. Internal vs. External Equity	Internal	External	Combination
2. Membership vs. Performance Emphasis	Membership	Performance	Combination
3. Efficiency vs. Growth Emphasis	Efficiency	Growth	Combination
<u>Pay Administration</u>			
4. Restrictive vs. Open Communication	Restrictive	Open	Mixed
5., 6. High vs. Low Centralization			
Participation	Low	High	Moderate
Authorization	Low	High	Moderate
7. High vs. Low Formalization	High	Low	Moderate
8. High vs. Low Standardization	High	Low	Moderate

Figure 4: Proposed Variance in Pay Policy by Strategic Organization Type

production based incentives. Prospectors were seen as emphasizing general skills, hiring at all levels of organization and pursuing entrepreneurial performance objectives. A compatible pay design for Prospectors might emphasize external equity, performance rewards and pay incentives based on creative or innovative behavior. The Analyzer, with human resource policies that combine aspects of the other two types, might be expected to have a mixed pay design. Support for these patterns is also found in Livernash, 1957; Doeringer and Piore, 1971; Galbraith, 1977; Lawler, 1981; Salscheider, 1981; Ellig, 1982; Kerr, 1984; and Milkovich and Newman, 1984.

With regard to pay administration factors, the proposed pattern of variance is an extension of each type's administrative style. Defenders are more centralized, formalized and standardized. Therefore, their style of pay system administration might be expected to follow suit. Prospectors are described as having more decentralized, informal and nonstandardized as well. The pay administration of the Analyzers might be expected to represent a middle ground between the other extremes.

EMPIRICAL INVESTIGATION OF PAY POLICIES

Procedure

A survey based on mailed questionnaires was considered the best way to cost effectively sample pay decisions in a large number of organizations. The questionnaire covered decisions on pay structure and level, mix, incentives and administration. It also covered decisions on business strategy, organization design and administration. A pilot group of fifteen compensation professionals reviewed the questionnaire. The members of this group represented a variety of industry and geographic backgrounds. They suggested improvements in the questionnaire, identified compensation directors as the most appropriate respondent group and provided a definition of middle managers. Respondents were asked to focus on middle management pay.

Target Population and Sample

One thousand firms in four digit, manufacturing, Standard Industrial Classification (hereafter, SIC) codes were selected as the study's target population. The COMPUSTAT data base (maintained by Investors Management Sciences, Inc.) was used to identify these firms. The four digits SIC codes were considered proxies for a firm's product market and strategic business unit. (A firm was assigned to a four digit SIC code based on the product market from which it drew the largest proportion of its revenues.) Only firms with the same SIC code between 1981 and 1984 were included in the target population. This was done to assure some stability in product market association. In addition, only firms with an average employee population of at least 100 over this same period were considered. It is more likely that organizations of this size would have pay policy covering middle managers.

Respondents for approximately 60 per cent of the firms in the population were identified through the annual membership directory of the American Compensation Association. The remaining 40 per cent were identified in the STANDARD AND POORS DIRECTORY (Vol. III, 1984). The survey response rate was 20$, resulting in a sample of 208 firms. This rate is typical of other studies using questionnaires of similar length (DeBejar, 1983).

As Figure 5 demonstrates, the sample was not representative. The sample firms had significantly higher net sales and employment levels than non participating firms. The distribution of firms across the manufacturing SIC codes differed also. One third of the sample firms were in machinery, except electrical and electronic/electrical equipment manufacturing.

Measures	Nonparticipants (N=797)	Participants (N=208)	Population (N=1000)
NETSALES (in thousands)			
MEAN	1338.76	2544.3	1564.00
STD	5571.57	6787.9	5826.70
NUMBER EMPLOYEES (in thousands)			
MEAN	11.35	20.09	13.00
STD	35.11	44.10	36.97
SID CODE DISTRIBUTION (%)			
20 Food and Kindred Products	5.6	8.6	6.2
21 Tobacco Manufactures	0.5	1.0	0.5
22 Textile Mill Products	1.9	—	1.5
23 Apparel and Other Products (Fabric)	—	—	—
24 Lumber and Wood Products (exc. Furniture)	1.9	0.5	1.6
25 Furniture and Fixtures	1.1	0.5	1.6
26 Paper and Allied Products	1.7	0.5	1.4
27 Printing, Publishing, and Allied Industries	5.0	2.0	4.4
28 Chemicals and Allied Products	8.9	7.6	8.8
29 Petroleum Refining	3.1	6.1	3.7
30 Rubber and Misc. Plastic Products	2.7	2.5	2.7
31 Leather and Leather Products	2.3	—	1.8
32 Stone, Clay, Glass, Concrete Products	2.7	5.1	3.2
33 Primary Metal Industries	5.7	6.1	5.8
34 Fabricated Metal Products exc. Machines, Transport	8.5	5.1	7.8
35 Machinery except electrical	16.0	20.3	16.8
36 Electrical and Electronic Machinery	15.6	18.3	16.2
37 Transportation Equipment	6.0	11.2	6.9
38 Measuring, Analyzing, Photo, Medical, Optical	6.8	4.1	6.3
39 Miscellaneous Manufacturing	3.9	0.5	3.3

Figure 5: Sample Representativesness

3. Does the pay level (actual average rate paid) for your unit tend to exceed the pay
    levels (actual) of your competitors?

1	2	3	4	5
Seldom; this unit tends to set pay levels below those of its competitors; the unit compensates employees in other ways.		Sometimes; but more often, the unit simply tries to meet competitors' pay levels.		Usually; the unit tends to set pay levels above those of its competitors.

Figure 6: Example of Pay Level Item on Questionnaire

Questionnaire Measures

Pay Decisions. The decisions identified in the literature were used to
develop measures of pay policy. Pay structure, level and incentive measures
were based on five point, anchored scales. For example, a pay level item was
phased as shown on Figure 6.

Measures of pay mix reflected the percentage that base salary, benefits
and incentives each represented in a middle manager's total pay. Pay
centralization measures represented the number of lower level managers who
participated in, or authorized, ten different pay decisions (ranging from
compensation philosophy to budgets). Communication measures involved the
number of formal channels over which seven kinds of pay information were
circulated. (These ranged from policy manuals to formal grievance
procedures.) Measures of pay formalization involved twenty different items
such as, "There are established guidelines on how to conduct wage surveys.
To what extent does this statement represent your pay policy?--(1) very
little; (3) moderately; (5) to a great extent." Seventy pay policy decision
were measured.

In general, questions were written so that the higher the scale score (5
is high), the more likely that the associated decision would represent a
highly developed internal labor market (internal promotion, job specific
skills, and so forth) and a centralized, formal and standardized style of pay
administration.

Measures of Strategic Type. Questionnaire measures of strategic type were
based on the Miles and Snow descriptions of Defenders, Prospectors, and
Analyzers. There were four measures--one on product market definition;
another on the business unit's reputation for product market innovation; a
third on the area of expertise or the function from which top management was
drawn; and the fourth, on the organization's general structure and
administrative style. In general, the higher the score (5) on these scales,
the more likely the organization was a Defender.

An index of an organization's overall business strategy was developed by
adding each firm's scores on the four questionnaire measures of strategic
type. These sums were then averaged, and the means and standard deviations
were calculated. Defenders were defined as firms with an average score more
than one standard deviation below the mean (less than 2.67); and Analyzers
were defined as firms with scores that fell within one standard deviation of
the mean (inclusive).

Control Measures. In addition to the measures on pay and strategic type, the
survey questionnaire included measures of respondent characteristics and
business unit age. The COMPUSTAT data base also included measures of
employment size, net sales and other industry characteristics. These

measures were used as control variables in sample analysis.

Levels of Analysis. The study survey was designed to compare pay policy across organization strategic types. The Miles and Snow typology was chosen as a measure of strategic type primarily because it allowed this kind of comparison. Theoretically, Defenders, Prospectors and Analyzers can be identified in all product markets. Strategic types might thus be compared without further stratification of the sample by product market. The primary unit of analysis in this study was organization strategic type. Within strategic type, measures of pay were limited to decisions concerning middle management. The middle management group was selected because their pay typically reflects a broader range of policy decisions than that of lower level employees, yet is considered less confidential than executive pay.

ANALYSIS AND RESULTS

Summary Profile of Sample Measures

The sample descriptive statistics indicated that the measures of pay decisions were normally distributed. Design decisions were slightly skewed toward a higher emphasis on internal equity, membership pay and incentives based on cost control performance criteria. The administration decisions indicated that sample firms tended to centralize pay decision making and standardize pay policies. Their pay administration was only moderately formalized. Overall, there was not a lot of variance in the sample pay measures. Measures of strategic type were also slightly skewed toward higher scale scores; that is, toward the Defender strategic type.

Measures of Pay Policy

Measures of pay decisions were factor analyzed for the entire sample. The resulting seven factors selected to represent these decisions are presented in Figure 7. The factors accounted for 61.1% of the variance in the sample.

The first four factors to emerge in the analysis were very like the proposed pay policies on participation, authorization, formalization and standardization identified in the literature review (compare Figures 2 and 7). The survey measures most closely related to these factors were those on participation in pay decisions, authorization of pay decisions, the regulation of pay policy and uniformity in the application of pay policy. The factor on external competitiveness covered survey measures on pay level decisions (Factor 5 in Figure 7). The membership versus performance factor covered decisions on pay mix and the efficiency versus growth factor covered decisions on performance criteria used for incentive awards. These are Factors 6 and 7 in Figure 7.

Pay scales were then developed from the seven factors that emerged in sample analysis. Each of the pay scales might be interpreted as follows: High scores on participation (1) and authorization (2) scales indicate that lower level managers are involved in discussing and approving a variety of pay decision; high formalization scores (scale 3) indicate that the business unit's pay structure and level decisions are made and implemented in a regulated fashion; and high standardization scores (scale 4) suggest that pay policy is uniform across divisions or departments. High scores on the external competitiveness (scale 5) imply that the pay level policy of the firm is closer to leading than lagging its competitor' pay levels; and high scores on the membership versus performance scale (6) suggest an emphasis on membership rewards (base salary and benefits) in pay mix decisions. Finally, a high score on the efficiency versus growth performance scale (7) indicated a concern with growth oriented performance criteria.

Emergent Pay Policy Factors	Factor Scale Description	Variance Explained %	Cumulative %
1. Participation	Level of managers partici- pating in pay plan decisions	18.8	18.8
2. Authorization	Level of managers approving pay plan decisions	12.2	31.0
3. Formalization	Degree to which pay plan design and administration is regulated	7.4	38.4
4. Standardization	Similarity of pay plans across business units	6.5	44.9
5. Degree External Competitiveness	Degree to which units pay level leads the competition	6.2	51.2
6. Membership v. Performance	Degree to which pay mix emphasizes membership rewards	5.1	56.3
7. Efficiency v. Growth	Degree to which performance rewards are based on cost criteria	4.8	61.1

Figure 7: A Seven Factor Model of Pay Policy Decisions:
Summary of Factor Analysis Results

<u>Analysis of Pay Policy Variance by Strategic Type</u>

The next step in the analysis was to classify each of the sample firms
as a Defender, Prospector or Analyzer. The firms were placed according to
their scores on the overall index of business strategy. The pay scales
described above were then compared across the three groups of firms. The
results of descriptive comparison are presented in Figure 8.

The pattern of pay scale difference across Defenders, Prospectors and
Analyzers was very like the pattern suggested in the literature review
(compare Figures 4 and 8). Defenders, for example, had lower scores on
efficiency versus growth performance scales. This suggests a concern with
cost based performance criteria. Prospectors, on the other hand, had higher
scores on this scale. This suggests a concern with growth oriented
performance criteria. Analyzers scores fell mid-scale. These descriptive
statistics suggested some support for the patterns of policy variance
derived from the literature.

The significance of mean differences in these scales across types was
also analyzed. The results suggest that when viewed as a composite of all
seven pay scales, policy did differ across strategy types. (These comparisons were done using multi-variate analysis of variance techniques.)
However, when analyzed individually, the means of only three scales differed
significantly by tape. (These comparisons were done using one-way analysis
of variance techniques, controlling for the firm's level of employment.)
These were the participation (1); author-ization (2); and efficiency versus
growth performance (7) scales. Overall, these results suggest that while
differences in pay policies do exist among strategic types, the differences
are not always significant.

DISCUSSION AND CONCLUSION

<u>The Two Basic Questions Investigated</u>

The first question this study investigated was, "Can a set of important
organization pay decisions be identified and measured?". The literature
identified these decisions and suggested that they might be related to more
aggregate pay policies. Measures of these pay decisions were developed and
used in a survey of middle management pay policy in 208 manufacturing firms.
These measures were factor analyzed and the emergent factors compared to the
pay policies suggested in the literature. The comparisons were favorable,
and the factors, once scaled can be used as measures of pay policy. These
measures are an improvement over those previously available. They are based
on an integrated search of the pay literature, and represent a broader range
of pay decisions than has been studied to date. They were quantified, and
based on a large sample of firms. This will make their replication easier.

There were some intriguing issues surrounding these measures, however.
Several pay structure, incentive, and communication decisions ere not
clearly related to any of the factors that emerged in analysis. In the case
of pay communication and incentive decisions this could be attributed to
problems with the questionnaire measures. Despite pilot testing, the survey
responses to these items were confused and sometimes inconsistent. Since
the questions designed to measure pay communication and incentive decisions
were based on the available literature, this suggests that a more
qualitative investigation may be needed. It should emphasize both the
organizational definition and range of these decisions.

In the case of pay structure decisions the problem is not so clear.
The survey respondents did not appear to be confused regarding the pay
structure items. And the items covered the domain of decisions discussed in

	Defenders(N=35)			Analyzers(N=136)			Prospectors(N=37)		
	Mean	Std.	Range	Mean	Std.	Range	Mean	Std.	Range
Pay Policy Scales									
(1) Participation	56.1	29.3	109.8	60.4	22.1	118.9	63.9	26.3	108.3
(2) Authorization	57.8	21.6	118.3	53.9	16.2	88.4	59.3	15.7	53.1
(3) Formalization	5.7	1.3	5.2	5.2	1.4	6.9	5.1	1.5	5.7
(4) Standardization	5.8	1.7	5.7	5.9	1.4	6.1	5.6	1.1	4.1
(5) External Competitiveness	.94	.20	.87	.93	.23	1.2	1.1	.24	.87
(6) Membership vs. Performance	2.95	.28	1.1	2.95	.34	2.1	2.97	.51	2.8
(7) Efficiency vs. Growth	1.3	.59	1.4	1.7	.61	2.7	1.9	.76	2.7
Business Strategy	4.2	.26	1	3.3	.33	1	2.2	.41	1.5
Business Age	51.7	36.4	96	53.3	29.2	94	44.8	31.2	97
Net Sales *	4989	12259	59922	2070	4490	28070	1944	5667	34350
Number of Employees *	17.9	34.2	187.9	21.9	44.6	366.9	23.9	62.0	364.6

* Numbers in thousands

Figure 8. Variance in Pay Policies for Defenders, Analyzers and Prospectors

the literature. Indeed these were the decisions considered crucial to an
organization's internal or external pay equity orientation. While the
results are specific to this sample, it is possible that some unidentified
pay structure decisions need to be included in the measurement of this
construct. Again, more in-depth case study may be called for.

The second question this study investigated was, "Do pay policies vary
systematically with differences in business strategy?". Simple comparisons
of pay scale means across Defenders, Analyzers and Prospectors supported the
notion that pay policy does indeed vary with strategic type (see Figure 7)
in this sample. The patterns of variance observed were similar to those
proposed in the literature review. Moreover, when differences in the joint
distribution of all seven pay scales were tested across strategic types, the
results were significant.

When individual pay scales were compared across strategic types,
however, only the participation, authorization and cost versus growth
performance scales were significantly different. The most straightforward
interpretation of these findings is that, in this sample, the only
significant variation in pay policy for middle managers was related to
differences in the degree to which pay decisions are centralized. While the
other scales did vary as the literature would suggest, that literature was
based on case studies and speculation. Also, the case studies were not
always specific to a particular employee group pay.

There are several other possible interpretations. The results may be
due to error in the measurement of either pay decisions or strategic type.
The questionnaire measures used in this study were new. Case studies were
suggested to improve pay measures. Sample firms could also be retyped using
another measure of business strategy. Pay policy variance could then be
reanalyzed to see if the pattern across types remains the same. Further,
the full range of policy variation may not be observed in a sample
restricted to manufacturing firms. A more heterogeneous sample may be
required.

<u>Conclusion</u>

This study set out to identify and develop measures of important pay
policies and to investigate variance in these policies across organizations
with different types of business strategy. Both these objectives were met.
The measures of pay policy developed were an improvement over those
previously available in the literature, although they need to be replicated.
The results also provided some empirical support for the notion that pay
policy might vary with business strategy. The overall pattern of variance
identified here may provide a step toward a descriptive measure of "fit"
between pay policy and business strategy.

Earlier in this paper the importance of pay policy "fit" was related to
the concepts of congruency and contingency. Pay policy that is congruent
with organization design and administration is believed to enhance employee
perceptions of pay equity and thus, motivation to perform. One measure of
pay policy congruency would be the strength and the direction of the
association between detailed measures of organization strategy, design and
administration and similar measures of pay policy. The pay measures
identified in this study provide a foundation for further investigation.

Pay policy that is contingent on business strategy is believed to
improve the link between pay and the employee behaviors needed to support
that strategy. One way of measuring pay policy contingency would be to
identify profiles of policy differences that are associated with different
types of business strategies. This study's identification of patterns of

pay policy like those proposed in the literature suggests that such measures
are feasible.

Measures of pay policy congruency and contingency are important to the
development of the notion of pay policy "fit". They are required to test
the question of more practical interest--"Does pay policy that "fits"
business strategy improve organization performance?". The results of the
present study represent a necessary first step in examining the implications
of pay policy "fit" for organization performance.

REFERENCES

Belcher, David W. Compensation Administration. (Englewood Cliffs, NJ:
   Prentice-Hall, Inc., 1974).

Burns, Tom and G.M. Stalker, The Management of Innovation, (London,
   England: Tavistock Publications, 1961).

Chandler, Alfred D. Jr. Strategy and Structure, (New York, NY: Doubleday
   Books, 1962).

Debejar, Gloria and George T. Milkovich, Human Resource Management and
   Business Strategy Survey. (Ithaca, NY: New York State School of
   Industrial Relation, Cornell University, 1983).

Doeringer, Peter B. and Michael J. Piore, Internal Labor Markets and
   Manpower Analysis, (Lexington, MA: Heath-Lexington Books, 1971).

Dyer, Lee and Roland Theriault, "The Determinants of Pay Satisfaction,"
   Journal of Applied Psychology, No. 5, (September, 1976) pp. 596-604.

Ellig, Bruce R. "Compensation Elements: Market Phase Determines the Mix,"
   Compensation Review, Third Quarter (1981) pp. 30-38.

Galbraith, Jay R. Organization Design, (Reading, MA: Addison-Wesley, 1977).

Kerr, Jeffrey, "Diversification Strategies and Managerial Rewards: An
   Empirical Study," Working Paper, Southern Methodist University, Dallas,
   Texas, 1984.

Lawler, Edward E. III, Pay and Organization Development, (Menlo Park, CA:
   Addison-Wesley, 1981).

Lawrence, Paul R. and Jay R. Lorsch, Organization and Environment: Managing
   Differentiation and Integration, (Boston, MA: Graduate School of Business,
   Harvard University, 1967).

Livernash, Robert E. "The Internal Wage Structure," in George W. Taylor and
   Frank G. Pierson (Eds.) New Concepts in Wage Determination, (New York,
   NY: McGraw-Hill, 1957).

Lorsch, Jay R. and John J. Morse, Organizations and Their Members, (New
   York, NY: Harper and Row, 1974).

Lorsch, Jay R. and Stephen A. Allen, Managing Diversity and Interdependence:
   An Organizational Study of Multi-divisional Firms, (Boston, MA: Graduate
   School of Business Administration, Harvard University, 1973).

Mahoney, Thomas A. Compensation and Reward Perspectives, (Homewood, IL: Richard D. Irwin, 1979).

March, James G. and Herbert A. Simon, Organizations, (New York, NY: John Wiley and Sons, 1958).

Miles, Raymond E. and Charles C. Snow, Organizational Strategy, Structure, and Process, (New York, NY: McGraw-Hill, 1978).

Miles, Raymond E. and Charles C. Snow, "Organizational Strategy, Design, and Human Resources," Working Paper, University of Pennsylvania, 1983.

Milkovich, George T. and Jerry M. Newman, Compensation, (Plano, TX: Business Publications, Inc., 1984).

Saischeider, James, "Devising Pay Strategies for Diversified Companies," Compensation Review, First Quarter (1981) pp. 14-22.

Salter, Malcolm S. "Taylor Incentive Compensation to Strategy," Harvard Business Review, Vol. 51 (1973) pp 94-102.

Zey-Ferrell, Mary (Ed.) Readings on Dimensions of Organizations: Environment, Context, Structure, Process, and Performance, (Santa Monica, CA: Goodyear Publishing, 1979).

HUMAN RESOURCE COSTS AND BUSINESS STRATEGY: STRIVING FOR

COMPETITIVE ADVANTAGE IN THE PHARMACEUTICAL INDUSTRY

Ira T. Kay* and Martin Leshner**

*The Hay Group, Inc.
 One Dag Hammarskjold Plaza
 New York, NY 10017

**AMEV Holdings, Inc.
 New York, NY

INTRODUCTION

Control over staffing levels and costs is a critical component in the
competitive positioning and resultant profitability of many industries.
Ideal staff size in a rapidly changing business environment is a major
concern to most managers. Staff levels are a function of many variables,
including the strategic thrust of the organization. Simply reviewing
current business plans to determine optimal staffing levels is not
sufficient. It is also important to track historical data that reflect the
effects of different strategies and economic situations on staff size, or
make comparisons with competitor staffing levels against their strategies.

We have found that within any industry there is great variability in
personnel costs, often with no apparent justification. Understanding the
components of these costs and linking them to the business strategies is an
important step for all businesses given the impact of human resource costs
on profitability. The information needed by most companies to develop
optimal human resource cost strategies to maintain competitive advantage and
appropriate margins is generally unavailable. This paper presents the
findings of a recent study of the pharmaceutical industry which analyzed
human resource cost structures in detail. These data are compared with
strategic and organizational data for the pharmaceutical industry in order
to determine the relationship between these important factors and optimal
staff levels. While this work represents the findings of the pharmaceutical
industry, we believe the results are applicable to other industries as well.

THE PHARMACEUTICAL INDUSTRY

By most measures, the pharmaceutical industry is considered the most
financially successful industry in the United States. The results of a
study on 1983 Return on Equity and Five-Year Growth in EPS (_Business Week_,
March 221, 1984) reveal that the pharmaceutical industry's ROE was 19.6%,
compared with 11.5% for all industries; and the five-year growth in EPS was
10%, compared with 0% for all industries.

In general, the pharmaceutical companies are positioned for maintaining their high levels of financial performance over the next five to ten years. This is even more valid for the domestic pharmaceutical units (DPU) within the pharmaceutical companies primarily because the strong dollar has hurt international sales. In addition, may international pharmaceutical companies have medical equipment units that are becoming less profitable.

However, there are issues facing the domestic pharmaceutical industry which create both opportunities and challenges. The favorable demographic situation in the United States, particularly the large aging population, creates tremendous potential for growth; it also creates increased competition. The health care cost containment movement and the significant number of patent expirations that will occur over the next three to five years also create significant challenges. Therefore, despite a high level of current and historical financial performance, this industry has significant motivation to develop and implement effective competitive strategies. Two key aspects of these strategies include the development of major new drugs (anti-arthritis, antibiotics, etc.) and effective cost management. One might predict the more traditional "smokestack" industries to be extremely cost-sensitive; nevertheless, the pharmaceutical industry is equally sensitive to this issue if only to avoid the problems that other traditional industries have faced during the past five to ten years. While human resource (HR) costs obviously are not the only costs incurred by the DPUs (e.g., chemical compounds, capital equipment, G&A), they do represent 20% of sales and are generally considered to be the most controllable expenditure.

HOW THE SURVEY WORKS

The survey had the following specific objectives:

o   To compare human resource cost and staffing levels for line and staff organizations for a selected group of domestic pharmaceutical units; and

o   To develop the linkages of financial performance, product diversity, business strategy and organizational effectiveness with human resource costs.

The methodology used to perform this analysis is called the Human Resource Cost Strategy (HURCOS) model. HURCOS is a three-step consulting process which utilizes data from a variety of human resource areas. The first phase of the process consists of a series of on-site interviews and tailored questionnaires to gather essential data on: _business strategy_ - the relationship between market attractiveness, competitive strength and strategic business objectives; _organizational structure_ - an understanding of how business diversity and corporate strategy effect optimal organizational structure; and _human resource practices_ - the areas of compensation, benefits and human resource planning.

In the second phase, HURCOS draws comparisons between each company and its strategic competitors. Human resource cost and productivity data are gathered from the strategic competitors - all on a strictly voluntary and confidential basis. The data are structured to fit the organization of the sponsoring client. Using this information, each organization's competitive standing is measured on several key human resource cost and productivity dimensions.

The final phase of the study links business strategy to human resource

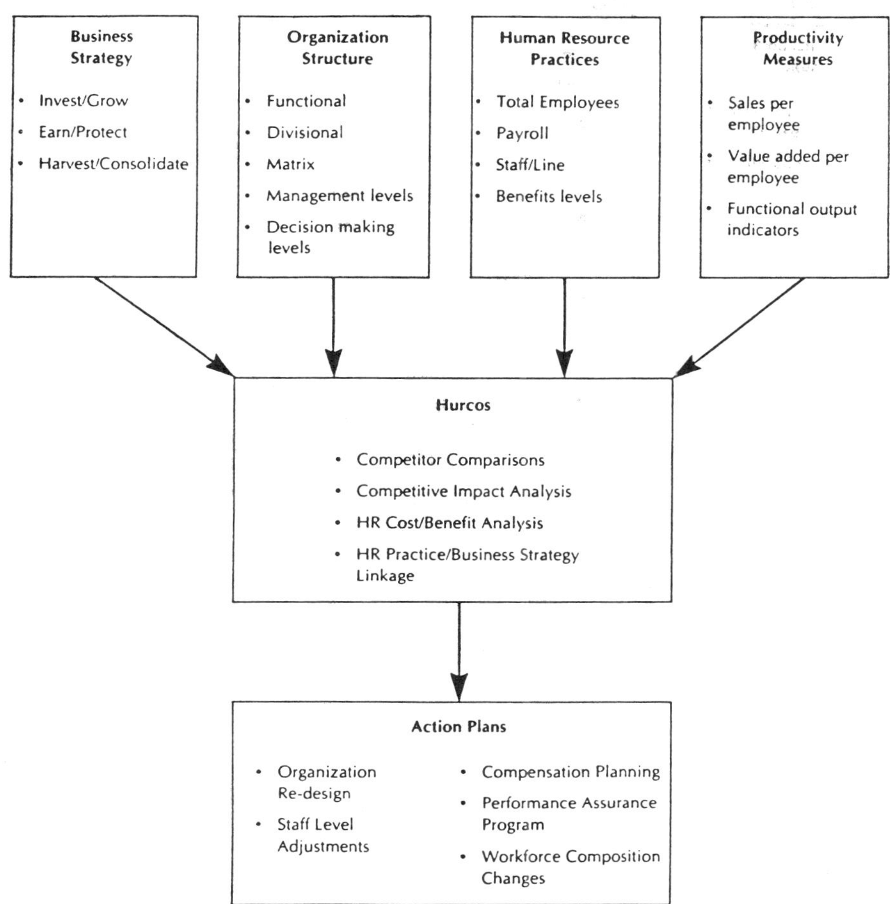

Figure 1: The HURCOS Process

cost structure. With the competitive dimension and human resource analyses complete, significant industry trends are assessed, and the human resource cost structure that is linked to the strategic goals is then identified. Subsequent recommendations for change include organizational streamlining, compensation planning, work force composition changes, staffing adjustments, performance assurance programs and/or benefits planning. Figure 1 illustrates this model.

The fundamental concept of the model show that a particular company's human resource cost structure emanates directly from its business strategies and organizational structure. For example, a company organized in a matrix, with overlapping accountability and jobs, would tend to have higher human resource costs than a company which is organized in a functional manner. (For a more detailed analysis of this linkage, see "Organization, Diversity and Performance," by Cassano/Nathanson, <u>Wharton Magazine</u>, Summer 1982). Furthermore, we would predict that a company with a complex business strategy would have higher costs then one with a simpler strategy. The cost structure can then be broken down into staffing levels, compensation patterns and the composition, i.e., the percentage of executives, exempt employees and nonexempt employees.

SURVEY PARTICIPANTS, HR COSTS AND PROFITABILITY

<u>Survey Participants</u>

The survey participants include 11 of the U.S.'s largest pharmaceutical manufacturers who are outstanding financial performers. We have not listed the company names to protect their confidentiality. We used revenue levels for the DPUs which were available from the individual companies, and, like profitability, are proprietary and therefore confidential. It should also be noted that complete data were collected for nine of the eleven companies and that partial data were used for various components of the analysis.

<u>HR Costs and Profitability</u>

Human resource costs are defined as payroll plus benefits covering all line and staff, exempt and nonexempt employees. It includes regular pay plus overtime and bonuses. The fundamental question facing organizations regarding cost structure is whether reducing their human resource costs will in fact increase their financial performance. Given specific types of strategies and organization structures, and one organization may explicitly desire to have higher costs provided they comprise a short-term investment which will generate higher profitability over the long term. It is, therefore, a pragmatic decision as to whether human resource costs are positively or negatively associated with financial performance.

In reorganizing or reducing their head counts, most companies make the explicit assumption that reducing their cost will increase their financial performance, certainly in the short run and probably in the long run. However, this probably depends upon the fundamental structure and strategy of the particular industry and may in fact vary with different industries. Defining high-cost companies as those that are above average and low-cost companies as those that are below average, we can draw the following conclusion: in the pharmaceutical industry, companies with <u>low human resource costs have high levels of financial performance</u>. Table 1 below presents the relationship between human resource costs for both staff and line employees and one-year and three-year corporate return on equity.

Table 1

Relationship Between Human Resource Costs and Return of Equity

Total Employees Human Resource Costs	Average Corporate Return on Equity (1983)	Average Corporate Return on Equity (1981-1983)
High Cost Companies	14.4	14.6
Low Cost Companies	22.7	21

Functional Staff Human Resource Costs	Average Corporate Return of Equity (1983)	Average Corporate Return of Equity (1981-1983)
High Cost Companies	13.9	14.6
Low Cost Companies	20.7	19.5

We believe that there are two reasons why human resource costs are
associated with financial performance in the pharmaceutical industry.
First, and most obvious, high expenses in any form, including payroll and
benefits, would tend to reduce profits. Second, and perhaps equally
important, is that organizations with limited head count, and which are
generally "lean," are probably more responsive to the marketplace in their
capacity to monitor the marketplace and adopt their strategies.

HUMAN RESOURCE COST STRUCTURE - RESULTS

One appropriate measure of human resource cost is as percentage of
total revenue. Figure 2 presents the primary findings of this survey.These
results are for both line and staff organizations and are quite startling in
their implications: the company with the highest human resource costs is
73% higher than the lowest cost company. As discussed in Section IV, the
implications for profitability are of utmost significance. We also examined
the human resource cost structure for staff functions.

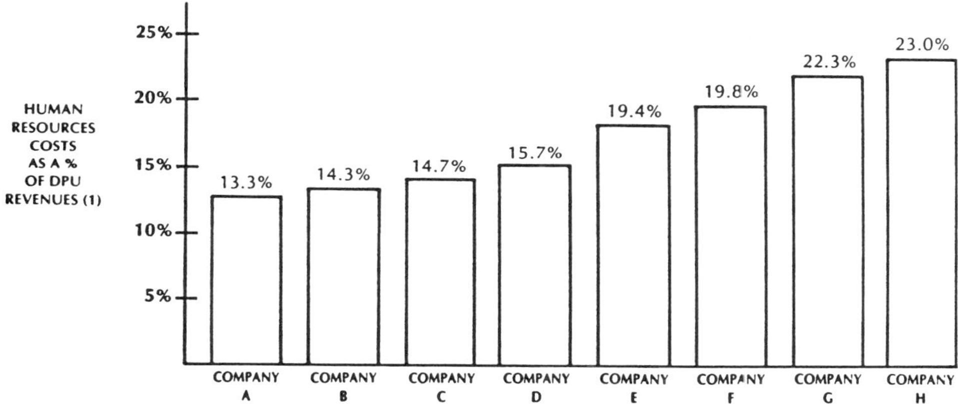

Figure 2: Domestic Pharmaceutical Unit Human Resource Costs: Line and Staff

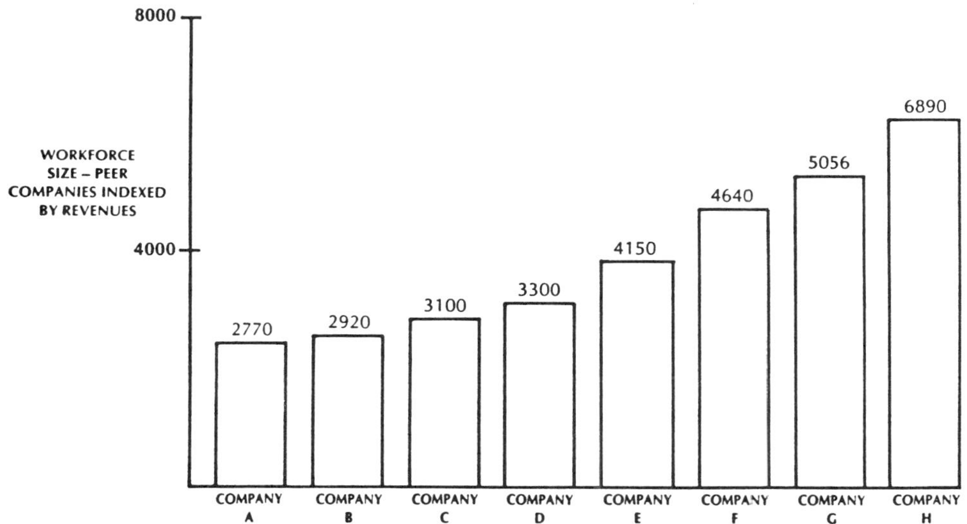

Figure 3: Total Domestic Pharmaceutical Unit Headcount

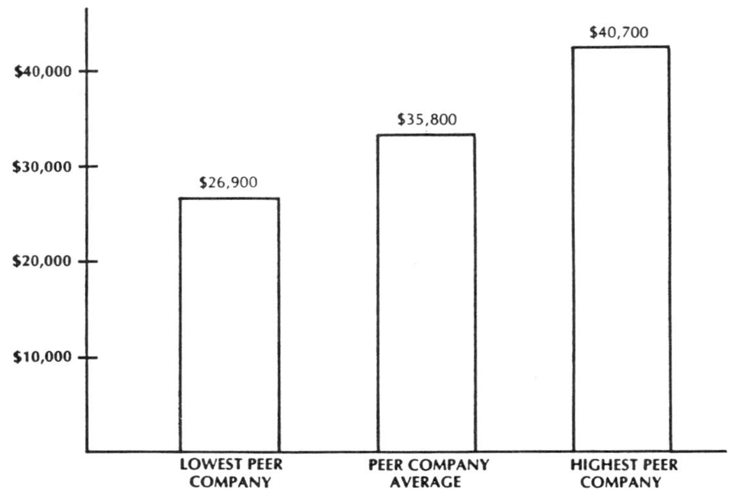

Figure 4:   Payroll Per Employee (Exempt and Non-Exempt)

The next question relates to accounting for these differences in human resource costs. Our model suggests that there are three potential areas that could account for these differences:

o   Head count Levels

o   Compensation Levels

o   Composition

Figures 3, 4, and 5 present the results of the analysis of head count, compensation and composition. However, analysis of these results reveals that the only statistically valid positive relationship is between HR costs and head count (R=.94). In fact, those companies with lower human resource costs overall tended to have <u>above-average</u> compensation levels. We conclude from this that low-cost companies pay very well, manage their head count

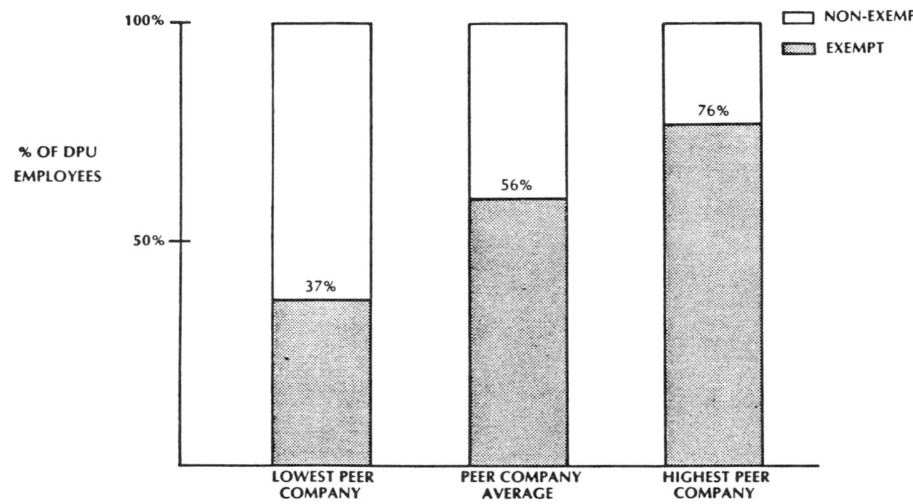

Figure 5:   Employee Mix

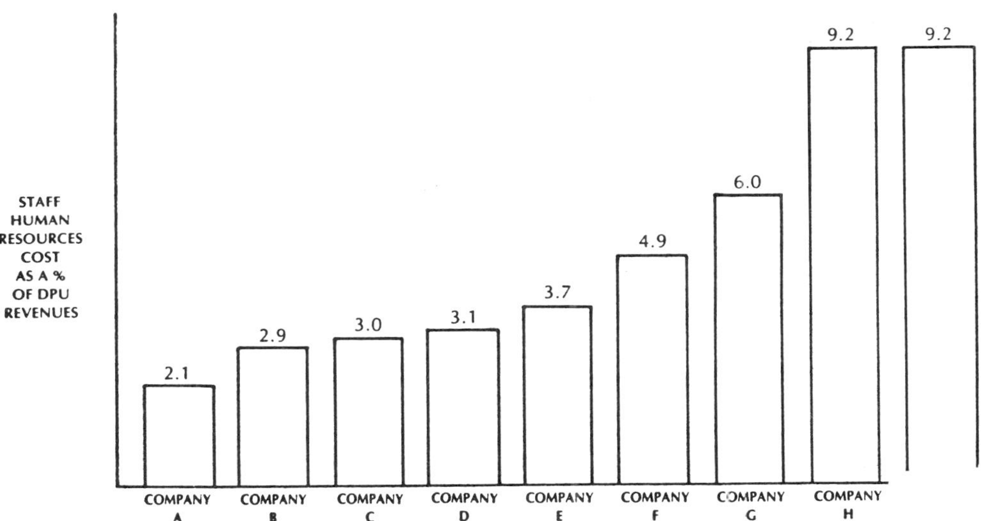

Figure 6: Staff Human Resource Costs

extremely carefully and demand high levels of performance. It is interesting to note, however, that while there is positive statistical significance only with head count, there is significant dispersion from highest to lowest in all three measures, namely 150% for head count, 51% for compensation and 105% for composition. The key conclusion is that the primary factor which influences human resource costs is head count.

These staff functions were: marketing support, market research, medical affairs, medical communications and education, civic relations, human resources, planning, information systems and the control function. Other functions (research, purchasing, etc.) were excluded since these functions were not present in all DPUs.

Figure 6 presents the results of these analyses for the survey participants. As was the case for the line and staff human resource cost results, the strongest explanatory factor for human resource cost is head count levels. High head count levels yielded high human resource costs.

ORGANIZATION STRUCTURE AND BUSINESS STRATEGY

In general, our research has shown that high organizational complexity is associated with high human resource costs. Organizational complexity is a function of a number of factors, including management layers, divisional self containment, span of control, etc. One striking finding in examining the organization structures of the DPUs of major pharmaceutical companies is the similarity among their organizations. We believe that this is explained by a number of factors, including: the similar business strategies (as defined below) among these companies; the need to be responsive to the Food and Drug Administration; and the basic simplicity of these organizations, namely production and sales units with modest levels of staff support. The implication for human resource costs is that since there is little or no variation in organizational complexity among the strategic competitors, little or no relationship to human resource costs was found.

The relationship to business strategies is somewhat different. We examined the relationship between a number of strategic variables and human resource costs. Two measures which were significantly related to human

resource costs were _revenue growth_ and the _diversity of the product line_.
The prediction would be that those companies which grow rapidly would have
levels of staff cost, as the staff growth might lag behind revenue growth.
In addition, one might predict that those DPUs with relatively concentrated
product lines (i.e., revenue from major projects as a percent of total
revenue), such as Smith-Kline and Tagamet, would have relatively low human
resource costs. There are economies of scale in the sales, production and
staff areas from supporting a relatively narrow product line. The specific
results of this analysis are presented below in Table 2.

There appear to be relationships between these two strategic measures
and human resource costs. While these results are associative, and not
causal, there are significant implications for management. For example, a
company with high human resource costs may not be able to easily reduce its
human resource costs without pruning its product line; as another example, a
company that is looking for modest growth should manage its human resource
costs extremely diligently.

HUMAN RESOURCE PLANNING IMPLICATIONS

The implications of this study are significant for the pharmaceutical
industry as well as other industries which may or may not be performing well
at present. Specific strategic measures are related to human resource
costs, and those human resource costs are related to profitability. When
companies are evaluating changing their competitive strategies, _they should
consider the human resource cost implications_.

Those companies which enjoy relatively low staff costs have both an
opportunity and a challenge. The _challenge_ stems from line management's
desire to increase staff levels. The _opportunity_ is to maintain high levels
of profitability primarily through maintenance of a growth strategy or a
concentrated product line. They must also remember the important linkage of
human resource cost to profitability. It becomes important for high-growth,
high-profitability companies to understand the possible need for staff
reductions as their markets decline or as their competitive strategies
change.

Those companies that have relatively high levels of human resource
costs are equally in a bind. Their human resource costs may be a result of
either explicit strategic plans or from historical accidents of diversified
product lines and relatively low levels of growth. In order to modify human
resource costs, the solution is more complex than simply reducing head
count. The reason is that those higher levels of people are probably needed
to support a relatively broad product line. This makes the challenge of
managing human resource costs - a critical strategic challenge facing all
industries, and the pharmaceutical industry in particular - that much more
difficult.

Table 2

Human Resource Costs and Domestic Pharmaceutical Unit (DPU) Revenue

Human Resource Costs	DPU Revenue Growth 1981-1983	Average Revenue From Large Products as % Of Total DPU Revenue
High Cost Companies	37%	55%
Low Cost Companies	56%	75%

SUMMARY

This article shows that human resource costs vary significantly among companies in the same industry and that they have a direct relationship to strategies. The authors conclude from this that there are optimum human resource costs for a given strategy. A particular company could have too many or too few resources for a given strategy. Companies need to be knowledgeable about this relationship conclude that the ideal human resource cost structure requires a review of internal data and a review of relevant strategic peers.

SECTION 3:

EMPLOYEE RESPONSES TO ORGANIZATIONAL STRATEGIES

This section looks at strategic human resource planning from the point of view of employees and their responses to organizational plans, strategies and change. This reality testing provides a perspective from the employee approaches to their lives and careers.

Griggs and _Manring_ take a novel human development approach to flesh out the issues. Ten major technically driven organizations collaborated in a study aimed at determining the key factors related to motivation and retention of engineers and scientists. The results of the study demonstrate that the nature of the work itself, organizational processes, which determine how work is allocated and evaluated, and the sense of having a career, are regarded as more important than traditional monetary and non-monetary reward and recognition practices.

Portwood and _Price_ focus on the impact of proposed changes on existing human resources. Human resource forecasts deal most often with positions, rather than people. Individual reactions are discounted, or are assumed to be random, and therefore inconsequential. Rarely do forecasts include a systematic survey of employee perceptions, expectations, and aspirations as part of a comprehensive analysis of current inventory. Managers planning strictly on the basis of these position-based forecasts have thus, at times, had to cope with unanticipated employee responses, including productivity, resistance to suggested shifts in location and/or career paths, and even sharply increased rates of retirement and turnover.

Gaertner discusses executive career patterns and organizational adaption to change". Interview and documentary data from three organizations are used to analyze the way in which organizational careers in general and the career experiences of executives in particular are related to an organization's ability to adapt to change. While the results are tentative, and based on only three cases, they give insights into the ways in which organizations adapt to increased uncertainty in their environments and the role that career patterns can play in the process of adapting to such change.

WHAT MOTIVATES TECHNICAL PROFESSIONALS TO CONTRIBUTE

THEIR BEST EFFORT AND MAINTAIN THEIR COMMITMENT TO THEIR ORGANIZATION?

Walter H. Griggs and Susan L. Manring

Griggs - Manring & Associates, Inc.
2725 Derbyshire Road
Cleveland Heights, OH 44106

BACKGROUND

In pursuit of a competitive edge, technically-driven organizations continue to strive for ways of increasing the contribution and satisfaction of technical professionals. A recent study sponsored by Technicare Corporation, a Johnson & Johnson company, has provided a much sharper focus on cost effective ways of increasing the utilization and reducing wasteful turnover of technical professionals.

There were several characteristics of this study which made it unique:

o There was active involvement of ten organizations and extensive participation of over 900 engineers and scientists in determining the key factors relating to contribution, satisfaction and retention.

o The mix of organizations represented a wide array of technologies, employed and industries served. There was,in addition, a considerable range of age and stage of organizational maturity represented.

o The methodology for collection and analysis of the data is a mathematically-sophisticated measurement technology based on an operations research model known as goal programming.

o The data were collected and analyzed so as to permit an understanding of differences based on age of respondents and organizational culture.

o The study recognized the interdependence among the factors relating to job content, organizational climate and managerial processes, career development, and extrinsic rewards. (Monetary rewards refer to the "extra" financial incentives, rather than base salary.)

o The scope of the study assured an adequate basis for designing and testing recommended approaches in a wide range of organizational environments.

METHODOLOGY

Measuring subjective opinions, such as the attitudes of engineers and scientists, can be highly unreliable. When there is concern that the outcome of a study may be used to change the professional life of the respondent, there is a great temptation to respond so as to manipulate the outcome in some way.

Many different approaches have been taken to resolve the problem of reliability. Perhaps the most effective and acceptable contribution derives from sampling theory. Most survey questionnaires which are to be converted into numerical values fall into one of two categories: assignment of value to a statement, and comparison of two alternatives with each other. These can be thought of as scaling and comparison.

A Likert type scale, for instance, has been shown to have considerable reliability in terms of scaling the opinion of one item against another, but the responses to the individual questions may be somewhat less reliable.

The method of comparing the alternatives against one another, which is known as "paired-comparison", has been available for many years. In order for the results to be valid, it isn't necessary that every respondent be familiar with the entire list of things under consideration, and that they compare all of the things with every other thing under consideration. If, for example, one hundred things are being considered, this means that each respondent must make 4,950 comparisons.

The paired-comparison methodology has not until recently been popular, due to the necessary length of the questionnaires and computational problems with the results. Both of these problems have been overcome with Objective Judgment Quotient (OJQTM), the powerful method used in this study.

In 1947, Thomas E. Bartlett, then teaching in the Schools of Engineering at Purdue University, determined that the published methods of scoring the results of the paired-comparison methods were erroneous because they were flowed by the "vote-counting" methods common to many evaluation studies. The weakness of the vote-counting method is that the results are determined solely by how many times the item is picked over others. The method does not give differential weights to the nature of the individual pairings.

To resolve this problem, Bartlett utilized an operations research model known as goal programming, which was developed by Abraham Charnes and W.W. Cooper, to arrive at a logical solution to incomplete sets of comparisons. This technique was to become the basis for OJQ (Bartlett, 1974). The essence of the technique used in OJQ is to minimize differences of opinions among all respondents. This is achieved by computing those scores which are most consistent with all rater comparisons. Unlike statistical procedures, with OJQ, only a linear weight is given to any differences of opinion or random error. This has the effect of taking into account all dissenting opinions without allowing such outliers to influence the final result unduly.

Since 1970, OJQ has become one of the standard methods for performance evaluation. Its uses have been expanded into such areas as organizational diagnosis, strategic planning, attitude surveying, job analysis and product image studies.

Used as the survey technique for this present study, OJQ provided better reliability using much smaller sample sizes than would have been necessary with other techniques. OJQ resolves the issue of "social desirability", i.e., participants responding to a questionnaire so as to manipulate the results toward an outcome that is socially desirable, by placing preferences in the context of comparison with all other items. For example, as we shall discuss later, the financial incentive items were paired in comparison with all other items of the questionnaire.

Another feature of the OJQ process which made it practical for this study is that while the scoring is different from what most administrators and respondents are used to, it is so natural that expensive administration is not required. Even when questionnaires are poorly distributed in a less than ideal environment, the results will be acceptable. The level of significance in this study is accurate to four figures.

MAJOR FINDINGS

In the aggregate, the key source of motivation, satisfaction and retention of technical professionals is the nature of job characteristics, organizational processes, and career development. These factors were regarded as more important than traditional monetary and non-monetary reward and recognition practices. The rank order of these items, however, varied by the age of the respondents and organizational culture.

Age appears to have the greatest effect, demonstrating the need for an adult development perspective in planning organizational interventions. This perspective would take into account that there are predictable changes that occur in individuals with respect to their orientation toward self and work at different points in their lives. (See Figure 1 for the distribution of the high leverage items which ranked in the upper quartile across age groups.)

Differences across the participating organizations demonstrate that each organization has its own culture which affects the priority issues identified by its professionals. Further, these cultural differences suggest that for individual organizations to use reward and recognition practices effectively, they must be able to measure how well the rewards match the value system of the organization. (See Figure 2 for the distribution of high leverage items which ranked in the upper quartile across the participating organizations.)

The traditional monetary and non-monetary reward and recognition practices generally did not rank in the upper quartile. These practices appear to be supporting mechanisms for validating the professionals' sense

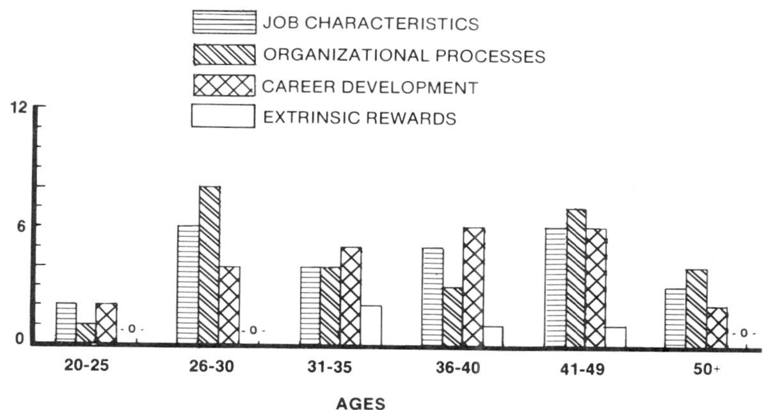

Figure 1: Distribution of High Leverage Items Across Age Groups

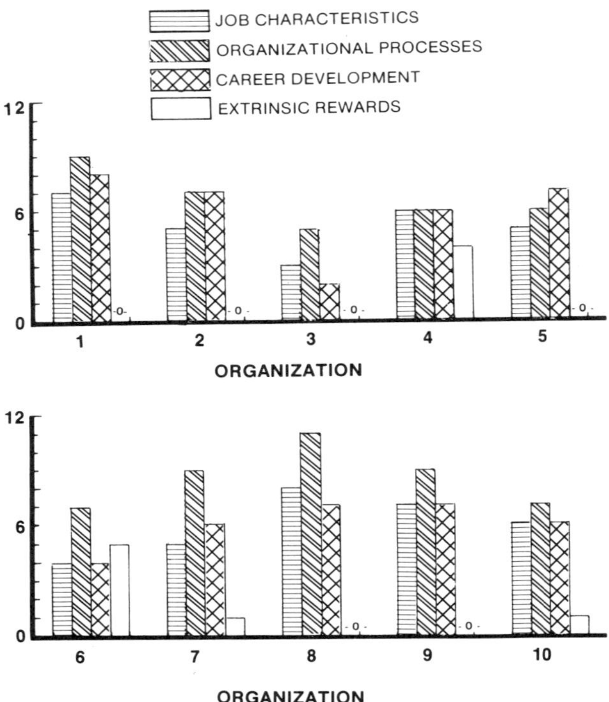

Figure 2: Distribution of High Leverage Items Across Organizations

of value to the organization. Therefore, while useful as symbols, they in themselves do not generally contribute significantly toward motivation or retention.

PRIORITY ISSUES

Originally, the questions asked by the participating organizations, and by technically-driven organizations, in general, were:

1. What are the most and least important reward and recognition practices for motivating and retaining technical professionals?

2. How important is having a well-articulated technical career ladder as distinct from the managerial ladder?

3. How useful are non-monetary incentives., e.g., patent or publication awards, service awards, etc.?

4. How important are financial incentives and what are the most effective forms of financial incentives?

Because age is major variable, the key action levers should be based on an understanding of how individuals' orientations toward their work, organization and career, and toward monetary and non-monetary incentives change over time. The following is a discussion of the high leverage issues across age groups in the four categories: (1) job characteristics, (2) organizational processes, (3) career development factors, and (4) extrinsic rewards.

<u>Job Characteristics Issues</u>

The high leverage job characteristics which ranked in the upper quartile are the following:

o   Seeing a meaningful end product or result from work

o   Having freedom to use personal judgment and initiative

o   Being busy and challenged within individual capacities

o   Having enough time to do quality work

o   Having broad job and/or project scope

o   Having influence and decision-making opportunities

o   Having clear/well-defined tasks and output goals

o   Working on crucial, relevant organization problems

The key job-related issues change with age. For example, the job characteristic most salient for the 20-25 year olds is the need to see an end product or results from their efforts. This item ranked at the 100th percentile, indicating that respondents in this age group consistently ranked it highest. The other job characteristic which is important for this group is ·the need for freedom to use personal judgment and initiative.

Since these are the "apprenticeship" years, the job needs to confirm this age group's ability to transfer academic training into practical application. And further, their work must justify faith in their good judgment and sense of their own professionalism.

For other age groups, specifically, 26-30 and 41-49, job characteristics are also of critical importance, but for different reasons. For the younger group (26-30), the apprenticeship years are over, and the need for challenge, scope and autonomy become central in validating the person's sense of competence and feeling of having graduated from apprenticeship.

For the older group (41-49), the refocus on their jobs reflects the need to reconcile their choice (or perhaps lack of choice) to remain in the technical track. The issue for them is validation of continuing technical competence and the ability to contribute significantly to organizational goals.

The two groups in between (31-35 and 36-40) share the same concerns, but also reflect an increased need for more clarity about goals and criteria for performance. At the same time, they appear to have an increased need for visibility in their organizations.

The finding from this study run counter to the prevailing myth that older professionals tend to lose interest in their jobs. We found that is important for this age group to be busy and challenged, to have broad job or project scope and to have decision-making and influence opportunities.

<u>Organizational Process Issues</u>

The high leverage organizational process issues which ranked in the upper quartile are as follows:

- o Having opportunities to participate in choice of work

- o Receiving minimum supervision and maximum latitude in deciding how to get things done

- o Having opportunities to do innovative work

- o Having state-of-the-art tools and equipment to work with

- o Swapping ideas or working out solutions with colleagues

- o Having open channels of communication

- o Being consulted by colleagues when affected by decisions

- o Having budget to carry on a special project

- o Influencing decisions that affect future company business

- o Feeling senior colleagues care about other's opinions

- o Having a system of flexible hours.

There is agreement across the age groups about the importance of having opportunities to participate in the choice of project work. Beyond this issue, the youngest age group, 20-25, reflects little consensus on what is important. This is understandable considering that they have little organizational experience and generally want a chance to prove that they can successfully negotiate entry into the adult world of work.

After five or so years into their careers, the 26-30 age grouped has many organizational concerns. Having passed through the apprenticeship years, they now want the status of independent contributor. Further, they are in the period of greatest concern about whether they have made the right choice about their profession, as well as whether the current organization is right for them.

In addition, to wanting to participate in their choice of project work, the 26-30 age group is concerned about the following: having maximum latitude in deciding how to get things done, having opportunities, support and recognition for doing innovative work, having budget to carry on a special project, and working with state-of-the-art tools and equipment. Having open process of communication and sense of colleague ship with peers and senior professionals are also important.

If the concerns that the professional experiences in his or her late twenties are satisfactorily resolved, the focus shifts during the 30's toward concern for visibility in the organization and recognition as a competent member of the professional group. Access to projects where the professional can make a clear and valuable contribution is of critical importance.

Most of these items are of concern for the 41-49 age group. And, they are particularly concerned about being consulted by colleagues when affected by their decisions. This age group also places a high value on having a system of flexible hours.

The 50+ age group shows relatively few concerns about organizational processes, except that they want minimum supervision and maximum choice over their work. They also want influence opportunities and show concern about being able to influence the future course of the business.

<u>Career Development Issues</u>

The high leverage career development issues which ranked in the upper quartile are as follows:

o Having individual expertise utilized and recognized

o Receiving direct, timely and usable feedback

o Having promotions/titles based on proven contribution

o Having abilities and contributions recognized by seniors

o Knowing individual strengths are matched to opportunities

o Pursuing company-related personal technical interests.

o Having individual efforts highly visible to management

o Having opportunities to move into management

o Developing expertise in more than one technical field

o Having equivalent of executive compensation levels

o Understanding how people get promoted

The strength of concern about career development varies across age groups in way that argues strongly for an adult development perspective when designing appropriate organizational responses to career issues.

For all ages it is important to have individual expertise utilized, recognized and rewarded. We interpret this to mean that technical professionals value feeling a part of the mainstream and being recognized as important contributors.

The youngest group, 20-25, has only one other concern which ranked in the upper quartile: receiving direct, timely and usable performance feedback. Providing this feedback is perhaps the fastest way for an organization to facilitate the professional's development and contribution.

The major issue for those in their early to mid-30's is to be confirmed as competent technical contributors. The potential for uninterrupted productivity is high when the professional feels both continually challenged and visible enough to senior colleagues and management. This age group wants direct and timely feedback and to know that individual strengths are matched to opportunities for promotions or transfers.

Career issues become more focal as the professional moves into the late 30's. The questions arise, "How close am I to my advancement timetable?" - "How am I doing compared to my peers?" - and finally, "What new areas should I pursue?" Professionals in this age group are concerned that promotions are based on proven contributions, and they also want to know that their individual strengths are matched to opportunities for promotion or transfer. This is a period when the possibility of effective dialogue with one's supervisor is critical in sustaining satisfaction and motivation in the technical career track. This is the only age group for whom having opportunities to move into management is a high priority issue.

Much has been written about the mid-life transition of the 40's. Some of the key issues are to become more realistic about one's achievements, to

reappraise one's choices, and for professionals, the need to reevaluate the
technical vs. managerial orientation. Early and productive reconciliation of
these issues is important for both the individual and the organization.

Our study indicated that professionals in the age group 41-49 have
either decided to remain technical, or they have become reconciled that
managerial opportunities are precluded for them. In either case, there is a
need for having individual efforts highly visible to management. This is the
only group for whom having the equivalent of executive compensation levels
for the technical career ladder is a high leverage issue.

The 50+ age group values having opportunities to pursue personal
technical interests relating to company goals. This is a way of leaving an
important "legacy" with the organization, and it could also contribute to
innovation in the organization.

Incidentally, the mentoring function, "Having opportunities and recognition for guiding and developing the efforts and capabilities of others", which
was ranked low, could become a potential new skill building area for the
senior professionals, providing the organization recognized its importance.

Technical vs. Managerial Career Ladder

A major question which is frequently discussed is whether technical
professionals prefer technical work or really want to move into management.
Two items on our questionnaire, which were ranked in relation to all other
items, were aimed to get at this concern: Having a well-articulated
technical ladder, comparable to opportunities in management and having
opportunities to move into management. With very few exceptions, these
career ladder items were not ranked in the upper quartile when compared with
other items. (See Figure 3 for the comparison of preferences for the
technical vs. managerial career ladder across age groups.)

Young professionals enter organizations, frequently having been told as
students that, if they are to become really successful in their careers, they
must move into management. This is reflected in this age group's stronger
preference for the managerial track (66th percentile) vs. the technical
ladder (43rd percentile), as Figure 3 show. However, interest in having a
well-articulated technical career ladder, comparable to opportunities in the
organization for just a few years. It then remains at about the same level
of interest for ages 26-49.

The heightened interest in managerial opportunities during the early
20's and again in the late 30's and 40's seems reactive: first, for the 20-
25 age group, to expectations derived from professional education about what
it means to be successful (e.g., move into management); and secondly, for the
older age groups, in reaction to the perceived lack of opportunity on the
technical career ladder and the perception that one can climb higher and see
farther on the managerial ladder.

Extrinsic Reward Issues

This study suggests that the value of extrinsic rewards may be largely
symbolic and therefore more useful in supporting other organizational
processes. The following summarizes our finding about extrinsic rewards,
focusing first on the non-monetary rewards and secondly on the financial
incentives.

a. Non-Monetary Rewards

While we expected that the non-monetary extrinsic rewards would receive

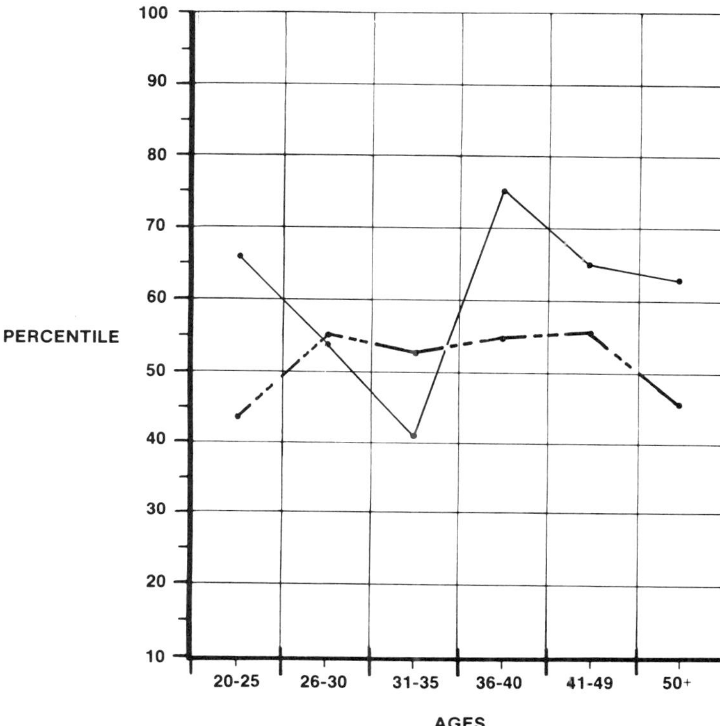

Figure 3: A Comparison of the Preferences for the Technical vs. Managerial
Career Ladders Across Age Groups

lower ratings than job characteristics, organizational processes and career
items, we did not expect them to be rated as low as they were. The low
impact non-monetary reward items which ranked in the lowest quartile are as
follows:

o Being inducted into company's Hall of Fame

o Having lunch/dinner with project team and immediate
   manager after special achievements

o Receiving awards for trade secrets

o Being encouraged to publish papers in technical journals

o Delivering papers at professionals meetings

o Receiving awards or recognition in formal ceremonies

   In general, the findings suggest that the cost-effectiveness of the non-
monetary extrinsic reward practices should be questioned. We would caution,
however, that arbitrary removal of existing practices can create strong
negative consequences.

If the special lunch or dinner with management were held, for example,
it would be important to structure the occasion so that it accomplishes
several objectives which meet other needs of the professionals: (1) provides
recognition to the group and individuals in a timely way after the
achievement; (2) becomes a forum for management to update technical
professionals on the state of the organization and its direction; and (3)
provides opportunities for questions and answers and general discussion of
mutual concerns.

b. Financial Incentives

In our early work with the participating organizations, we discussed the
relative importance of financial incentives. Several questions emerged, to
be answered through our research:

1. How important are financial incentives?

2. What are the most effective forms of financial incentives, e.g.,
    cash bonuses or stock options?

3. Should these (cash or stock) incentives be based on individual
    contribution, company performance, or some combination of the two?

4. Should they be given to recognize individual or task team efforts?

We learned from the respondents that, in general, financial incentives
are weak motivators. However, a cash bonus based on individual contribution
has some appeal, particularly for professionals in their 30's and 40's. It
is not just the money itself which is important here. We believe the
emphasis is on receiving recognition for individual contributions.

Generally, technical professionals do not relate to company performance
as a measure of their contribution as directly as managers do. In a
sub-sample which compared managers to professionals ranked all forms of
financial incentives lower than the managers did, except for receiving a cash
bonus based on individual contribution. For this item, the professionals
ranked it considerably higher than managers did.

In general, there is less interest in receiving any kind of stock
option, compared to cash bonuses, as an incentive to stay with one's
organization and contribute. No forms of stock incentives were ranked in the
upper quartile by any age group.

Neither special income awards based on the individual's contribution to
team success or based on the project team contribution is a particularly
powerful incentive, although it is worth noting that for the 31-35 age group,
financial awards based on project team contributions ranked in the upper
quartile (78th percentile). This fits with the importance of working out
solutions with colleagues for age group.

ACTION RECOMMENDATIONS

Organizations have been asking several critical questions on how to
increase the motivation, satisfaction and retention of technical
professionals. Many of these questions have been focused on how to use
extrinsic rewards, both monetary and non-monetary,more effectively. This
study indicates a need to understand the interdependence of both the
extrinsic rewards and the intrinsic factors of the job itself, organizational
processes, and career development issues.

We believe there is an overriding question that organizations need to
address:

What are the conditions under which technical professionals can maximize
their contribution and satisfaction, and remain committed to their
organization?

In the following sections we discuss our action recommendations in each of
the four areas outlined in this research.

Job Design Recommendations

Because challenge and growth are key issues for technical professionals,
there is a compelling argument for viewing jobs and organizational settings
as the context in which people continue to learn and grow. We have found
that viewing jobs and organizations as learning environments makes it
possible to talk about people, jobs, and organizational processes in the
language of experiential learning (Kolb, 1984). Applications of this model
in organizational settings have demonstrated the value of measuring the
degree of match between job demands and the learning and challenge needs of
the person (Kolb and Wolfe, 1981).

We suggest that this approach would provide more creative responses to
technical professionals' needs for increasing job challenge and scope, in
ways which would also increase the professionals' contributions to their
organization. The implementation of this recommendation should involve task
teams comprised of professionals, technical managers, and human resource
managers who are specialists in job design. While there is considerable
precedent for modifying jobs to match levels of individual competence, this
recommendation is founded on two important principles which makes it
different from much previous work in this area: (1) job design is based on a
proven theory of adult learning and (2) technical professionals as well as
managers are involved in the process.

Organizational Process Recommendations

We believe that technically-driven organizations can expect a high
payoff from a renewed focus of three target areas for organizational
development: (1) organizational communication, (2) team building, and (3)
management development. The specific recommendations in these areas are
discussed below, as they relate to enhancing the contribution and retention
of technical professionals.

a. Organizational Communication

The traditional employee communication process tends to be a top-down
message-sending orientation. While this is important, and certainly
necessary to provide an overall sense of organizational direction and unity
of purpose, it is only a partial view of what organizational communication
requires.

Organizational communication requires the use of two other elements of
the communication process, in addition to top-down message sending: (1) the
management of the symbols which communicate how the organization values its
professionals, and (2) the development of an organizational climate for open
communication upward, downward and laterally.

Several of the high leverage organizational processes identified in this
study are examples of organizational symbols: having a system of flexible
hours communicates trust in the professionals. Providing state-of-the-art
tools communicates the organization's investment in maintaining technological
leadership. Having a budget to carry on special projects communicates both

trust in the individuals who are involved and the organization's valuing of
creativity and innovation. The public valuing of innovation and risk taking
is a powerful organizational symbol which can be key in both recruiting and
retaining technical professionals.

The development of a climate for open communication means the
establishment of norms about how people relate to each other. Organizations
which are committed to fostering discussions based on mutual trust enhance
the possibility of effective team work and less organizational game playing.

For those organizations which do not have a well-articulated communication strategy, we recommend that a task force comprising technical professionals, managers and human resource specialists be formed to create such
a strategy as well as a plan for implementation that addresses the specific
communication requirements of the organization. The process used to develop
this strategy should model open channels of communication and high levels of
participation, and demonstrate a commitment to organization dialogue.

b. Team Building

The professionals in this study ranked several items relating to
collegiality and team work very high. An added benefit in building effective
work teams is the learning it provides for technical professionals. During
the process of team building, professionals learn a great deal about how to
relate more effectively to each other. This kind of learning is critical in
developing the people skills that technical professionals need and often
lack. In addition to developing people skills, team building also gives
professionals a sense of belonging. It is this sense of belonging that
enhances the professionals' commitment to remain with the organization over
time.

We recommend that organizations recommit themselves to active team
building, using a design that is oriented toward: (1) interpersonal skill
building for technical professionals, as well as (2) the creation of
productive team environments.

c. Management Development

From our interviews with professionals, we found that a major reason why
technical professionals leave organizations is a difficult relationship with
their supervisor. We believe that the root of this problem is "bossism". A
consequence of technical professionals' education is that they are trained to
be critical. While this is a very useful trait in scientific problem
solving, it is dysfunctional in interpersonal relationships, and it is very
counter-productive in managing professionals.

Often the prevailing assumption of managers is that their job is to
control subordinates' behavior in order to reach organizational goals. This
conflicts directly with the needs of professionals for autonomy and self-
direction. Alternatively, those managers who are more oriented toward
facilitation, as opposed to control, can have a powerful effect on increasing
the rate of learning for subordinates.

We recommend that a new emphasis be placed on management development
which focuses on the nature of the interaction between the supervisor and
subordinate. The objectives of this development should be two fold: (1) to
help technically-trained managers acquire a more facilitative style, which is
compatible with the professionals' need for self-expression and growth, and
(2) to create a system where managers and professionals together can define
the optimum mix of supervision and latitude in deciding how to carry out
project assignments.

<u>Career Development Recommendations</u>

It is very costly, to both organizations and individuals, when technical professionals feel that they must leave their present organization in order to meet their career objectives. Most often this assumption is based on very incomplete knowledge about what opportunities are available within the professional's organization.

Technical professionals need an understanding of what career opportunities exist, and they need accurate and timely feedback on their performance in order to know where they stand.

In order to respond effectively to these issues, a career development program should be based on three primary principles:

1. It must be contribution-oriented. By this we mean the essential dialogue between the manager and professional must focus on how to enable the professional to increase his or her contribution to the organization.

2. It must be grounded in an understanding of the audit development process which recognizes that the needs of individuals for challenge and continued learning change over time.

3. It must require that both managers and professionals be equally prepared in advance of career discussions. This means they each need to learn the same language and concepts relating to career choices.

We believe that an approach to career development which is based on these principles will provide a vehicle for the effective integration of the job design and other organizational development activities which we have discussed above. As career development discussions focus on planning for the increased contribution, learning and satisfaction of technical professionals, the primary subject matter will be the characteristics of the job and the organizational processes which support performance.

<u>Extrinsic Reward Recommendations</u>

We recommend that organizations examine more critically what is the specific effect of extrinsic reward and recognition programs over against the costs. Our major concern is the unintended "ripple effect" consequences of the financial incentives, in particular. While professionals, in certain age groups, value cash bonuses as recognition for individual contribution, the measurement of the individual contribution is very difficult and furthermore, difficult to defend to those not receiving the bonus. The question to be raised within organizations is the extent to which these rewards are perceived as being equitably issue may be a problem is some organizations.

If an organization wants to offer financial incentives based on individual contribution, we suggest that there be an explicit process which involves the technical professional in identifying the criteria for measuring contribution.

Future planning for extrinsic rewards needs to be significantly better targeted to the needs and interests of different age groups of technical professionals and to the culture of the organization.

CONCLUSION

This study has provided a wealth of data which can be used in two essential ways: (1) the data provide a well-grounded analysis of many areas

of organizational concern relating to increasing the contribution and
retention of technical professionals, which can be used as the basis for
planning interventions and (2) the data provide a base line against which
organizations can measure the effectiveness of planned interventions to
increase the contribution and retention of technical professionals.

With the participation of ten organizations and over 900 technical
professionals, we believe this study clearly demonstrates that innovation and
organizational effectiveness are best served - not just by rewarding
technical professionals following their achievements - but by fostering the
conditions which enable and inspire technical professionals to contribute
their creative efforts.

REFERENCES

Bartlett, Thomas E. and Leonard R. Linden. "Evaluating Managerial
  Personnel", Omega: The International Journal of Management Science.
  Vol. 2, No. 6, (1974) pp. 815-819

Kolb, David A. Experiential Learning: Experience as the Source of Learning
  and Development. (Englewood Cliffs, N.J., Prentice Hall, Inc., 1984).

Kolb, David A., Donald M. Wolfe, et al. Professional Education and Career
  Development: A Cross Sectional Study of Adaptive Competencies In
  Experiential Learning. Final Report. National Institute of Education.
  (NIE Grant No. NIE-G-77-0053, 1981).

EMPLOYEE RESPONSES TO ORGANIZATINAL STRATEGIES:

THE FORGOTTEN VARIABLE IN HUMAN RESOURCE FORECASTING

James D. Portwood* and Karl F. Price**

*Dept. of Human Resource Adminsitration
 Temple University
 Philadelphia, PA 19122

**Towers, Perrin, Forster, and Crosby
 Centre Square West
 1500 Market Street
 Philadelphia, PA 19102

INTRODUCTION

In today's turbulent business environment, organizational success and even survival often depend on tiemly, appropriate responses to shifting external conditions. Human resource forecasting is a key element in this response system, alerting management to possible adjustments in staffing levels and skill mixes which may be necessary as part of any strategic redirection. Such information is critical to the development of action plans for effecting orderly, efficient transitions in human resource structures and policies.

One potentially relevant factor which human resource forecasters often fail to consider in making their predictions, however, is the reaction of existing employees to proposed changes. Human resource forecasts deal most often with positions, rather than people. Individual reactions are discounted, or are possibly assumed to be random, and therefore, inconsequential. Rarely do forecasts include a systematic survey of employee perceptions, expectiations, and aspirations as part of a comprehensive analysis of current inventory. Managers planning strictly on the basis of these position-based forecasts have thus, at times, had to cope with unanticipated employee responses, including lowered productivity, resistance to suggested shifts in location and/or career paths, and even sharply increased rates of retirement and turnover.

The purpose of this paper is to demonstrate, using a representative case study, the importance of employee attitudes and career preferences on the outcome of organizational planning and change efforts. The case also provides several examples of constructive organizational responses which may be utilized when data on such attitudes and aspirations are available. The primary focus here, however, will be on reasons why, and areas where, employee perceptions may have a significant impact on the accuracy and reliability of projections generated by traditional human resource forecasting and planning systems.

THE ISSUE

The risks associated with ignoring individual responses to organizational plans was expresses very well by Eddie C. Smith, in a speech to the Human Resource Management Association of Chicago (1984). He concludes that:

"Most organizations today, with which I'm familiar, are considering strategies which will require considerable internal change if they are to be implemented successfully. Unfortunately, very few of them realize it. As I'm sure you realize the, [primary] problems [associated with this type of change] are not technical or logistical, they are emotional and political and, thus, much harder to solve."

The problem is that most traditional HR planning models (See MacCrimmon, 1971) fail to consider what influence such emotional responses and political dealings may have on the size, composition, and distribution of the current work force as it is projected into the future. Employees confronted with perceived undesirable alternatives due to strategically dictated change may react in a number of disfunctional ways (e.g., quitting, enlisting support from others to prevent or delay change, seeking to block transfers, etc). All this is likely to lead to significant departures from the planned pace of change, as well as the numbers and types of employees one may have expected to have available.

The extent to which human resource planning depends on predictable labor force behavior is clearly demonstrated in a recent article by Guy Miller (1980). He begins by suggesting that HR forecasts (on which such plans are based) are primarily a function of historic labor flow trends, taking into account turnover, terminations, retirements, and transitions and transfers of various types. The implicit assumptions underlying such trend, analysis appear to be; (1) that individuals will generally continue to behave and make personal career decisions in much the same fashion as in the past; and (2) that they will willingly acquiesce to changes in projected task requirements and career paths dictated by shifting organizational demands.

These assumptions, however, neglect the finding (See Hall, 1976) that individuals' career related decision making does not occur in a vacuum. Rather it is substantially influenced by the context and conditions experienced by the employee. As changes occur which alter these contexts and conditions, employees often rethink their personal relationship with the organization, and may make radical changes in their own career strategies. This appears to be especially likely among key individuals with special talents, for whom numerous external career options are available.

Some planning models have suggested that individual level information be included in the HR forecasting and planning process (See Milkovich and Mahoney, 1978). Empirical evidence (Schwartz, 1985) indicates, however, that steps which might assist organizations in assessing and managing individual responses (i.e., Inclusion of data relevant to person-position matching as part of the HR information system, communication through formal career counselling programs, and integration of individual career and successive planning activities) are rarely incorporated in existing HR planning systems. The absence is especially noticeable in what Schwartz characterizes as "traditional systems." This type represents a significant majority (60%) of the organizations described in his research.

The reluctance to include employee job attitudes and/or career preferences in the forecasting process may result from a perception that such

attitudes, and behaviors that spring from them, are isolated independent
events. If this were true, it might be argued that, while change may create
mismatches between career aspirations and career realities for some, it would
likely provide others with new opportunities. The result would be to cancel
out any effect at the aggregate level. Since forecasting is interested only
in aggregate trends, individual career decisions would be irrelevant to the
process.

There are forces at work, however, which are likely to make individual
reactions non random. It has been suggested by several theorists (For
example see Wanous, 1980) that individuals engage in self selection, choosing
organizations and positions which they feel provide them opportunities for
career goal attainment. Assuming applicants are responding to similar
aspects of the job, this process should tend to shape and narrow the
diversity in aggregate employee attitudes and preferences. Parallel
socialization through common experiences may further restrict employees'
preferred alternatives.

While this limited focus is an advantage to the organization in its
attempts to reward and control employees, it becomes a distinct liability
when significant change is required. If the change is at variance with
established preferences and expectations, current employees may independently
come to very similar and potentially disruptive conclusion relative to their
relationship with the organization. Each individual's decision may also be
reinforced by the observation that others have reached the same conclusion.

Having data on individual attitudes available may not allow the
organization to prevent such responses, but it can assist planners in several
way. First, forecasters might wish to qualify their estimates of human
resource availability and necessary staffing efforts based on likely employee
responses to various change strategies. Second, planners faced with choices
among alternative strategies may wish to consider which plan would be least
at variance with existing employee attitudes and preferences. Finally, in
cases where disruption is unavoidable, it make give planners and managers
sufficient warning to allow for discussion of issues with employees prior to
implementation. The organization in the case study outlined below did have
such data available, and was able to make use of it in these ways as part of
a change effort.

THE STUDY

The reserch on which this paper is based was originally undertaken to
study the development of managers' work attitudes and career strategies from
organizational entry through their first two years on the job. During the
course of the study, conditions arose requiring significant changes in the
entry level position on which the study focused. Availability of attitudinal
data from job incumbents allowed the organization to consider the impact of
proposed changes of these employees' reported career strategies, and to
consider likely responses among this group. Specific descriptions of the
organization, sample population, target job, and situation ultimately leading
to the observed job change appear below:

The Organization - The study was conducted in a large mid-western
Commercial Bank. While the bank accommodates individual customers, the firm
is involved primarily in providing a range of credit and financial services
to corporate clients. Like most institutions of this type, it has offices in
major U.S. cities and several locations abroad. An aggressive expansion into
this broader market over the last ten years has resulted in the hiring of a
large number of client representatives. These representatives are
responsible for obtaining and servicing corporate accounts. It was from new

hires in this area that work and career attitude data were collected.

The Sample - The study involved over 200 representatives hired over a
three year period. As the primary external contact for the Bank's commercial
customers, these representatives are given a great deal of responsibility and
face a rather diverse set of tasks. In keeping with the importance of this
position, considerable effort is devoted to recruiting and developing the
very best talent. Search is, therefore, limited to graduates of a selected
number of quality universities, and only the highest performers from those
institutions. These individuals are then further developed in an extensive
training program.

With such selective recruiting and intensive indoctrination it was not
surprising to find striking similarities among the sample population relative
to their prior experiences, work and career attitudes, and self perceptions.
A significant majority (60%) had graduate degrees in some area of business
administration. Almost half (49%) had had prior work experience in financial
institutions.

Study participants generally demonstrated an intense career orientation.
The availability of career options in this position was most frequently cited
as the primary reason for accepting the job. Subjects also reported
considerable job search activity, with 81% seeking and receiving other job
offers before deciding upon their present position. Finally, more than 90%
reported that they had begun formulating specific career strategies at the
time of entry (data were collected shortly after the new hires entered the
organization).

Participants also could be characterized as generally self confident and
assured. More than 70% reported being confident that they could carry our
their career plans and reach career objectives. Approximately 80% expected
to have a great deal of personal control over their career. There was also
general agreement (+80%) that they were well prepared to carry out the
responsibilities of their current position. All these finding indicate a
great deal of similarity in how these individuals view themselves, the job,
and their career prospects.

The Job - At the beginning of the study period, the account
representative's position was very client-centered with each representative
having primary responsibility for all dealings with specific corporate
customers. Since the bank offers both credit and financial services (e.g.,
foreign exchange, letters of credit, etc.) to such clients, representatives
had to be both sales persons (promoting bank services) and financial analysts
(checking the credit worthiness and analyzing credit needs of their account
organizations). In this structure, junior account representatives generally
handled smaller corporate customers while senior responsibilities were given
primary responsibility for the larger more complex accounts.

Both junior and senior representatives, however, were doing essentially
the same job and carried the same responsibilities. This horizontal
integration of tasks made it possible to gain wide exposure to bank
operations, engage in a variety of activities, and obtain a great deal of
responsibility early in one's career. It was, in fact, these aspects of the
job which subjects cited as additional reasons (other than career options)
for accepting the account representative's position. This job structure,
however, was destined to change over the course of the study period as a
shifting market environment forced a re-evaluation of the bank's strategic
direction.

The Situation - The bank's philosophy had always been to establish
stable long term relationships with corporate clients, emphasizing personal

contacts and quality service. The focus had also generally been on the
lending business, with financial services provided as a secondary activity.
This strategy required that account representatives be viewed by customers as
their primary adviser and problem-solver in financial matters. All
representatives were, therefore, expected to be in frequent contact with
clients, prepared to analyze situations and provide solutions (usually loan
or credit arrangements).

Since the client base spanned the range from small business operations
to huge multinational corporations, there were many potential customers and
requirements for a large number of account representatives in the field
calling on current and prospective customers. There was also a fairly clear
path for advancement as representatives gained experience and acquired
responsibility for more complex and/or more specialized accounts.

During the course of the study, however, market conditions underwent a
dramatic change. Deregulation of the banking industry had at once made the
credit markets more turbulent and competitive while opening up opportunities
to provide a range of new and lucrative financial services (stock brokerage,
more sophisticated money management techniques). These shifts, coupled with
an increasingly turbulent economic environment (leading to a rise in problem
loans both at home and abroad), resulted in a sharp decline in the
profitability of the credit portion of the business, and pressures for
tighter control of loan portfolios. In this new environment larger companies
represented a more stable credit risk, and were more likely to need the new
more profitable financial services which the bank was able to offer.
Ultimately these forces led to a strategic re-evaluation.

THE CHANGE

At the organization Level - The strategic re-evaluation resulted in
several shifts at the organizational level. Most obvious was the transfer of
smaller (and generally less profitable) accounts to a subsidiary, thus
leaving the bank free to concentrate on it's larger clients, and the
promotion of new products to this "upper end market." Also occurring was a
shift in emphasis away from writing loans as the primary activity, toward
sale and delivery of financial services. these new trends also signaled some
significant changes in the responsibilities of many account representative.

At the Job Level - The emphasis on large clients signifi-cantly reduced
the client base and therefore the need for account representatives engaged in
client contact activities. Larger clients, however, required more attention,
and their credit needs were generally more complex. This incresed the need
for, and problems associated with, credit contact for at least the first
several years of their tenure with the bank. lost was the horizontal
integration of tasks and opportunity for early client responsibility which
originally attracted many individuals to this position.

Expected Impact - Forecasts, employing the traditional position based
approach, suggested little if any HR impact resulting from the change. The
number of account representatives needed would remain essentially the same
(even though new representatives would now not attain full account
responsibility for several years). Skill requirements would also the same in
the long run. While the junior account representatives' job would now be
much more analytical in nature, marketing skills would still be necessary as
the individual moved up in later years to the position of senior account
representative and team leader. According to this scenario, no major shifts
in number of types of personnel would result from the change, and therefore
no response from the HR department was called for.

What became evident in analyzing employee career attitudes and self

perceptions, however, was that many of the current junior account
representatives were not likely to see the new intermediate career path as
either to their liking or their advantage. If even a portion of these
employees were spurred to action by the change, it was clear the human
resource department would indeed be involved, despite the initial forecast
predicting otherwise.

EMPLOYEE ATTITUDES AND CAREER PERCEPTIONS

The attitudes and preferences of junior account executives appear to be
at variance with the new reality of their position in several areas. First,
an analysis of personal career planning beliefs and reported strategies
suggests these employees are not likely to be either patient or particularly
flexible in pursuit of their career goals (See Table 1). They generally
believe in the value of career planning and are very committed to the idea
that personal involvement is necessary for goal attainment. They are not,
however, prepared to abandon their own goals as a price for progress. These
feelings are emphasized by participants' expectations. Confronted with this
situations newly hired account representatives might be expected to resist
the change, or at least express considerable dissatisfaction.

Other factors which could possibly create trouble are employees'
expected pace of career movement, their focus on the first position as a yard
stick for assessing career status, and their short time horizon in career
planning. Participants expect to move within the first 3-4 years, while
plans now call for junior account executives to remain part of analysis
support teams for 5=+ years. The analytical nature of their position will be
counter to these individuals' expressed desires for broad responsibility.
Finally, a short planning horizon is likely to discourage them from looking
past this first placement to the more agreeable prospect of moving up to the
senior representative position. Taken together these opinions suggest a high
probability of frustration growing among junior executives over what they are
likely to see as inadequate and misdirected career progress. If so, the last

Table 1

Participant Beliefs/Behavior Relative to Personal Career Progress

Belief/Behavior	Mean Score 1-5 Scale Except Where Noted*)	% Reported (Scale Noted)
-Progress Depends on Personal Planning	4.65	97.1 (Agree or Strongly Agree)
-Best to Go Along with Organzational Plans	2.45	55.1 (Disagree or Strongly Disagree)
-Expected Influence on First Placement	3.65	71.3 (A Great Deal or A Very Great Deal)
-Criticality of First Placement	4.06	74.5 (Important or Very Important)
-Time in First Placement	± 3.5 years*	87.9 (less than 4 years)
-Planning Horizon	± 4 years*	87.6 (less than 5 years)
Probability I May Have to Look to Attend Career Goals	2.95 (1-4)*	65.1 (Some or High Elsewhere Probability)

item in Table 1 indicates that at least some individuals would consider
seeking opportunities elsewhere.

While friction appears certain to arise over the change in career
path, the Bank also has to face the fact that junior executives' expectations
as to specific job content are going to be severely challenged, especially in
the anticipated amount of client contact. Since considerable evidence exists
to suggest that employees' initial job expectations are highly associated
with job preferences (See for example Portwood and Miller, 1976),
representatives' disaffection with this change is also likely to be high.

This would certainly seem to be the case given that 84.5% of
participants expressed a preference for positions with direct client contact
vs. ones without. This theme is also carried through (as suggested above) in
junior executives' job expectations. As Table 2 indicates, the group
generally expects to often make contributions, gain recognition, experience
challenge, and grow personally as a consequence of marketing related
activities. In each case, the feeling is that marketing activities will
provide more opportunity for these outcomes than analytical aspects of the
position. Loss of marketing responsibilities will thus likely be perceived
as reducing the possibility for personal need satisfaction in several key
areas.

The damage, however, goes beyond loss of immediate need satisfaction.
Tables 3 & 4 indicate that representatives see customer contact as a major
portion of their job and they generally expect to be given primary
responsibility for many aspects of their relationship. Perhaps more
importantly, they also see client contacts as critical for their career
progress in the Bank. For such career oriented individuals, this may be the
most difficult aspect of the change to accept. For them delaying customer
contact may mean an unacceptable delay in their career timetable.

Such delays, along with failure to allow involvement in (and to
support) personal career plans are among the factors most closely associated
with expectations that individuals may have to look elsewhere to satisfy
career goals (See Table 5). Also associated with this feeling are

Table 2

Participant Expectations for the Account Representatives'
Position (Next 3-5 years)

Expectations Relative to Marketing Responsibility	Mean Score* Marketing vs. Analytical	% Reporting Often Or Very Often
–Make a Significant Contrbution to the Bank	3.70 – 3.59	65.7
–Gain Recognition Through My Efforts	3.46 – 3.21	49.2
–Will be Involved in Challenging Work	4.02 – 3.85	79.4
–Will Experience Personal Growth	4.21 – 4.05	80.9

*Answers on a 1-5 scale (Rarely – Very Often)

Table 3

Participant Expectations Relative to Task Requirements
(Next 1-3 years)

Task Requirements	Percent of Time Spent On	% Reporting Most Important to Perform Effectively for Career Progress
Administrative Duties	20.3	4.5
Analytical Responsibilities	31.4	32.8
Knowledge Skill Acquisition	11.2	13.4
Selling and Customer Service	30.2	46.3
Managing Subordinates	5.2	1.5
Other	2.7	1.5

Table 4

Participant Expectations Relative to Degree of
Responsibility for Client Contact Activities

Areas of Responsibility	Mean Scores (1-5 Scale, No Resp.-Sole Resp.)	% Expecting Primary or Sole Responsibility
-Developing New Business Through Customer Calls	4.10	73.5
-Selling Financial Services	3.78	71.6
-Serve as Client's Financial Advisor	3.30	47.8
-Coordinate Customer Contacts from Other Bank Departments	4.08	74.6
-Provide Customer Service and Follow-up	4.13	86.6

expectations that more time will be spent in credit analysis and less in
client contact. Since the proposed change will have negative affects on all
the aspects mentioned Table 5, it is not unreasonable to project a likely
increase in turnover rate, request for transfer, and other withdrawal
behavior.

One final interesting trend revealed in the attitudinal date was the
emergence of two distinct subgroups in the sample relative to their self
perceptions and subsequent career preferences and strategies. One implicit
assumption on which the original projection of no HR impact was based, was
that all account representative were equally willing nand able to carry
either of the two major responsibilities of the position (Marketing and

Table 5

Factors Associated With Perceived Likelihood of Having
to Pursue Career Goals Elsewhere

Factor	Degree of Association
Expected Tenure in First Placement Progress	.254**
Degree of Personal Impact on Career	-.213*
Perceived Organizational Support for Personal Career Plans	-.186*
Precept of Time I Expect to Spend in Credit Analysis	.242**
Percent of Time I Expect to Spend in Selling/Customer Contact	-.197*

*Sig .05
**Sig .01

Analytical). The only change according to the original scenario was one of
timing and emphasis. Representative would of course get to use both skills
in the long run.

What was not anticipated was that individuals do not see themselves
as equally in both areas. In fact it tends to be more an issue of one or the
other skill dominating. The correlation between two questions asking about
perceived competence in marketing and analytical areas produced a significant
negative relationship (-.186, sig$\geq$ .05). Even more interesting this
"marketing vs. analytical orientation" carried over into representatives'
preferences in, and approach, to the job.

Table 6 outlines several areas where expectations based on orientation
diverged significantly. Not surprisingly, marketing oriented individuals are
much more focused on the marketing aspects of the job, both for need
satisfaction and as a basis for career success. The projected job change is
thereform likely to impact this type of individual most severely. It may lso
mean they are more likely to exit the Bank taking their marketing skills and
their desire for client contact with them.

ORGANIZATIONAL IMPLICATIONS

Armed with the additional information on employee attitudes provided
by this study, the Bank was able to initiate a thorough analysis of likely
employee responses as implications of the strategic redirection began to
emerge. Since external conditions dictated the job change go through
substantially as planned attention focused on what the impact might be on
junior executives' behavior.

It was agreed that mismatches were incritable, with the likely result
being loss of commitment and possible turnover or transfer for some. those
who stayed might also be expected to exhibit greater anxiety, uncertainty,
and need for information and reassurance. It was also concluded that if

Table 6

Participant Job Expectations: Association with
Marketing and Analytical Orientation

Job Expectations/Desires	Correlation With Analytical Orientation	Correlation With Marketing Orientation
Make a Significant Contribution to the Bank		
Marketing Area	-.177	.251**
Analytical Area	.161	.021
Gain Recognition for		
Marketing Efforts	-.212*	.213*
Analytical Efforts	.185*	.064
Will Have Challenge		
In the Marketing Area	165	.301**
In the Analytical Area	192*	.107
Will Be Able to Grow Personally		
Through Marketing Work	.101	.184*
Through Analytical Work	.232*	-.123
May Experience Difficulty		
In the Marketing Area	.054	-.189*
In the Analytical Area	-.374**	.174
Desire Position with Significant Client Contact	-.102	.188*

employees' perceptions of personal competence were correct, the Bank stood to lose a disproportionate number of those representatives with a skill base in marketing. While this would have no immediate effect, it would likely pose a problem in the long term. The bottom line for the Bank would then be a work group that was smaller and less balanced in terms of skills than the one which might have been predicted without the additional information.

ORGANIZATIONAL RESPONSE

The most immediate need for the Bank was to consider ways to hedge against any losses in the current work force, while insuring that new hires would be more compatible in their expectations with the new realisties of the position. Being aware of possible problems in advance allowed the Bank to adjust both the number of recruits they projected hiring, and the recruiting approach they used. This shift was especially important given the significant investment each recruit represented, and the fact the the recruiting cycle is approximately one year in length. Delays in making these changes could have meant difficulties continuing on into succeeding years.

For those already on board, the Bank initiated changes in their training program to emphasize more clearly the skills be used in the new position, along with more intense counselling for those having difficulty with, or questions concerning, the new job structure. Opportunities for transfers to other Bank operatins were also considered for interested junior executives.

Finally the implications of losing a higher proportion of marketing oriented individuals selectively were considered, and steps taken to monitor turnover for any trend of this nature. The feeling was that evidence of a growing skills imbalance would have to be countered with additional recruiting (possibly at senior levels) and "down stream" training as remaining account representatives approached promotion to senior representative.

Insufficient time has elapsed since the change to fully assess implications of the shift and subsequent organizational responses. The one piece of hard evidence is the turnover rate, which is more than twice as high for the '84 recruiting class (12 of 68, 17.6%) as for the '83 group (7 of 81, 8.6%) over the same period a year earlier. In addition, four individuals from the '84 class have accepted transfers to other bank divisions. Of the 16 individuals leaving or transferring, 11 exhibited a marketing orientation. Anecdotal evidence from interviews with HR and training staff also indicates that the predicted anxiety and demand for information among trainees is also occurring.

While there is no way of knowing, turnover and anxiety might have been worse without Bank efforts to inform and counsel junior account representatives. Conversely it could be argued that some recruits may have left who would have stayed for now, but would have left later after the full extent of changes became clear. In either case, the Bank is better off for having anticipated the difficulty.

CONCLUSIONS

The reported perceptions of current account representatives, and preliminary evidence of responses to the change, suggest that organizations can not simply ignore individual responses to shifts in the individual-organizations relationship. Such individuals will expect to hold their employer to the "psychological contract" (See Schein, 1970) which they feel they have negotiated.

The primary question relative to such attitudinal analysis in the HR forecasting process is therefore not "Should it be done?", but "How can it be made more precise and useful?" One major difficulty with the analysis conducted in this case was that it predicted negative responses would occur, but provided no information on the magnitude of such responses (i.e., levels of turnover, numbers of marketing vs. analytically oriented individ-uals leaving, etc.) Such trends should be predictable, however. Marketing research, for example, depends on sampled consumer attitudes and some experience with calibration to project likely sales figures. One would think that with some practice it might well be possible to do the same with employee attitudes. Employees are in a sense consumers of the jobs organizations have to offer.

Perhaps such analysis would not be cost effective for all employees in all organizations. Walker's (1980) observation, that in banks, total personnel costs are second only to the cost of capital, seems to suggest, however, that in this case at least it would be advisable for key employees such as those studied here.

REFERENCES

Hall, Douglas T., Careers in Organizations, (Pacific Palisades, Calif.: Goodyear Publishing Co., 1976).

MacCrimmon, Kenneth R., "Improving Decision Making and Manpower Management Systems," "Business Quarterly," Vol. 35, No. 3 (Autumn, 1971), pp. 29-41.

Milkovich, George T. and Mahoney, Thomas A., "Human Resource Planning Models: A Perspective" Human Resource Planning, Vol. 1, No. 1, (Spring, 1978), pp. 19-30.

Miller, Guy E., "A Method for Forecasting Human Resource Needs Against Internal and External Labor Markets," **Human Resource Planning**, Vol. 13, No. 4 (Fall, 1980), pp. 189-200.

Portwood, James D. and Miller Edwin L., "Evaluating the Psychological Contract: Its Implications for Employee Job Satisfaction and Work Behavior," **Proceedings of the 36th National Academy of Management Meetings**, Taylor, R.L., O'Connell, M.J., Zawacki, R.A., and Warrick, D.C., eds, August 14, 1976, pp. 109-113.

Schein, Edgar H., **Organizational Psychology** 2nd Ed., (Englewood Cliffs, N.J.: Prentice-Hall, Inc. 1970).

Schwartz, Robert H., "Practitioners Perceptions of Factors Associated with Human Resource Planning Program Success," Human Resource Planning, Vol. 8, No. 2 (Summer, 1985), pp 55-66.

Smith, Eddie C., "Observations on SHARPS Implementation," Human Resource **Planning**, Vol. 7, No. 1, (Fall, 1984), pp. 63-66.

Walker, James W., **Human Resource Planning** New York: MacGraw-Hill Book Co., 1980).

Wanous, John P., **Organizational Entry** (Reading, Mass.: Addison-Wesley Publishing Co., 1980).

EXECUTIVE CAREER PATTERNS

AND ORGANIZATIONAL ADAPTATION TO CHANGE

Karen N. Gaertner

School of Business Administration
Georgetown University
Washington, DC 20057

INTRODUCTION

Work organizations in the United States have been buffeted by
significant change in their environments during the past few years. There is
reason to believe that these changes in technological, competitive,
regulatory, and social domains will continue to present critical challenges
to organizations. An important task for any firm under these circumstances
is to develop managers who are capable of leading the organization through
this turbulence, adapting to uncertainty, and creating change internally in
anticipation of change to come from without.

In this paper we address adaptation to change as experienced by three
organizations, noting their strategic and structural approaches to change as
will as the career paths characteristic of the organizations and the specific
career experiences of top managers. In the sections to follow we present a
framework that guides the analysis, then describe the three organizations,
and finally draw conclusions regarding some of the more important actions
taken to ensure adaptability under changing business conditions. Information
about the three organizations was obtained through semi-structured interviews
with the top management group (approximately twenty executives per
organization), career histories for all these executives, organization
documents such as corporate histories, annual reports, and organization
charts, and unstructured interviews with other employees as needed, for
clarification, detail, and nuance. In all three cases, a few facts have been
altered in order to protect the confidentiality of the organizations
participating in the study.

ENVIRONMENT, STRATEGY, STRUCTURE, AND CAREERS

Recent research such as Miles and Snow's (1978) work has focused on the
links among business strategy, organizational environments, and
organizational structure. Though results are mixed, there is a general
tendency for high performing organizations to show evidence of congruence
among strategy, structure, and environmental demands. For example, Hambrick
(1983) finds that high performance requires a good "fit" between firm
strategy and environmental characteristics, more proactive, innovative
strategies generally fitting better in turbulent environments. Similarly,
Burns and Stalker's (1961) classic research regarding the relationship
between organizational structure and technical change in the environment

argues for decentralized, flexible, "organic" structures in changing
environments and more centralized, rule-governed, "mechanistic" structures in
stable environments.

What is not well-researched is the way in which managerial careers fit
with strategy, structure, and environmental characteristics, or more
generally, the way in which careers contribute to organizational
effectiveness under varying circumstances. By managerial careers, we mean
relatively enduring patterns of socialization, training, and mobility
(usually position or assignment changes), which may take place within one
organization or across many organizations (Gaertner, 1980). In this view
managerial careers are a process through which people move and develop in
order to assume greater amounts of responsibility.

Research in this area is sparse, but demonstrates the potential
usefulness of this line of inquiry. For example, Hitt, Ireland, and Palia
(1982) find that the importance of different functions (e.g., accounting,
marketing, production) varies with the organization's strategy. Thus a
"manufacturing-driven" company will place strategic emphasis on manufacturing
systems and production efficiency <u>and</u> is likely to be run by people with a
manufacturing background.

In addition to this structural view of careers, there is recent research
that links personality characteristics of executives with organizational
effectiveness. For example, Gupta and Govindarajan (1984) find that managers
who are willing to take risks (within the context of their jobs) and who have
a high tolerance for ambiguity perform better than others. Similarly,
Miller, Dets De Vries, and Toulouse (9182) find that managers with a more
internal locus of control tend to develop more innovative, proactive
strategies than others, and that these strategies are most appropriate in
relatively dynamic, heterogeneous environments.

Despite these scattered results, however, the observation made by
Galbraith and Nathanson (1979) is still valid. They noted, "there is a great
deal that needs to be done in examining which... career process(es) best fit
different product/market strategies and different structures." (p. 265) This
research begins to address that question.

The framework that guides the research is shown in Figure 1. Here we
see that the appropriate strategy and structure for an organization will
vary, depending upon the environment conditions in which the organization
competes. Organizations operating in relatively stable environments are
likely to place strategic emphasis on internal operational efficiency and
"safe" rather than innovative operations. In order to implement this
strategy, a fairly rigid, rule-governed (or tradition-bound), centralized,
functionally oriented, mechanistic structure and culture are likely to be
found. Organizations operating in more uncertain environments are likely to
pursue more market-oriented strategies that emphasize innovation and revenue
enhancement as means toward success. The appropriate structure for this
strategy is likely to be more decentralized, flexible, product or customer
oriented, organic, and ad hoc, supporting risk-taking and change. These
relationships are not universals, but they are supported by research in the
field.

What is not well-known from research are the relationships suggested by
columns 4 and 5 in Figure 1, the fit between patterns, the personal
characteristics of people moving through those careers, and the larger
context of environment, strategy, and structure. This paper addresses that
issue in two ways. First, we explore the relationships between the structure
of managerial careers and the environment, strategy, and structure
of the organizations, as suggested in Figure 1. We expect to find

Environmental Conditions	Strategy	Structure	Career	Executives' Characteristics

Stability
Little
  Uncertainty
	Reactive
	Not innovative
	Cost-focused
	Operations-
	  driven
		Centralized
		Undifferentiated
		Rule-governed
		Risk-averse
			Structured
			Concrete
			Intra-
			  functional
			Few entry
			  ports
			Promotion
			  from within
			Slow moving
				Operations or
				  finance exp.
				Administrative
				  orientation
				External locus
				  of control
				Risk averse
				Low tolerance
				  ofambiguity

Unstable
High
  Uncertainty
	Proactive
	Innovative
	Revenue-focused
	Market-driven
		Decentralized
		Differentiated
		Flexible
		Risk-taking
			Ambiguous
			Inter-
			  functional
			Many entry
			  ports
			Hiring from
			  outside
			Fast moving
				Marketing
				  experience
				Action
				  orientation
				Risk-taking
				High tolerance
				  of ambiguity
				Internal locus
				  of control

Figure 1: Relationships Among Environment, Strategy, Structure,
and Executive Careers

organizations operating in a stable environment to have structured, concrete
career patterns, a strong tendency to promote top managers from within, and
a top management cadre with experience in operation or finance. Similarly,
organizations operating in an uncertain environment are expected to hire
managers from outside, have ill-defined or changing internal promotion
patterns, and be run by managers with a more external focus, probably
expertise in marketing or research and development.

The second question we address is the way in which organizations adapt
to a change in their environments, moving from the top panel of Figure 1 to
the bottom panel. Moreover, we are interested in the importance of career
patterns and executives' career experiences in producing such change, since a
common response to change or adversity is to change the top management team
(Allen, Panian, and Lotz, 1979; Brown, 1982). We know that organizations
structured as in the bottom panel are likely to perform best in turbulent
environments, but by what process do organizations change their internal
strategy, structure, culture, and career patterns when confronted with the
need to move from a placid environment to a turbulent environment? We pursue
these questions in the sections to follow. The discussion is summarized in
Figure 2.

THREE CASES OF ORGANIZATIONAL ADAPTATION TO CHANGE

CONSUMCO

a.   <u>History</u>

CONSUMCO is a multi-billion dollar consumer goods firm. Its roots go
back to the mid-1800's, yet its current form is the result of a recent

	CONSUMCO	SLEEPCO	INFOCO
Environment			
Turbulence	mod-high	moderate	high
Munificence	moderate	moderate	low
Rate of Innovation	moderate	low-mod	high
Strategy			
Proactivity	moderate	low (mod-high)*	high
Driving Function: Past	operations	operations	R & D
Present	marketing	operations	marketing
Structure			
Divisional-Functional	mixed	functional (divisions)*	functional
Decentralization	moderate	moderate	low
Differentiation**	low	high*	moderate
Executive Careers			
Internal-External Source	external	internal	external
Variability Among Executive	high	low	low
Dominant Functional Experience	none	operations	marketing
Concreteness of Career Patterns	low	high	low
Age of Executives	40-50	50-60	30-45
Job Security	low	high	low

* parent company when pertinent
**different cultures in different divisions

Figure 2:   Summary of Company Characteristics

acquisition that nearly doubled the company's size. Prior to the
acquisition, CONSUMCO was considered a conservative, stable, even stodgy
organization, though extremely profitable. In Miles and Snow's (1978) terms,
this was a classic "defender" organization. It was dominant in its markets,
not prone to introduce new products, and it sought to improve profitability
by reducing costs rather than increasing revenues. The structure was
mechanistic and rule-governed. Many functions were centralized, and most
decisions were made at the very top of the organization. The cultural
emphasis was paternalism and risk-avoidance. As one person said, there was a
strong feeling that, "It worked for us then so it will work for us now." The
firm had well-defined career paths within functional areas, nearly always pro
moted managers from within, almost never fired employees. In other words,
the old CONSUMCO fit the top panel of Figure 1 very well.

The company CONSUMCO acquired was rather different. Managers there were
described as "street wise" and "willing to shoot from the hip." Though the
company operated in some of the same markets as CONSUMCO it did not dominate
most of them. This, combined with a broader range of products, led the firm
toward less strategic complacency than was evident at CONSUMCO. This
noncomplacent stance was reflected in numerous reorganizations, a cultural
emphasis on change, and top level executive development that was widely
described as "a revolving door." This firm was operating more toward the
lower half of Figure 1 than the top half, though its strategy could best have
been described as erratic and its structure, changing. Top management career
patterns reflected these strategic and structural characteristics, especially
in marketing (though there were more stable, concrete patterns within the
sales and manufacturing operations).

CONSUMCO today is a mix of these two cultures, though it is dominated at
the top by people from the more "street wise" predecessor organization. At

the time of the acquisition, significant new competition in its markets
successfully ("We killed 'em," said one manager), which lent credibility to
the more aggressive, risk-oriented way of doing business characteristic of
the acquired firm.

CONSUMCO is now more marketing driven and less operations and sales
driven as competition has become more intense. The culture is now described
by most executives as one that emphasizes adaptability and flexibility,
melding the old "shoot from the hip" culture of the acquired firm with the
more cautious, conservative approach of the old CONSUMCO. In other words,
the company is realigning its strategy, structure, and culture in the bottom
panel of Figure 1. However, as discussed below, its career patterns and
general approach to human resource management are still more erratic than
many managers wish.

b.   Structure

CONSUMCO is organized in a mixed functional -divisional structure.
There are three big product groups (division), each with its own marketing,
manufacturing, finance, and personnel functions. Sales and distribution for
two of the three divisions and research and development for all three are
centralized as functional areas, serving all the divisions. This mixed
structure is intended to allow the divisions to develop their own marketing
strategies for their own markets, hire the appropriate human resources to
carry out those marketing strategies, and craft their manufacturing
capability to meet the market plan. At the same time it is intended that
cost efficiencies be realized through centralized functions. This structure
reflects a natural tendency for organizations to reduce costs during times of
intense competition. It also, however, reduces the organizations flexibility
in responding to its environment. In other words, this structure is not
completely consistent with that suggested in the bottom panel of Figure 1.
Whether it will be satisfactory in the long run probably depends upon the
level and frequency of competition in CONSUMCO's markets.

c.   Career Patterns

Career patterns are erratic at CONSUMCO. Adaptation to change was
accomplished, in part, by numerous personnel changes, including many outside
hires at high levels. There is a belief that people from the old, more
stable environment are not appropriate managers for the new, more competitive
environment. Thus, in all areas, career patterns have been disrupted with
outside hires, unusual lateral transfers, and termination. The current
situation, as one person noted, is that the company is "running lean with
nobody in the que." Another, less gently, said "We have been ruthless [with
people] in the past, probably too ruthless." CONSUMCO also does relatively
little college recruiting (though it plans to increase this activity). As a
result there are few stable "entry ports" that initiate internal career
patterns leading to the general manager level. Most managers with whom we
spoke hope that this is a transitional phenomenon. They feel that more
internal mobility is desirable and should be achieved as soon as the
organization finishes hiring the necessary people who will enable it to
compete effectively in its market.

When asked about the firm's greatest strength, the overwhelming response
was its flexibility and adaptability, characteristics very consistent with
the culture described in the lower half of Figure 1. Flexibility is
facilitated by, among other things, the variety in experience of top
managers. The dozen top people come from finance, manufacturing, research
and development, personnel, sales, and marketing. This mix creates more
variety in approaches to problems, sometimes causing conflict but also
promoting creative solutions to the conflict. As one person said, "This is

not like [his former company]. There, everyone at the top is from the same
mold. They all stand around, patting each other on the back, telling each
other what a good job they are doing while their business erodes. Here we
are all different, so we don't run into that problem."

d.   Summary

The old CONSUMCO reflected the top panel of Figure 1, including the
hypothesized relationship between career patterns and the organization's
strategy and structure. The new CONSUMCO is moving toward the bottom half of
the figure, with a more proactive (though hardly high risk) strategy, a more
decentralized structure, and a culture that emphasizes adaptability and
change. However, it is not possible to say what form career patterns have
(or will have), as they are in a state of disruption. In other words, though
personnel changes were a key element in the firm's ability to adapt to
change, existing career patterns (that are supposed to prepare people for
future positions) were a hindrance.

SLEEPCO

a.   History

SLEEPCO is a multi-billion dollar division of a lodging corporation that
operates hotels throughout the world. SLEEPCO is very profitable and has
experienced steady, fairly rapid growth during the last twenty-five years.
Top management sees new competition in their markets developing during the
next decade, as well as a need to segment their markets and develop niche-
specific products. These insights are fairly recent, and not particularly
consistent with the way in which the hotel business has been run in this
company in the past.

SLEEPCO, while facing changing environments and experiencing steady
growth, has not faced any significant jolts from the environment. This
division promotes almost exclusively from within, hiring graduates from
highly respected university-based hotel management programs. Strong, well-
entrenched norms about careers in this division exist. Managerial career
patterns include developing experience and expertise in all of the functions
of hotel management and rotation from one hotel to another, increasing in
size and complexity. Mobility from entry level to top management in SLEEPCO
is not rapid, but it is very regular. Employees in this division are
relatively closely knit and a strong "old boy" network operates. In sum,
SLEEPCO is similar in orientation to the old CONSUMCO, functioning in the top
half of Figure 1.

b.   Structure

As would be expected, this rigid structure and strong normative
orientation do not lend themselves to internal innovation. The way in which
SLEEPCO innovates is through reliance on corporate staffs. The parent
company, like CONSUMCO, is organized in a mixed functional-divisional
structure, though there are fewer centralized functions in the parent. One
of these functions, however, is charged with making the risky real estate
deals that result in new hotels. Another staff group is charged with new
product development. Thus, the central concept for adapting to change is a
willingness to redefine the organization's "technical core" (Thompson, 1967),
allowing stable businesses to operate as the technical core, "buffered" by
staff-level groups charged with managing risk and creating change. SLEEPCO
is the technical core, running a relatively routine, well-known business,
while the corporate staffs are the buffer, interacting with the environment,
creating opportunity, and managing change.

c.   Career Patterns

The risk associated with this type of structure and mix of cultures is that SLEEPCO will continue to train people, through career pattern mobility, to run only part of the business. SLEEPCO is not training people who can make a contribution to the parent company in accepting and managing risk. Indeed, as time goes on, the cultures may become so different between SLEEPCOand the other parts of the parent company that they may become incompatible.

SLEEPCO's parent organization has a commitment to developing executives internally. There is a corporate willingness to "create jobs in order to add talent to the bench." In contrast to CONSUMCO where there is little concern about the talent on the bench, SLEEPCO's parent has begun to cluster jobs around promising employees rather than wait for an opening in the structure, in order to develop and keep their best people.

This corporate-level activity of creating developmental situations for high potential future executives is also a source of cultural conflict between SLEEPCO and the parent. When high potential candidates are identified in, for example, the planning function, there is a desire to rotate them through SLEEPCO so that they can get hands-on experience with the largest and most profitable division in the company. Yet the rigidly defined career patterns and closely knit culture in SLEEPCO present a problem. There is a great deal of resistance to these high potential candidates. As one person said, "We moved one fellow into [SLEEPCO] but they blocked and tackled him when we put him in place. He left." One executive summarized the situation as he said, "[SLEEPCO] is the best at what we have done and the best at what our problems are."

d.   Summary

SLEEPCO, by itself, probably would not perform well in a turbulent environment. It is structured to function in a stable environment. However, in partnership with the parent organization, and through removing the more uncertain aspects of the hotel business from SLEEPCO, the division is able to continue to contribute substantially to company growth and earnings. Though there are signs of tension in this partnership, this sort of arrangement has the potential to provide the parent company with both the ability to adapt to change while simultaneously operating efficiently under stable conditions.

INFOCO

a.   History

The last of the three organizations is the smallest and youngest. Barely 20 years old, this billion dollar division operates a variety of information management and data transmission services to industry. As part of a Fortune 500 parent organization, INFOCO is bound by some of the policies and procedures of the parent, including a strong reliance on strategic planning. At the same time, it is rather different from most of the other divisions of the parent in that it does no manufacturing. In fact, according to one executive, the parent company admits to "not understanding" the division, and the division, in turn, "has done little to endear itself to [the parent]."

INFOCO is almost completely self-contained, unlike SLEEPCO. The division experienced very rapid growth until about five years ago, when the basis of its business was supplanted by new technology. As one person said, "We made money but never knew how or why. It was like a giant faucet that rained money on us. When it started to dry up we had no way of knowing why."

During this period the company was organized in a matrix-type structure, products were prepared exactly to customer specifications, somewhat unrelated businesses were acquired, and the company's unique technological capability drove the business. Career patterns did not exist, and the company was so loosely structured that it was ill-prepared to deal with changes in the needs of its customer base. In other words, INFOCO was operating in the bottom half of Figure 1, but to such an extreme that it did not have the structures and disciplines in place to help it monitor and anticipate changes in its environment. By 1982 the division was performing poorly, due in part to a business recession, to its unsuccessful new business ventures, and to continuing changes in its technological environment. These problems led to a new president being appointed in 1982, the eighth in its history.

This president has many years of parent company general management experience but no experience in the technology that forms the historic base of INFOCO. The top management team, put together in the last three years, is more similar to the president than to long term INFOCO employees. Only one of the ten has significant INFOCO experience. The others tend to be young (30's) and <u>not</u> technically trained. Thus the president hired people who were similar to each other but not similar to older INFOCO employees. This approach is consistent with the "outside hiring" notion presented in the bottom part of Figure 1 but not consistent with the "variety of experience at the top" notion. Nor is it similar to CONSUMCO's approach (great variety among top managers) that accounts for some of CONSUMCO's adaptability and flexibility.

During the first two years of the president's tenure there were three major reorganizations, two major layoffs, and a major strategic redirection. The layoffs were necessary in order to implement a new strategic direction away from the business as it was in 1982 and toward a new technology and a much more focused, niche-driven, market-oriented set of products. In order words, the company took some very bold, proactive strategic steps ahead of its competition in order to get back on track and "win in this environment."

b.   <u>Structure</u>

INFOCO is organized functionally at the top with product groups within each function. This, of course, is not consistent with Figure 1. Marketing and sales are separate from research and development and, as might be expected, the firm is grappling with coordination problems inherent in trying to market and sell new customer-oriented products out of one department with the R&D creators of the products in another department. This, together with some historic animosity between marketing and R&D and the new strategic emphasis on marketing rather than R&D, leaves INFOCO with an operational challenge in the coming months.

c.   <u>Career Patterns</u>

The situation at INFOCO seems to provide a test for the notion that a good general manager can manage anything. In the other two organizations, the people running the business are a product of the business or of a business in their industry. In the case of INFOCO, most top executives were not schooled in the industry. Only now is INFOCO beginning to staff their lower and middle level positions with people experienced in the industry (though not from INFOCO).

There are no internal career paths leading to top positions within INFOCO, though the parent company generally promotes executives from within. The resident of INFOCO has never been an insider. Nor are there many lateral outlets for INFOCO employees to move to other parts of the parent firm. Thus, careers are truncated and, as one person noted, "The division loses

some of its most ambitious employees early in their careers because there is
no place for them to go."

As with CONSUMCO, there is some willingness among managers to begin to
address the need for developing managers who can be promoted internally. One
person went so far as to say that the critical task now is to, "...leave the
organization alone. It has been jerked around too much lately. People need
some stability." Others echoed this view, saying that their primary focus
was to heal the organization and to keep the critical mass of experienced
talent from leaving the company.

d.   Summary

INFOCO is different from the other organizations because it never has
operated in a truly placid environment, though the firm's technological
advantage perhaps made it appear so in the past. It is the only one of the
three organizations that is moving from a matrix-type structure to a
functional structure, and it is the only one that had no career paths in
place from the past that could have been a factor in adapting to change. In
many respects INFOCO is now structured like organizations in the top panel of
Figure 1, those operating in a stable environment. Yet INFOCO's business
environment is not stable. In fact, the most recent reorganization
represented a move away from a purely functional structure to the current,
more product-oriented functional form. When asked why the division was not
organized by product throughout, the prevailing opinion was that the R&D
group needed to stay together to avoid losing its critical mass. There is so
much emphasis on cost reduction now that a purely product-oriented structure
is not considered a viable alternative because of the extra expense incurred
in duplicating R&D human resources.

DISCUSSION AND CONCLUSIONS

At the beginning of this paper we identified two questions that would be
addressed, one regarding the relationship between organizational careers and
structure and strategy and the other regarding the way in which organizations
adapt to changes in their environment (and the role that careers play in
adaptation).

As summarized in Figure 3, we can begin to answer these questions, based
on the evidence from the three cases:

First, with respect to the "fit" between the structure of career paths
and the structure and strategy of the organization, it appears that in stable
environments, career patterns are as suggested in Figure 1. That is, using
the old CONSUMCO and the current SLEEPCO, we saw that centralized, well-
defined, mechanistic structures tended to have well-definded, concrete career
paths. Moreover, long-term (if not lifelong) employment characterized these
two organizations, consistent with a strong policy to promote from within.
In other words, existing career patterns did a very good job of preparing
future executives for the status quo.

With regard to careers in organizations operating in more dynamic
environments, our results are less instructive, partly because these
organizations were all in the process of adapting to their new, more
uncertain environments. Certainly the evidence suggests that more ambiguous
career paths with many entry points, as suggested in the bottom part of
Figure 1, is the direction in which these organization are going, but in
CONSUMCO and INFOCO it is not correct to say that systematic career paths
exist at all. Thus, while there was sentiment to begin more internal
mobility and executive development in both organizations, we do not know what
form, if any, career paths will take in the long run. Thus the question of

STUDY CONCLUSIONS

1. Stable environments and mechanistic organizational structures fit
    with concrete career patterns and internal promotion policies.

2. People are a key element in organizations' ability to adapt
    to change but existing career patterns are not.

3. New blood is required for organizations to implement significant
    strategic change.

4. A short-term need to cut costs can be counterproductive in
    the long run for organizations seeking to become more flexible.

5. The opportunity to manage a small but complete part of a business
    is useful for training general managers internally.

6. Organizational adaptability and flexibility is enhanced by a
    heterogeneous top management cadre composed of individuals
    with different career experience.

Figure 3: Conclusions

"fit" between strategy, structure, and career patterns in turbulent
environments remains open.

The second question we addressed was the process of adapting to a more
turbulent environment. In all of the companies, adaptation included
strategic change, extreme for INFOCO, moderate for the other two. All three
firms became more market-driven. Two of the three, CONSUMCO and INFOCO, also
chose to make structural changes. Interestingly, however, the structure in
place in CONSUMCO and INFOCO are _not_ those that the literature predicts will
allow the companies to be most adaptive. CONSUMCO has product divisions, but
with key functions centralized, some of the problems of coordination
characteristic of functional organized, some of the problems of coordination
characteristic of functional organizations plague them. INFOCO's main
business are functionally organized, and this company is experiencing some
difficulty coordinating marketing and research and development. Both
companies are placing a strong emphasis on cost cutting which seems to be
overriding the need for adaptable (but more costly) sub-units.

The third company, SLEEPCO, is the only one of the three organizations
to create adaptability as a staff function, allowing the operating divisions
to continue to run the stable part of the business. SLEEPCO may have chosen
this route because it was never as dominant in its markets as CONSUMCO and
INFOCO and therefore was never as complacent as the other two. It may also
be that SLEEPCO is not facing declining profit margins or serious threats, so
is able to take a more gradual approach to adapting to an uncertain
environment. In any case, SLEEPCO's response, together with its parent
company's actions to manage risk and uncertainty at the corporate staff
level, is more consistent with the approach suggested by the research
literature regarding effective adaptation to changing conditions.

Finally, while personnel changes were part of change in all three cases,
in none of them were internal career patterns used as a means of developing
managers who could cope with change and help the organization adapt. In
fact, just the reverse is true. One of the _primary_ means of coping with
change was not through strategy or structure but rather, through key outside
hires. At CONSUMCO and INFOCO considerable outside hiring took place (and
continues, to a degree).

At SLEEPCO there was no large-scale replacement of personnel, and career paths in SLEEPCO itself were left unchanged. However, "outsiders" to SLEEPCO, the corporate finance staff, were "brought in" to create the real estate deals that would form the basis of future profitability within SLEEPCO.

Several tentative conclusions regarding the way in which organizations adapt to change emerge from these three cases. First, all three firms are pursuing an outward looking, market-driven strategy that involves market segmentation, focused effort, and building from strength. This also implies that people with such a perspective, people who have some familiarity with marketing concepts, people who are outward looking, are likely to do well and to provide leadership under these conditions.

Second, the first point notwithstanding, having several career patterns that lead to the top of the organization is a positive contributor to an organization's ability to sense the need for and to produce change. Managers at CONSUMCO felt that the variety of experience at the top was critical to their ability to be flexible and adaptive. Employees at INFOCO are critical of the nontechnical background of top management (yet also realize that a marketing orientation is important in the current environment).

Third, it is apparent from these three cases that "new blood" is required for organizations to implement significant change in strategic direction. Whether internal career paths can train managers to be adaptive to change is not clear. None of these three cases presents that situation. However, the advice of several executives with whom we spoke is instructive. They argued that lower level managers, as they were moving through the organization, should be exposed to as much cross-functional experience and as many different management styles as possible in order to develop a broad perspective and personal flexibility.

Fourth, cost-cutting was one of the first responses to a rapidly changing competitive situation in CONSUMCO and INFOCO, yet the implications of cost cutting are not long term adaptive, both in terms of structure (centralization) and human resource depth ("running too lean"). As one person said, "We may have reduced costs too much. We could have problems executing the plan. We're in trouble if a key person leaves." Another expressed a similar concern about getting below a critical mass of experiences people in some areas. Structurally, the most flexible, adaptable organizations are decentralized and organized by product or customer or market rather than function. This is not INFOCO's structure and at CONSUMCO the product divisions are very large and, as noted, lacking two key functions.

Fifth, and finally, the solution pursued by SLEEPCO for adapting to change is intriguing, unusual, and worthy of further consideration. The parent has managed to be adaptive without being disruptive, at least in the short run. This, on the surface, appears to be a promising solution to the problem of balancing the need for adaptability with stability, the need for risk-taking with the need for predictability, the need for adventure with the need for security. Whether this strategy will backfire as different cultures emerge within the parent is not yet clear, though this is certainly a risk.

At the same time that we can derive several questions unanswered. First, it is not clear how much change a competent work force can tolerate before it becomes too distracted and demoralized. Organizations, as collections of individuals, benefit from success and continuity. Too much change and/or too many strategic refinements deny a work force the sense of stability and predictability from which competent performance may emerge. Many employees at INFOCO felt that the firm had experienced too much change

and uncertainty to be able to function effectively. Similar feelings were
expressed at CONSUMCO, though not as strongly.

     Second, as noted above, we do not have much evidence regarding the ways
in which change-oriented career patterns can be institutionalized in
organizations. Career patterns usually imply stability and repetition that
can run counter to the need for flexibility. Certainly in these three cases
we saw examples of career patterns not contributing to an organization's
ability to adapt to change. Because one of the primary purposes of career
paths is to train and develop future managers, we are left with a question
about the efficacy of traditional career mobility in organizations facing
turbulent environments.

     Several of the executives with whom we spoke did offer ideas about
career structures that could encourage flexibility and adaptability. One
such suggestion had to do with the legitimization of risk-taking. At
CONSUMCO one manager said his unit had made a $10 million mistake and, "To
the organization's credit I didn't get canned. What they did was a clear
signal that they encourage risk-taking, though you certainly have to manage
the risk." Another manager said that his job was to encourage his
subordinates to take calculated risks and then to manage the failures while
his subordinates managed the success. Yet another said he had "tweaked the
com[ensation] system" in order to reward the new activities he was stressing.

     Another component of adaptive career patterns is inclusion of the
opportunity for young managers to run a small part of the business. This
requires an organizational structure with small operating divisions rather
than large ones, each focused around a small number of related products or
services. Under these circumstances high potential employees are given
practice in running an entire operation on a small scale. SLEEPCO's parent
is doing some of this, as is INFOCO's.

     The last unresolved issue from these three cases is the extent to which
outside hiring is desirable. CONSUMCO's top management expressed the need to
hire from outside, as they have done, but the _desire_ to being much more
promotion from within. INFOCO has done the same. SLEEPCO is buffered by the
parent and does nothing but entry-level hiring.

     The literature suggest that internal promotion practices contribute to
the retention of good employees, as these employees develop company loyalty
in anticipation of future promotions (Smith, 1979; Anderson, Milkovich, and
Tsui, 1981; Rhodes and Doering, 1983; Scholl, 1983). However, these studies
fail to take account of the effect of changing business conditions on the
efficacy of internal promotion patterns. Certainly the evidence from these
three cases suggests that the benefits of internal promotion patterns are
fewer under conditions of change. Unfortunately we have no way of saying, at
this point, how much outside hiring is good. Clearly, this is an area in
need of more research.

     This study has provided some preliminary conclusions regarding the way
in which managerial career patterns, or the lack thereof, can affect an
organization's ability to adapt to change. The conclusions are clearly
tentative, as they are based on only three cases and, within those cases, on
rich but unsystematic interview data. In order to begin to develop stronger
conclusions we need to extend the study to more organizations and to develop
methods of systematic data collection from a wider group of employees in each
organization. Weaknesses notwithstanding, these data have given us insights
into the way in which organizations adapt to increased uncertainty in their
environments and the role that career patterns can play in the process of
adapting to such change.

REFERENCES

Allen, M.P., Panian, S.K., and Lotz, R.E. "Managerial Succession and Organizational Performance: A Recalcitrant Problem Revisited." Administrative Science Quarterly, Vol. 24,No. 2 (June, 1979) pp. 167-180.

Anderson, J.C., Milkovich, G.T., and Tsui, A. "A Model of Intra-Organizational Mobility," Academy of Management Review, Vol. 6, No. 3 (October, 1981) pp. 529-538.

Brown, M.C. "Administrative Succession and Organizational Performance: The Succession Effect." Administrative Science Quarterly, Vol. 17, No. 1, (March, 1982) pp. 1-16.

Gaertner, K.N., "The Structure of Organizational Careers", Sociology of Education, Vol. 53, No. 1 (January, 1980) pp. 7-20.

Galbraith, J.R., and Nathanson, D.A., "The Role of Organizational Structure and Process in Strategy Implementation," in D.E. Schendel and C.W. Hofer (eds.) Strategic Management. (Boston: Little Brown and Co., 1979).

Gupta, A.K. and Govindarajan, V., "Business Unit Strategy, Managerial Characteristics, and Business Unit Effectiveness at Strategy Implementation." Academy of Management Journal, Vol. 27, No. 1 (March, 1984) pp. 25-41.

Hambrick, D.C., "Some Tests of the Effectiveness and Functional Attributes of Miles and Snow's Strategic Types", Academy of Management Journal, Vol. 26, No. 1 (March, 1983) pp. 5-26.

Hitt, M.A., Ireland, R.D., and Palia, K.A., "Industrial Firms' Grand Strategy and Functional Importance: Moderating Effects of Technology and Uncertainty", Academy of Management Journal, Vol. 25, No. 2 (June, 1982) pp. 265-298.

Miles, R.E., and Snow, C.C., Organizational Strategy, Structure and Process. (New York: McGraw-Hill, 1978).

SECTION 4:

STRATEGIES FOR PRODUCTIVITY MANAGEMENT

In this section emphasis is on strategies and methodologies which can
be employed for productivity management of human resources. There has been
much written around the issue. On the other hand there has been a lot less
written concerning strategies and methods which have some promise of leading
to productivity improvement. The three papers in this section home in on
ways that may have some promise.

Mactaggart indicates that improvements in productivity can be brought
about by developing a planning framework which focuses on critical aspects
of human resource management. The paper presents strategies for allocating,
deploying and using the organization's human resource as part of its
fundamental process of managing change. The paper is set in the context of
Canada's federal public service using numerical examples coupled with the
discussion of methods of strategy development.

The next two papers by Bolda discuss productivity issues relating to
strategies for making training and sourcing decisions based on productivity
considerations. The papers review procedures used by personnel researchers
at General Motors. The first paper is a pilot study aimed at forecasting
cost-benefits associated with proposals for job training and retraining of
factory workers, both skilled and unskilled. The second study involves
maintenance and tool room jobs. Attention in this study is turned to which
source of job entrants will be the most productive. Both studies used task
teams which included manager-judges to help set the basic parameters and
then checked the results using theoretical methods refined from the
personnel research literature.

STRATEGIES FOR MANAGING PRODUCTIVITY IMPROVEMENT

R.V. Mactaggart

Public Service Commission of Canada
Ottawa, Ontario K1A DM7

INTRODUCTION

Productivity improvement seems certain to remain a catchword of the eighties. Whether stated as a `search for excellence' or giving `value for money' it is a concept which is as much in vogue in the public as in the private sector. No matter how it is expressed it ultimately resolves into the need to do more with less. In human resource terms, planning to do more with less means that payoff must come from the better use which it is planned to make of the organization's work force. The real and continuing purpose of human resource planning is therefore to obtain a better return on current an projected payroll expenditure.

Acceptance of the purpose as stated above has considerable significance for the type of planning that is done and how it is done. In the first place it means that a human resource planning strategy must be developed by corporate management, at the apex of the organization where responsibility rests for all strategic planning. In the second place it means that development of such a strategy will integrate human resource and planning at all levels of the organization. Integration takes place because line managers need to know corporate management's plans for the deployment and utilization of human resources before finalizing their own objectives and priorities. Thirdly, it means that the human resource planning strategy must seek to improve the ratio between human resource inputs and the outputs which are obtained from their efforts, which is the essence of productivity.

METHODS FOR PRODUCTIVITY IMPROVEMENT

There are basically two ways to tackle productivity improvement. One is to deal at the level of individual employees and to study ways of increasing their outputs. This is the "work smarter, not harder" approach which often leads to task simplification by applying time and motion methods. The second way deals with total outputs and studies how the organization's complete work force is deployed in relation to where those outputs are produced. This is the strategy approach, and it involves analyzing structures, policies, systems and functions so as to establish what amounts of human resource input are used where they are used, and what obstacles may be barring their optimum use. A comprehensive productivity improvement programme will combine aspects of both approaches. Whatever, the approach, the quantity of human resources that is, and will in future be needed, depends primarily on two factors:

1. The volume of outputs which are to be produced.

2. The levels of efficiency which can be obtained in
    producing those outputs.

Both factors are of major strategic concern, and must be planned by
corporate management. First they must plan for a given level of demand for
goods or services and how to meet it. They must also plan to involve
employees in efforts to become more efficient, and the human resource
planning strategy should be the primary instrument for directing such
efforts. The strategy which is adopted must at least encourage all levels
of management to find better ways of allocating and scheduling work, of
applying technology to speed up processes, and of streamlining
administrative tasks.

The first step in developing the strategy is to identify which outputs
are produced for the direct benefit or consumption of external clients and
users. It is value of those goods and services which are delivered beyond
the boundaries of the organization that constitute the best measure of its
return on resources employed. The next step is to determine which parts of
the organization directly produce the outputs for external consumption. In
some units the greater part of their human resources will be committed to
that production, while in others only a small part, or even none at all,
will be involved. Resources which are deployed in functional units such as
finance, personnel and data processing belong in the latter category, and
contribute only indirectly to the value of what the organization creates.
Note that production is not used in a narrow manufacturing sense, but
depends on the mission and mandate of a particular organization. In the
public sector it could refer to the delivery of social benefits, the testing
of materials or the granting of loans to small businesses. The productive
functions could therefore be as varied as financial audit or applied
research, again depending on where and how their outputs are used. A third
step is to compare the inputs of human resources which have measurable
outputs against those whose outputs are not, and perhaps cannot be
quantified. Completion of these tasks marks the end of the developmental
stage of human resource planning. Its results can be displayed so as to
separate the direct, or productive system, from the indirect, or maintenance
and support system. They will often show that few units in the organization
fall exclusively into either system, and even they may not always fit into
the classical descriptions of `line' and `staff'. Analysis of the results
will also show that every unit of the organization, regardless of the
nominal system it belongs to, uses a proportion of its resources in
seemingly unproductive tasks. Sharing information, reviewing data, checking
results can all serve purposes, and a modicum of such overhead activities is
unavoidable, but they should not be allowed to absorb more than a small
proportion of available resources.

The development stage defines and sets the scene for what should be
continuing trusts of the corporate strategy. One of the thrusts is to
deploy more resources into the direct or productive system, making it
possible to increase outputs; the other is to change the mix of activities
in favour of those with measurable outputs, making it possible to monitor
efficiency. These two essential features of the human resource planning
strategy pave the way for specifying its short term objectives. The
preliminary work that has been done also lays the groundwork for preparing
an organization plan, because it pinpoints areas where units could be re-
structured to give a better concentration of functions and tasks, and
perhaps give some economies of scale. The next step is to decide on
realistic objective which the human resource planning strategy should be
able to achieve within a specified time frame.

Selecting objectives is always a matter of judgment, but it can be made easier by finding out how the current breakdown of tasks and activities has changed over time. It make little difference whether the existing ratio between direct and indirect systems is 80:20 or 50:50; nor does it matter greatly whether the split between measurable and non-measurable functions is 60:40 or 70:30. What is important is to retain the initial separation that was done, so that the same organizational units are classified in the same way and remain on the same side of the line separating the productive from the maintenance system. The number of employees on both sides of the dividing line is then tabulated in an historical time series, covering all functions and units, and a similar time series is compiled on the proportion of payroll expended on each activity.

Completion of the foregoing tasks (which can be undertaken by staff specialist) presents a concise and comprehensive picture of the way in which the organization has been evolving. It brings a disciplined look to bear on the past and present deployment of resources, raising questions about its current efficacy. Closer study of the expansion or contraction of functions will reveal those situations where transfers of responsibilities and activities have been a factor, and those where they have not. The results may on occasion cause some surprises, even if total strength and the relative value of the payroll have not changed dramatically during the period under review. Surprising or not, attention can now be directed to changes which were the result of known shifts in programs and outputs, and to those which occurred because of internal policies and procedures (or were even due to plain empire building). Corporate management has to decide to what extent the changes are still appropriate, and whether they are consistent with the future shape of the organization. It is those decisions which dictate the scale of the strategic deployment which is planned.

HUMAN RESOURCE PLANNING STRATEGY

An example of a possible human resource planning strategy can be given by supposing that a five per cent increase is needed in the delivery of outputs to external clients (production from the `direct' system). For demonstration purposes it is supposed that the organization in question has 2,000 employees. Units in which more than half the work force is engaged in the direct production of goods or services for external users account for 60 per cent of total strength. Those units constitute the productive system, regardless of how they are linked organizationally. The remaining 40 per cent, 800 employees altogether, work in units where less than half of the human resource is committed to producing outputs for external users. The strategy statement would cover its broad intent, its immediate objectives and criteria for achieving them. On that basis it might be expressed as follows:

> Human Resource Planning Strategy: to increase by three per cent the number of employees working in key units with high priority operations. Achieving this goal will mean transfers and new assignments for about the same proportion of present strength, so should less than 70 employees. The incidence of these movements of personnel will vary between units, and has been calculated to ensure that the activities which will most benefits are those with measurable outputs in the productive system.

> Concurrently, all Responsibility Centre Managers would be directed to deploy resources within their respective units so as to reduce by five per cent the proportion of employees whose outputs are not presently measurable.

The strategy allows for any combination of measurable and non-measurable
activities. Depending on what the initial mix is, the internal
deployment may give rise to a temporary surplus in some units. Where
that happens the surplus would be reserved for redeployment as a
corporate resource. The manner in which the internal, or tactical
level, adjustments are effected will be decided by unit managers, each
of whom must prepare an appropriate operational plan. They should be
given a target date when they have to submit a combined operational and
human resource plan for approval. They must by then have systems in
place to record measurable outputs,and their success in planning for and
making the required changes will be judged by changes in the levels of
those outputs at subsequent reviewing dates. Outputs will also become
the key factor in assessing each unit manager's continuing standards of
performance. The organization plan can then be revised to show the new
establishment levels which the strategy is designed to produce. The
expected outcome of its application is summarized for the entire
organization in Table 1.

Application of the strategy brings about the redeployment of 66
employees, which is 3.3 per cent of the total strength of 2,000. In return,
the proportion producing outputs for external clients goes up from 60 to 62
percent, and the internal support level goes down from 40 to 38 percent,
which means a shift of four per cent in the proportion of resources deployed
in the `direct' system. Similarly, the spread between measurable and non-
measurable functions and activities widens by five percentage points. the
strategy identifies areas in which additional jobs will be created and what
sort of jobs they will be. It also begins the process of identifying what
number of people may need to be retrained and what sort of training they
will need.

The strategy does not rely on a rigid formula, so it has the
flexibility to develop options whose different impacts can be precisely
calculated. The options can be prepared by specialist, who need not assume
that there are superfluous jobs nor that any less than essential tasks are
performed. Their basic premises are that the mix of jobs being done changes
over time, with some tasks and activities becoming more important and others
less so, and that some of the work that is being performed offers immediate
scope for improvement. The more complex the range of tasks which an
activity includes the more it can be improved. What the adopted option
should do is to selectively favour managers who are output oriented, and it
should be slanted towards units which are predominantly producing goods and
services for external users.

The strategy does not deal with which tasks might be improved nor how.
That is left to the discretion of individual managers, and how they go about
it becomes a measure of their competence. They can of course use experts in
fields such as methods study, job design and office automation. They may
consult with specialists is proven techniques like work sampling or zero
base budgeting to analyze their operations. They can also involve
subordinates in the improvement process, perhaps leading to a more
participative style of management, or the introduction of quality of work
life incentives along with new applications of technology.

Decision making is always a matter of choices - between goals,
priorities and methods, among other - and the decisions about which
activities could or should be made more efficient are a matter of tactics,
which are dealt with in the next and final stage of human resource planning.
This is the stage when managers plan the training and development, the
staffing actions and the job revisions which are all needed to adapt to a
changing operational situation. This is when they begin to reach decisions
about performance and work assignments after reviewing employee capabilities

TABLE 1: RESOURCE UTILIZATION IN THE XYZ ORGANIZATION (2,000 employees)

Productive System: 1200 employees

	'External' Outputs		'Internal' Outputs	
	Meas.	Non-meas.	Meas.	Non-meas.
Deployments	600	200	300	100
Strategic	+26	+6	+7	+1
Tactical	+10	-10	5	-5
	636	196	312	96

Maintenance System: 800 employees

	Meas.	Non-meas.	Meas.	Non-meas.
Deployments	150	50	450	150
Strategic	-3	-3	-20	-14
Tactical	+3	-3	+8	-8
	150	44	438	128

Pre-deployment utilization

Direct	Indirect	Meas.	Non-meas.
600	150	600	200
200	50	300	100
300	450	150	50
100	150	450	150
1,200	800	1,500	500

Ratio: 60/40   75/25

Post-deployment utilization

Direct	Indirect	Meas.	Non-meas.
636	150	636	196
196	44	312	96
312	438	150	44
96	128	438	128
1,240	760	1,536	464

Ratio 62/38   78/23

and potential. This too is the time when they need to consider
subordinates' career interests, prepare succession plans, and study the
composite nature of the work force.

The outputs of this management activity which are most relevant in
human resource planning terms are the identification of impending shortfalls
or surpluses, deficiencies in knowledge and skill, and changes which are
desired in the overall profile of the work force. The specific human
resource planning effort is to define and select the means to deal with
those issues, and to move towards the underlying goals which managers want
to attain regarding the caliber and composition of the groups that they
manage. Its results form the basis of negotiations with the delivery
systems of personnel administration, so that the functional specialists can
plan their workload. This is done in terms of positions to be structured

and classified, employees to be transferred or promoted, new entrants to be
hired and placed, training to be given, candidates to be tested and
individuals to be counselled.

The basic strategy allows senior management to direct and control a
process to improve the way human resources are used. The process is a
continuous one, but it might not be the best way to deal with a situation
where significant downsizing must take place. Such a situation may result
from economic recession or be due to transferring work to another location.
In the public sector it is more likely to arise because of public pressure
to obtain value for money while at the same time mounting new or expanded
programs. A strategy is therefore needed which can be applied selectively,
without either curtailing existing operations or ruling out delivery of
essential new services, and which relies entirely n attrition to achieve its
objective.

CANADIAN FEDERAL PUBLIC SERVICE EXAMPLE

Attrition means leaving the outflow taps open while the inflow taps are
either closed or turned down. Using that simple concept it is quite
feasible to reduce the work force to any given level. What is theoretically
possible has to be balanced against what would be counter-productive, so the
strategy must strike a balance between inflow and outflow, and establish
where and in what numbers replacements should be allowed for employees who
leave. The balancing act is made more difficult by the fact that rates of
separation vary widely between occupational groups or categories of
employees. Canada's federal public service has six major categories.
Historically the attrition rate has been lowest from its Management Category
and highest from its Operational Category, which covers skilled trades and
general services occupations. Because of their different loss rates (both
voluntary and involuntary) a complete ban on hiring would lead to a much
faster rate of depletion from some categories and groups than from others.
Such a freeze would also have more impact on some departments, or branches
of the organization, than on others, because again of the different
composition of their employee groups.

In the following example the objective is to achieve a reduction in
strength of eight per cent. This arbitrary figure is used because the rate
of separations from the public service has been at least that high in recent
years. Four options are outlined and the answer to the question of when the
target reduction of eight percent would be met depends on which option is
adopted.

> Option 1: Target reduction of eight per cent in all categories. Losses
> from each occupational group must reach that level before an
> vacancies can be filled. Replacements can then be brought
> in only to the extent that the number of employees in each
> group level remains eight per cent below its starting
> strength.

The universal nature of this option makes it easy to apply and to
monitor. It also has the advantage that it does not undermine stability by
eroding the base of the organization. The risk of doing so and producing a
top heavy structure is due to the internal career advancement opportunities
which arise when vacancies occur at senior levels. The practice of filling
them by promotion exerts a pull function, causing a chain reaction and
triggering a series of appointments in all levels below. Without the rider
in this option a ban on replacement would have little or no effect, except
on the lowest levels where most external recruitment takes place. A
disadvantage of the option is that the time any unit takes to achieve the
objective depends on the distribution of its employees between categories.

Since the mix is unique to each department some would reach the eight per cent reduction much sooner than others. This would be a major drawback if the strategy was aimed to bring about successive levels of reduction, but would be less of a problem if a single cutback was planned.

> Option 2: Overall reduction of eight per cent from current strength, but it does not apply to specified "essential" groups. The number and size of the exempted groups will be compensated for by adding to the percentage cutback in the remainder. Beyond that, the embargo on replacements applies as in Option 1

The work force reduction programme which was implemented by Canada's federal government in 1979 made an exception of certain groups such as correctional staff in federal penitentiaries and nurses in veterans' hospitals. The drawback is that the reasons for the exemptions are always debatable and liable to change over time. For example, governments can (and do) bring in measures designed to reduce the number of offenders who are sentenced to prison terms. Fewer in detention might mean less need for prison staff but more demand for psychologists, sociologists and others supervising parole conditions. Hospitals too have been transferred to provincial from federal jurisdiction. This option would also have widely varying impacts on departments. Those having a large proportion of their establishment in exempt groups would be particularly constrained in all other areas. In other situations the temptation would exist to force fit some jobs into an exempt classification. An obvious case in point might be in financial administration which employs qualified accountants who could also meet the requirements for entry to the professional auditing group. If either group was exempted, the possibility would exist to change the classification of positions from one group to the other by emphasizing duties appropriate to the exempted group.

> Option 3: An average reduction of eight per cent it can vary between categories and groups within each department as long as the cutback in the department's total strength meets the target.

The flexibility in this option allows senior management to exempt certain groups which are critical to their own department's functions. A handful of specialists, all belonging to the same occupational group, might fill key roles in several areas of activity which would be jeopardized if any one of them left and could not be replaced. A disadvantage of the option is that it upsets the previously existing balance between groups, a balance which was presumably established to create an effective organization. Exemptions which were not carefully controlled could soon product a lopsided structure which would threaten a department's long term capacity to fulfill its mandate.

> Option 4: Target reduction of eight per cent of a pay band, regardless of the mix of occupations which it covers. Replacements can be brought in for losses from and occupational group as long as the total reduction remains at the eight per cent level among all those whose annual salaries place them in a particular income range.

Using pay bands instead of occupational categories and groups gives senior management much more latitude to cope with the particular circumstances which each department faces. It offers more flexibility because discrete pay bands, say at five thousand dollar intervals, tend to iron out the differences in attrition rates between occupational groups. The distribution of employees according to annual rates of pay provides a baseline which is uniquely fitted to each department, and allows managers to

change the mix of occupational groups to suit new conditions. It also paves
the way for better control over payroll costs, which is the theme of the
third strategy.

The selected work force reduction strategy might offer managers a
choice of options, and be stated as follows:

Strategy for Work For Adjustment: The purpose is to bring about a major
shift of human resources within the department. Its goal is to reduce
the number of employees by eight per cent, and to rely on attrition to
achieve that reduction. Either of two options (options three or four
which have already been described) may be used to implement the required
reduction. Branch implementation plans will be reviewed by senior
management on a given date. They should include details of the losses
which are expected to take place form each occupational groups as a
result of resignations, retirements and transfers during the course of
the next twelve months. It should also disclose any situations where it
is proposed to obtain replacements before reaching the eight per cent
rate of separations from any group or pay band. Vacancies can not be
filled in any occupational group where the total losses from the
category to which it belongs are not expected to reach eight per cent
within a year. The only exception which can be made is if a particular
group is exempted from the full eight per cent reduction, in which case
the plan must identify an compensating increase in losses elsewhere.

The impact of the two options in the work force adjustment strategy can
be considered by comparing two departments of similar size but with marked
differences in their composition. The distribution of employees between
occupational categories in these examples is shown in Table 2.

Department `A' has almost two thirds of its employees in administrative
and administrative support positions. Department `B' is much more dependent
on scientific, professional and technical groups,which constitute more than
40 per cent of its strength. The nature of each department's operations
dictates its mix of occupat-ional categories, and senior management's choice
of strategy would be very much influenced by how those operations are
structured so as to avoid the upheaval of any large scale reorganization.
They may find it easier to accommodate existing structural arrangements by
opting to reduce the numbers in each pay band, where there is a more even
distribution, as is shown in Table 3.

In both departments the $30-35,000 payband has the largest number of
employees, amounting to approximately 20 per cent in each case. Above that

TABLE 2: DISTRIBUTION OF EMPLOYEES BY OCCUPATIONAL CATEGORY
IN TWO SAMPLE DEPARTMENTS

	DEPARTMENT `A'		DEPARTMENT `B'	
	No.	%	No.	%
Management	64	2.6	99	4.4
Admin. & F.S.	668	27.0	493	21.9
Scient. & Prof.	240	9.7	360	16.0
Technical	561	22.6	615	27.3
Operational	31	1.3	69	3.1
Ad. Support	913	36.8	614	27.3
Totals	2,477	100.0	2,250	100.0

TABLE 3: DISTRIBUTION OF EMPLOYEES IN TWO SAMPLE DEPARTMENTS
BY SALARY LEVELS

| | DEPARTMENT `A' | | DEPARTMENT `B' | |
Payband	No.	%	No.	%
60	37	1.5	55	2.4
55 - 60	50	2.0	111	4.9
50 - 55	67	2.7	114	5.1
45 - 50	85	3.4	159	7.1
40 - 45	147	5.9	185	8.2
35 - 40	234	9.5	315	14.0
30 - 35	493	19.9	453	20.1
25 - 30	484	19.5	252	11.2
20 - 25	444	17.9	359	16.0
20	436	17.6	247	11.0
Totals	2,477		2,250	

level the numbers and proportions steadily diminish in each higher pay band;
below its, they taper off although not in strict descending order in the
case of Department `B'.

An eight percent reduction in strength leads to the same number of
losses, regardless of which option is used, but the options give scope to
modify the impact of the cutback in accordance with departmental priorities.
Department `A' might opt for a reduction by payband in order to protect its
minority of scientific and technical personnel. Among its more highly paid
employees (those with salaries above $45,000) the proportions are fairly
even. About 22 per cent of those occupying senior management and
administrative positions are included in the top four paybands, and about 21
per cent of those in scientific and professional positions are spread over
the same four levels. In Department `B' on the other hand, more than 56 per
cent of its scientists and technical specialists are in paybands above
$45,000, compared with less than 30 per cent of its senior management and
administrative staff. It might therefore opt for a reduction by
occupational category in order to avoid losing a disproportionate number of
its high earning professionals.

The varying incidence of losses in both departments is shown in the
Tables 4 and 5. The figures in the top row show the number under each
category heading by which that category would be reduced. The figures in the
extreme right hand column show the number opposite each pay band by which
that pay band would be reduced, and of course the reductions could be made
from among employees in any of the occupational categories whose salaries
place them in that pay band. Note that the total number of losses shown for
Department `A' in Table 5 differs by one in the row and column
calculations, due to rounding off to whole numbers.

As shown in Table 4, cutting back by category would mean reducing the
Management complement by five in Department `A'. If it chose instead to
reduce by payband its Management Category would be cut by a minimum of three
(all from the upper level Executive Group) and a maximum of seven, if its
most highly paid administrative and scientific staff were left untouched. In
the same way Department `B' would need to cut its Management Category by
eight. Or, as can be seen from Table 5, it could vary its reduction of
that category anywhere between four and thirteen by opting for payband
reductions. Similar tradeoffs between categories and paybands are possible
at all levels, depending mainly on how a department is structured.

TABLE 4:   IMPACT OF EIGHT PER CENT REDUCTION IN DEPARTMENT `A'

	Mgt.	Admin. & F.S.	Scient. & Prof.	Tech	Operat.	Admin. Support	Total
Losses	5	53	19	45	2	73	197

Payband			Strength				Losses
60 +	37						3
55 − 60	27	19	4				4
50 − 55		56	11				5
45 − 50		50	35				7
40 − 45		58	58	31			12
35 − 40		80	98	56			19
30 − 35		270	19	204			39
25 − 30		134	15	264	1	70	39
20 − 25		1	−	6	6	431	35
< 20					24	412	<u>35</u>
Totals	64	668	240	561	31	913	198

TABLE 5:   IMPACT OF EIGHT PER CENT REDUCTION IN DEPARTMENT `B'

	Mgt.	Admin. & F.S.	Scient. & Prof.	Tech	Operat.	Admin. Support	Total
Losses	8	39	29	49	6	49	180

Payband			Strength				Losses
60 +	51	1	3				4
55 − 60	48	9	54				9
50 − 55		22	91	1			9
45 − 50		82	55	22			13
40 − 45		62	73	50			15
35 − 40		43	53	218		1	25
30 − 35		222	24	204	2	1	36
25 − 30		50	7	109	25	61	20
20 − 25		2		11	31	315	29
< 20					11	236	<u>20</u>
Totals	99	493	360	615	69	614	180

It has already been said that a basic purpose of human resource planning
is to obtain a better return on payroll expenditure. If it is to do so it
may need a specific strategy to moderate payroll costs, because average
earnings tend to rise year by year - and not just due to inflation. The
upward movement is propelled by a number of forces which include more
complex operations and the use of increasingly sophisticated technology.
These forces combine with the higher incomes resulting from progression
along a learning curve to foster the reclassification of jobs. A strategy
to regulate the job classification and promotion processes could follow the
lines of the example cited in the work force reduction strategy and be based

TABLE 6: DEPARTMENTAL DEVIATION FROM TOTAL ORGANIZATION DISTRIBUTION

Pay ($000's)	Service Wide %	Dept %	SIGNIFICANCE (+)positive or negative(-)		
			HIGH	MEDIUM	LOW
60 +	1.1	1.3	(+)		
50 - 60	3.9	3.6		(-)	
40 - 50	9.2	8.8			(-)
30 - 40	20.0	23.8	(+)		
20 - 30	44.4	39.3	(-)		
< 20	21.5	23.2		(+)	
	100.0	100.0			

on the distribution of employees between different pay bands. The strategy
might be stated as follows:

Strategy for Payroll Cost Control: corporate plans call for a reduction
of eight per cent in current expenditure on payroll in present dollar
costs. The reduction will offset expected changes in base salary levels
and annual increases awarded to employees. The payroll has been analyzed
to compare the proportion of employees in each category and pay band in
each department with their distribution throughout the entire
organization. The purpose of the strategy is to bring these proportions
more in line, particularly in functional staff groups which form the
bulk of the maintenance and support system. At some pay levels this
will give room for an increase in the number of departmental employees.
At others, where the department substantially exceeds the average, it
will mean a decrease in the number at that level. Decisions on staffing
actions to fill vacancies will be governed by the extent of the
discrepancies which now exist between the departmental and service wide
proportions of employees in each pay band. The matrix in table six
highlights those which, from a corporate standpoint, are considered to
be significant.

Degrees of significance as shown in Table 6 are defined as follows:

HIGH: the departmental proportion differs from the public service one by
more than ten per cent.

MEDIUM: the departmental proportion differs by between five and ten per
cent.

LOW: the departmental proportion differs by less than five per cent.

The discrepancy at each pay scale level can have either a positive or a
negative value. These values form the criteria for implementation, and
apply as follows:

A. Positive value (departmental proportion is above norm)

Where the difference is:

1. High: no replacements until current payroll cost has been
reduced by the target amount

2. Medium: replacements may be obtained for one in every four
vacancies occurring as a result of losses

3. Low: one in every two of those leaving may be replaced

The number of employees in pay bands of high and medium
significance will decline as losses occur. The surplus which this
attrition generates will provide a reserve of person years
available for departmental allocation. Proposals may be made to
obtain additional person years from that reserve. Most (if not
all) of the requested positions must fall into pay bands in which
the departmental proportion of its employees is less than the
service wide average, i.e. has a negative value.

B. <u>Negative value</u> (departmental proportion is below norm)

Where the difference is:

1. High: replacements may be obtained for three out of every
four losses which occur

2. Medium: one in two of those leaving may be replaced

3. Low: no replacements until current payroll costs have
been reduced by the target amount

Note that the plan must show overall savings in a unit's payroll
costs will reach the target level of eight percent by a specified
date. Where replacements are permitted, priority should be given
to filling positions which are defined as productive in the
existing human resource deployment strategy (See earlier text).

The formula is intricate but the concept is simple and pragmatic. The
number of employees in each pay band can be itemized on as finite a scale as
is needed. Staff can compile lists of the groups and levels whose annual
rates of pay fall into each interval on the scale, and calculate their
probable loss rates, so that managers have complete information at hand when
they undertake their planning. Restraints on hiring replacements ensure
that corrections to an imbalance at any level proceed in a planned and
orderly way. If a negative balance existed in an upper pay bank (i.e. there
is a smaller proportion at that pay level than is found service wide) senior
management might want to monitor its intake, so as to avoid a sudden upsurge
of high salaried employees.

A single strategy such as has been outlined could not be used in all
situations, but the general principles can have universal application. The
example has been given would be appropriate, for instance, in the case of a
department which had the same distribution of employees as that shown above
in Table 6. The impact of the payroll control strategy on it is shown in
Table 7, which gives the percentage of replacements which could be obtained
at each pay band level.

TABLE 7: PAYROLL SAVINGS IN A DEPARTMENT WITH 10,000 EMPLOYEES

Annual salaries	No. of employees	Variance from norm	Percentage replaced	Expected losses	Savings ($000's)
60 +	130	(+)high	nil	7	437
50 - 60	360	(−)medium	25%	27	1,485
40 - 50	880	(−)low	nil	70	3,150
30 - 40	2,380	(+)high	nil	190	6,650
20 - 30	3,930	(−)high	75%	79	1,975
< 20	<u>2,320</u>	(+)medium	25%	<u>174</u>	<u>3,045</u>
Total	10,000			547	16,742

Total payroll for such a department would amount to approximately $284 million. The estimated reduction of $16.742 million is close to six per cent, which is the saving which could be expected within a one year period. Human resources planning and financial specialists would again need to collaborate to develop alternative strategies for senior management, and to establish the probable time frames within which they would achieve the desired level of payroll reduction.

SUMMARY

It is of paramount importance to what is proposed that one of corporate planning's main thrusts is seen to focus on the organization's use of its human resources. Signalling a change of direction in this way can be just an influential in productivity improvement as the development of a powerful methodology to support it. The approach which has been presented aims to establish the framework for such a methodology, relying on familiar elements of the management process to do so. Each of those elements offers a partial answer to questions of effectiveness, efficiency and economy. The set of strategies which integrates them covers human resource planning, work force reduction and payroll cost control An appropriate combination of these three strategies can form the foundation on which to build a system for more productive management,as the Auditor General of Canada termed it.

FORECASTING THE COST-BENEFITS OF JOB TRAINING

Robert A. Bolda

General Motors Corporation
9-118 General Motors Building
3044 W. Grand Boulevard
Detroit, MI 48202

INTRODUCTION

To say that there is a strong interest among U.S. managers in the use
of employee job training programs as quality and productivity intervention
devices is to understate the situation. On a national basis, industry's
commitments to training in "hard" skills, "soft" skills and remedial
training efforts are massive, and the availability of government and
community agency support for employee training and retraining stimulates
additional activity. Clearly, there is a ground swell of interest out there
for training.

Human resource professionals have a contribution to make in this area
by helping to structure decision processes regarding employee job training
programs while program designs and contents are in the developmental or
"proposal" stages. I envision HRP concepts and tools as being helpful in
answering three types of questions at the outset of deliberations: What are
the firm's training needs? What are the cost - in dollar terms - associated
with the various action options which seek to meet those needs? What is the
likely impact of each training option on individual employee performance and
productivity - also in dollar terms?

This paper reviews procedures used by personnel researchers in a recent
pilot study aimed at forecasting cost-benefits associated with proposals for
job training and retraining of factory employees, both skilled and non-
skilled, and summarizes the general results obtained. The data and certain
of the project details have been altered to preserve sensitive
organizational information without distorting the pattern of results.

METHOD

A Task Team of training experts, operating managers, technical experts
is manufacturing technology, and staff personnel was formed to provide input
on several early phases of the pilot study: definition of factory job
classification clusters, identification of training needs, development of
proposed training contents, cost estimation, and administration of a plant-
level questionnaire.

Job Clusters. The Task Team analyzed all of the factory job classifications
in place in several large plant locations and assigned the jobs to clusters
based on similarity of duties, pay rates, and skill requirements. Twenty

non-skilled clusters emerged, along with six skilled job clusters.

<u>Training Needs</u>. The Task Team developed detailed definitions of training needs for each job cluster, giving consideration to both current job duties and anticipated job content changes. The Team focused on current performance effectiveness and opportunities for enhancing job performance throughout the process of identifying specific training needs.

Two broad classes of training needs resulted:

> "Hand On" Needs – including such areas as metrics, gauge-reading, lubrication techniques, computer literacy, electronic trouble-shooting, tool technology, safe equipment practices, statistical process control, inventory control processes, and specific hands-on retraining

> "Other" Needs – including team-building skills, interpersonal skills, quality/product orientation, the business plan, communications and quality of work life

<u>Training Contents</u>. Members of the Task Team prepared detailed outlines of training time requirements associated with the training needs identifies for each cluster of jobs. The Team as a whole reviewed and revised specific training contents, and a set of final training outlines was developed for each cluster of jobs.

<u>Training "Duration" Estimate</u>. We recognized the need to obtain an estimate of the likely duration of training impact, i.e., to estimate the half-life of job training effects. The training expert members of the Task Team provided their collective judgement that the likely impact period for job training of the types under review is approximately 2 1/2 years.

<u>Costing Training Experiences</u>. Staff members familiar with training development and administration costs indicated that such costs aggregate to about $20 per trainee hour of exposure. This figure was applied to the suggested training program durations in each cluster training recommendations to obtain an aggregate training cost, assuming that it would be possible to administer all of the training programs in their entirety in a single year.

<u>Forecasting Training Impact</u>. Cost benefit forecasts require that projections of training <u>costs</u> and <u>incremental performance/productivity gains</u> resulting from training be estimable in a common metric, i.e., in dollar terms.

At least three approaches might be used to forecast training impact:

1. Surveys of the firm's own experiences with similar training programs might provide a basis for estimating a typical or expected gain due to training (Cascio, 1982). For this pilot study, no such data was available.

2. Surveys of the professional literature, called meta-analyses (Hunter and Schmidt, 1983), indicate that the typical training program reported shifts the performance criterion mean by about 4/10ths of a standard deviation. That is, the difference between pre- and post-training performance is typically positive and has a magnitude of about 4/10ths of a SD in the criterion distribution. This is a broad-gauge estimate, and in the author's view, not sufficiently precise to justify its use as a prime estimator. This approach will be called the <u>theo retical</u> method.

3. Training impacts might be estimated by comparing pre-training
indices of job performance with post-training job performance
indices forecast by a large number of informed managers. Hunter &
Schmidt originated a questionnaire for collecting supervisor's
judgments on the _Dollar Value of the Performance_ of job incumbents
whose performance is low, average and superior. Judges handle the
task reliably and indicate comfort in providing estimates which
reflect many facets of performance in one assessment -- quantity,
quality, absences, etc. That aggregate has a value to the firm,
and supervisors can render judgments which estimate the aggregate
value. This approach will be called the Judgment Method.

It should be noted that the Hunter-Schmidt research indicates that
(a) supervisors estimating the dollar value of performances of low,
average and superior employees tend to depict dollar value data as
normally distributed and (b) over a large number of studies, it has
been found that the SD of the dollar value of performance
distribution tends to be approximately estimable by taking 40% of
the annual wage paid on the job in question.

For this pilot study, the Judgment Method was used to estimate the
impact of job training, and the Theoretical Method was used a cross-check
device. Both methods provide an impact estimate in dollar value terms.

The Judgment Method involved the following procedural steps:

A. To make this phase of the project workable, six job classifications
were selected for study, representing over 80% of the participating
plants' work forces. Three non-skilled jobs were included: machine
operator, material handler, job setter; and three skilled jobs were
studied further: machine repair, tool & die, electrician.

B. Managers from several plants and divisions familiar with each of
the six study jobs participate in the forecasting study and each
was selected because of the long experience in supervising the
activities of employees in one of the six study jobs. A total of
92 managers took part. Each supervisor was asked to do three
things:

   1. Estimate the dollar value of the performance of the average
   employee currently on the job (i.e., estimate job performance
   dollar value before training).

   2. Thoroughly study the training contents recommended for
   employees in that job.

   3. Estimate the post-training dollar value of the performance of
   the average employee on that job, i.e., forecast the performance
   value of the average employee assuming that the suggested
   training had been success-fully completed about _six months ago_.
   Separate post-training estimates were given for the "hands on"
   and "other" training content packages.

RESULTS

Judgment Method. The impact of the proposed job training experiences on
employee productivity can be estimated in "dollar value of performance"
terms by comparing judgments of the current value of employee performance
with judgments of job performance values after exposure to each of the two
training packages. Table 1 displays data which illustrate the findings of
these analyses; actual data are not provided.

TABLE 1

MEAN DOLLAR VALUE OF JOB
PERFORMANCE ESTIMATES* PROVIDED FOR:

Job	Current Incumbents	Incumbents After "Hands ON" Training	Incumbents After "Other" Training
Tool & Die	$18.00	$20.50	$22.00
Electrician	19.00	23.00	21.00
Machine Repair	17.00	21.00	20.00
Overall Skilled Averages	18.00	21.50	21.00
Job Setter	17.00	19.50	18.00
Operate/Assemble	16.00	18.50	19.50
Material Handler	15.00	17.50	18.00
Overall Non-Skilled Averages	16.00	18.50	18.50

*As indicated in the text, the data here are not actual results by may be viewed as illustrative of those findings.

The manager-judge estimates of the dollar values of the performance of current job incumbents are in the first data column. Across all skilled jobs, the average estimate for current incumbents was $18.00/hour, and estimates rose to $21.50/hour and $21.00/hour for post-training under the "Hands On" and "Other" training experience packages, respectively. For the non-skilled job clusters, average current performance value as $16.00/hour and the post-training values rose to $18.50/hour for each training package.

The difference between current mean values and post-training values are statistically significant. Inter-rater agreement on estimates of current and post-training performance values as calculated by the intra-class method, and was in the high .80's.

Cost-benefits in the first year associated with implementation of each training package in each job cluster can be estimated in an approximate sense with this equation:

Net Gain

(1st Year) = (N) (MS/year (Y) - (N) (H) (C/hour)

where:

N = Number of employees in each job cluster who are trained (assume 100)

MS/year = Mean shift in dollar value of performance/hour associated with a particular training experience

Y = Number of working hours in a year (assume 2,000)

H = Number of training hours/trainee associated with a particular
    training program (assume 200 hours/trainee/training package)

C/hour = Standard cost of training on per-training hour basis
          (assume $20.00/hour)

The (N) (H) (C/hour) term is an incremental cost estimate

The cost benefit calculation for the Tool & Die job cluster associated
with the "Hands On" training package is as follows:

Net Gain = (100) ($20.50 - $18.00) (2000) - (100) (200) ($20.00)
(1st year)
          = $500,000 - $400,000

          = $100,000

In other words, a $100,000 gain in dollar value of performance is
projected for Tool & Die trainees in the first post-training year,
representing a 25% return on the $400,000 investment.

It would be more realistic to project an aggregate cost-benefit impact
across the expected duration of the positive training effect, which experts
in this study estimated at 2 1/2 years. That is, the firm benefits from 2
1/2 years of training effect,rather than the single year projected in the
$500,000 gross gain shown in the calculation above. Letting the symbol D
stand for the expected duration in years of the positive training effect,
the Net Gain equation can be rewritten in a more complete form as:

    Net Gain = (N) (MS/hour) (Y) (D) - (N) (H) (C/hour)

Applying this equation to the Tool & Die example above would result in:

    Net Gain = (100) ($2.50) (2000) (2.5) - (100) (200) ($20.00)

      = $1,250,000 - $400,000

      = $850,000

This equation can e applied to the data associated with each job
cluster and each training package. An aggregate of these result provides a
total cost-benefit analysis across jobs and training plans.

As an example, consider the skilled jobs as a whole. Using data from
the "Overall Skilled Averages" line in Table 1, a net gain can be calculated
for post-"Hands On" training performance as follows:

Net Gain = (300) ($3.50) (2000) (2.5) - (300) (200) ($20.00)

      = $5,250,000 - $1,200,000

      = $4,050,000

Applying this equation to the post-"Other" training experience produces
a net gain across skilled jobs of $4,300,000. Across all non-skilled jobs,
the net gain estimates are $2,550,000 for each of the two training packages.

Summing over skilled and non-skilled jobs and across both training
packages, the total net gain to the firm is $12,450,000, and the benefits of
that training are expected to accrue over 2 1/2 years.

Theoretical Method. A second projection approach was used as a sense-check on the net gains calculated from the Judgmental Method. The second technique, called the Theoretical Method, makes use of two observations reported by Hunter and Schmidt:

1. The standard deviation of the distribution of dollar value of performance associated with employee incumbents in a particular job can be roughly estimated at a value equal to 40% of the average wage paid to those incumbents, and

2. Meta-analysis of a large volume of published literature reporting the effects of job training indicates that the typical effect of training is to shift the performance distribution to the positive side by about 4/10's of a standard deviation in that distribution.

The following general equation can be used to project the net gain associated with job training:

$$\text{Net Gain} = (N)\,(SD\$)\,(d)\,(D) - (N)\,(H)\,(C/hour), \text{ where}$$

N, D, H, and C/hour are defined as in the earlier examples, and

SD\$ = standard deviation of the distribution of dollar value
    of employee performance; i.e., 40% of average wage paid,

d = The typical effect of training on performance in standard
    deviation, or standard score, terms; that is, .4.

Assuming hypothetical annual wages for skilled employees at about $40,000, a total theoretical gain calculation can be made summed across both training packages as follows:

$$\text{Net Gain} = (600)\,(\$16,000)\,(.4)\,(2.5) - (600)\,(200)\,(\$20.00)$$

$$= \$7,920,000 - \$2,400,000$$

$$= \$5,520,000$$

The results of the Theoretical Method approach provide a rough check on the reasonableness of the Judgment Method results. Note that the Judgement Method produced total net gain estimates across skilled jobs and across non-skilled jobs of $7,350,000 and $5,100,000, respectively. The counterpart estimates provided by the Theoretical Method approach are $7,200,000 and $5,520,000. The small margins of difference between corresponding estimates, particularly in the skilled area, suggests that the judges performed their tasks thoughtfully.

DISCUSSION

The human resources planning approach outlined in this paper was intended to link cost-benefit analysis with training design activities at an early point in the management review process, a connection which has been difficult to make because of the complexities associated with quantifying potential post-training gains in employee performance. The procedures used here for estimating gains in dollar value terms were suggested by the developing literature on utility theory and meta-analysis and do not represent major departures from the state-of-the-art in those areas.

The use of informed manager-judges to assess the value levels of current and post-training employee appears to be supported as a concept by two findings in this report: the reliability of the basic scaling method is acceptably high and differences in net gain estimates provided through a

theoretical model and a judgment-based approach were quite small. The human
resource manager should note that the cost-benefit projections based on
judgment data uniformly suggest that performance gains exceed costs and that
the margin of benefit over cost is very substantial -- larger, possibly,
than many human resource practitioners have previously conceived.

The human resource planner has a few new tools available to help in
quantifying the impact of employee training on productivity, and those tools
enable us to use cost-benefit analysis in a more informed manner than has
been possible in the past.

REFERENCES

Cascio, W.F., Costing Human Resources: The Financial Impact of Behavior in
    Organizations, (Belmont, CA: Wadsworth, Inc.,1982).

Hunter, J.E., and F.L. Schmidt, "Quantifying the Effects of Psychological
    Interventions on Employee Job Performance and Workforce Productivity,"
    American Psychologist, Vol. 38, (April, 1983) pp. 473-478.

INDIVIDUAL PRODUCTIVITY: A SOURCING ANALYSIS

Robert A Bolda

General Motors Corporation
3044 General Motors Boulevard
Detroit, MI 48202

INTRODUCTION

With increasing frequency, Human Resource functions are called upon to contribute to the enhancement of employee productivity through the design and implementation of selection and job training programs affecting the firm's factory work force. A quick inventory of the procedural and conceptual tools available to the practitioner to help in this process suggests some strengths and some weaknesses. From a techniques standpoint, the literature on selection and training is quite broad and constitutes an asset. From the standpoint of human resource planning, however, the tool box is less adequately stocked; two general types of deficiencies can be considered:

1. Needs analysis in the area of productivity is a particularly complex task. Objective indices of base period or current productivity levels in the classical metric of "output per unit of time" are not often available, particularly on paced or service type factory jobs. Where hard data are available, they are typically confounded by moderating operational factors which mask the effects of individual differences in employee productivity

2. The idea of estimating potential productivity gains for use in projecting the "benefits" side of the cost-benefit equation in dollar terms has proved to be an elusive objective in the literature.

Within the past few years, Hunter & Schmidt (1983) have published a series of papers on the utility of personnel programs which provide some useful insights in dealing with the two deficiencies noted here. It is the purpose of this paper to report on procedures and results of a pilot study recently undertaken to assess the productivity levels of several groups of plant employees in both relative terms and in dollar value terms. The groups represent three employment sources for craft jobs: two types of internal selection-training approaches and the external labor force. Certain aspects of the study design and data results have been modified to preserve the confidentiality of sensitive information; these changes do not distort the pattern of results.

THE SITUATION

Research interest centered on two families of factory jobs having

roughly similar levels of responsibility, rates of pay, personnel
requirements, selection processes and training programs. One family included
several maintenance department jobs, and the other family encompassed several
toolroom jobs. Large numbers of employee incumbents work in each job family.
Incumbents enter maintenance and tool room jobs from three sources:

Source A: By completion of a formal selection-training process

Source B: By completion of an informal selection-training process

Source C: By direct hire from the external work force

PROCEDURE

Using special questionnaire techniques, a large number of experienced
managers provided two types of judgments regarding employee performance/
productivity: (1) "dollar value of performance" judgments on the current
employee incumbent group, and (2) paired comparison judgments relating to the
productivity of "average-performing employees" in seven source-categories of
particular interest to us.

Dollar Value of Performance Judgments

The Hunter-Schmidt research cited earlier indicates that the judgments
of informed supervisors of job incumbents can be used to scale employee
productivity on a "dollar value of performance" continuum. Judges estimate
the dollar value of the output of employees in a specific job at three points
on that continuum: the average performing employee (the employee whose
performance is at the 50th percentile of the group); the superior performing
(whose performance is at the 15th percentile of the group). A questionnaire
was designed to collect dollar value judgments from 106 maintenance and
toolroom management people. In particular, each manager was asked to
estimate the dollar value of the performance of employees who perform at the
15th, 50th, and 85th percentiles. Mean dollar value estimates were
calculated for each of the three percentile judgments and for each job
family.

Paired Comparison Judgments

Participating managers were asked to provide comparative productivity
judgments on seven categories of maintenance and toolroom workers. The
categories were developed in the following manner.

First, it should be noted that maintenance and toolroom employee
incumbents may enter jobs from one of three sources:

Source A: "Graduates" of a formal, four-year, on-the-job training
           program having specific outside educational experience
           requirements; a common, valid selection process is used in
           selecting candidates for appointment to trainee status.

Source B: "Graduates" of an unstructured, longer, on-the-job training
           program, having less formal outside educational requirements;
           selection for trainee status is driven by traditional
           upgrading criteria.

Source C: Direct hire from the external labor market of an individual
           whose experience and job history background are equivalent to
           those of successful "graduates" of Sources A or B. Selection
           criteria center on establishing that equivalency.

Second, it was recognized that productivity comparisons of these
sources might be affected by varying amounts of employee in-plant job
experience. Accordingly, a two-level experience dimension was added to each
of the sources to provide contrasts between employees recently "graduated" or
hired, and those with several years' in-plant experience on the job. Third,
it was decided to include in the evaluation set a comparison with employees
in the same types of jobs who worked for other employers in the plant
communities.

Having identified these seven groups, or source-categories, of
workers,it was decided to ask experienced managers to scale the comparative
productivity of the average-performing incumbent in each source-category.
The final set of seven categories to be compared and studied was as follows:

1.   "The average employee who has just completed the (Source A)
     program"

2.   "The average employee with several years' experience after
     completion of the (Source A) program"

3.   "The average employee who has just completed the (Source B)
     program"

4.   "The average employee with several years' experience after
     completion of the (Source B) program"

5.   "The average newly-hired (Source C) employee"

6.   "The average (Source C) employee after several years' experience
     with the company"

7.   "The average experienced tradesperson who works for another local,
     non-affiliated employer in the area"

The same group of 106 managers participated in paired comparison ratings
of these seven categories (i.e., the six internal groups and the single
external reference group). In this procedure,the seven items to be rated are
arranged in pairs so that each item is paired with each other once. The
judge is asked to read each pair and select that item which, in the judge's
experience, is the _more productive_ of the two. Each judge enters 21 such
judgments, and relative differences in productivity between the seven source-
categories are developed by tabulating the numbers of "votes" given to each
category.

RESULTS

<u>Paired Comparison Rating</u>.

Paired comparison ratings of productivity were summarized by totalling
the numbers of "more productive" votes assigned to each source category by
the manager-judges. These frequencies were converted to normalized scale
values along a standard scale having a mean of 50 and a standard deviation of
10; i.e., a scale value of 70, say, would indicate a high productivity
source, scaled at about two standard deviations above the mean (Guion, 1965).
The reliability of these scale values was analyzed by studying inter-judge
agreement, and the resulting intra-class correlations were in the .90's.The
actual scale values obtained are not reported here for confidentiality
reasons, but the data displayed in Table 1 are illustrative of the types of
results which were found.

Table 1 displays productivity scale value data for each of the seven

TABLE 1

MEAN NORMALIZED SCALE VALUES* OF PRODUCTIVITY
BY SOURCE CATEGORIES

Source Category	Maintenance Employes	Toolroom Employes	Total Maintenance & Toolroom Employes
The average employee who:			
1. Has just completed the Source A Program	58	58	58
2. Has several years' experience after completing a Source A Program	67	66	67
3. Has just completed the Source B Program	41	41	41
4. Has several years' experience after completing a Source B Program	49	47	48
5. Is a newly-hired (Source C) employe	46	47	47
6. Is a Source C hire after several years' in-plant experience	52	51	52
7. Is an experienced tradesperson who works for another local employer	48	47	47

* As indicated in the text, the data displayed here are not actual results but may be viewed as illustrative of those findings.

source categories and for each of the two job families. The first source category, "The average employee who has just completed the Source A Program," was assigned a mean scale score of 58 in both the maintenance and toolroom contexts, indicating that such employees perform at a productivity level about 80/10's of a standard deviation above the mean productivity for all employees. Another illustration might be source category 3, "The average employee who has just completed the Source B Program." A scale score of 41 was assigned in both job families, indicating that this subgroup of employees is seen as performing at a productivity level 9/10's of a standard deviation below the mean productivity of all employees.

Because the scale scores assigned in the maintenance and toolroom families are very similar, the data sets were combined. The composite figures will be used hereafter.

The scale scores shown in Table 1 indicate that the judges made major distinctions between the source categories with respect to productivity. Newly-graduated and experienced graduates of the Source A Program occupy positions on the scale significantly greater than the others. It should be noted that the Source A Program involves both selection and training processes which are carefully conceived and administered. Source B

graduates, in contrast, are seen as significantly less effective immediately
after completion of the Program, and even after several years' experience
does not approach the productivity levels of the Source A people.
Interestingly, tradespersons working for outside employers are judged to be
near average on the scale score continuum.

The differences in productivity between employees recently placed and
those who have accrued several years' experience on the job are fairly
consistent across Sources, A, B, and C. Experience appears to add about
7/10's of a standard deviation to the productivity scale scores.

<u>Dollar Value Judgments</u>.

The scale scores referenced in the discussion on paired comparison
productivity ratings are relative measurements. In an attempt to provide a
more meaningful scale of measurement to the source data, the manager-judges
were asked to provide estimates of the dollar values of job performance of
employees in maintenance and toolroom jobs. That is,they were asked to
estimate a dollars/hour figure reflecting their evaluation of all employees
in the present incumbent groups. The specific task required the judge to
estimate dollar values for employees whose performances are at the 15th,
50th, and 85th percentiles, corresponding to low, average and superior
performers. The difference between 15th and 50th percentile judgments is
taken as an estimate of the standard deviation of the dollar value of
performance distribution for on-roll employees. Similarly, the difference
between 50th and 85th percentile judgments provides a second estimate of that
standard deviation. The general expectation is that the two SD estimates
will be approximately equal in magnitude, as one would probably find with
normal distributions.

The dollar value judgments were analyzed, and it was found that the
reliability of the final scale values, as assessed by studying the intra-
correlations of judges' responses, was in the .90s'. Once again,the judged
dollar values for maintenance and toolroom jobs were very similar, and are
combined into a composite hereafter.

Overall, the judges estimated that the dollar value of the performance
of average, or 50th percentile, employees is approximately $13.00/hour, a
figure fairly close to the average rate paid to jobs in the two families
under study. The dollar value result for low performers (15th percentile
people) was $8.00/hour, and the dollar value judged for superior (85th
percentile people) was given as $20.00/hour. In other words, the judges see
a difference in performance value between average and superior performers of
about $7.00/hour ($20-$13), or about 50%. The superior performer is seen as
providing work worth about 2 1/2 times as much as the low performer
($20 vs. $8).

It is noted that the two standard deviation estimates, $7.00 on the
upper side of the distribution and $5.00 on the lower side, were not
significantly different. Further analyses involving dollar value results
will be made using a composite of the two estimates, or $6.00/hour.

Table 2 displays the paired comparison ratings of source category
productivity and the dollar value judgment data graphically on a common
basis. One way to compare the results of the two sub-studies and to develop
insight into dollar value differences between source categories, is to
compare scale scores and dollar data at similar standard score, or standard
deviation unit points. For example, recent Source B graduates were assigned
a productivity scale score in the paired comparison task of 41, or 9/10's of
a standard deviation below the mean of the group. Since the dollar value of
performance judgments indicate that one standard deviation in the dollar

TABLE 2

GRAPHIC DEPICTION OF PRODUCTIVITY SCALE VALUES*
AND CORRESPONDING DOLLAR VALUE OF PERFORMANCE JUDGEMENTS*
(MAINTENANCE AND TOOLROOM COMBINED)

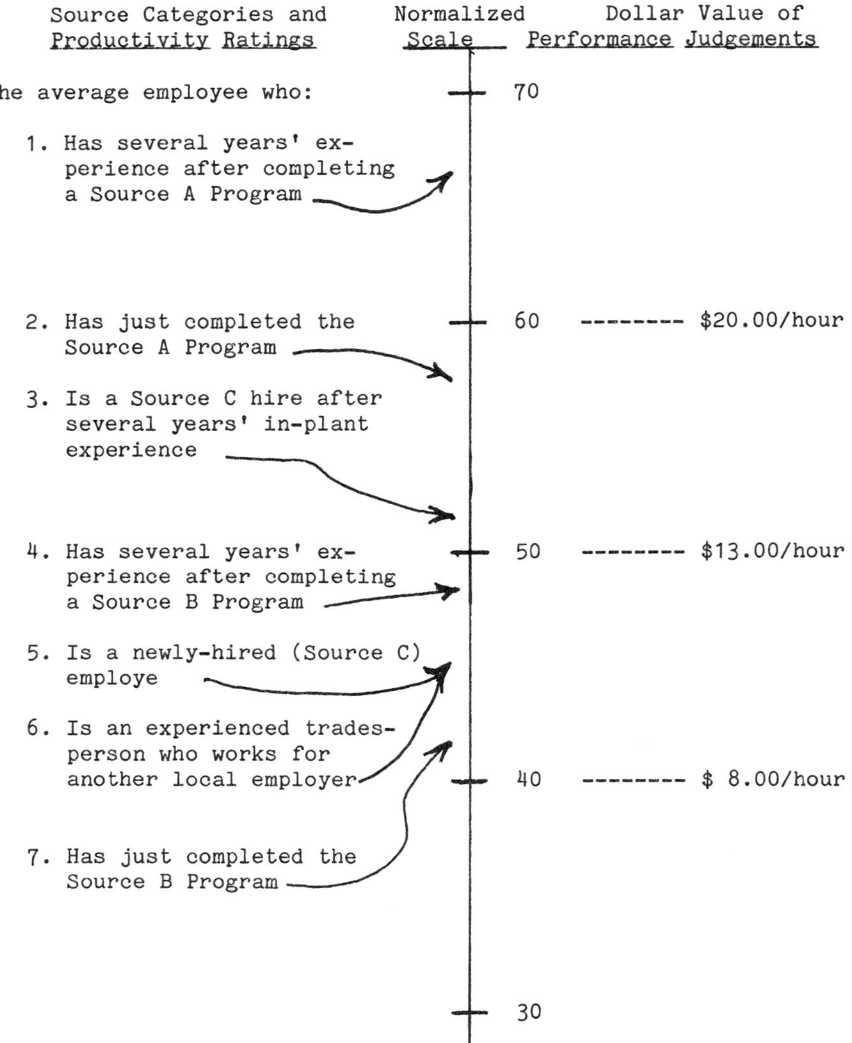

* As indicated in the text, the data displayed here are not actual
results but may be viewed as illustrative of those findings.

value of performance distribution is gauged at about $6.00/hour, then it
probably follows that the recent Source B graduate is performing at a dollar
value level of approximately $5.40/hour below the mean of $13.00/hour, or
$7.60/hour, ($13 - (.9) x $6.00)

DISCUSSION

Many human resource planning professional find it useful to take
inventory of resources at an early point in project activity. In the

author's view, an assessment of "where we are now" is an essential first step in planning that has to do with productivity enhancement. This paper has outlined a study undertaken to assess employee productivity as related to employment sources: programs involving different selection standards and processes and equally different training models. The specific conclusions drawn from these data might be summarized as follows:

- There are sharp differences in the job performance/productivity of employees who entered maintenance and toolroom jobs from different selection-training backgrounds.

- The more carefully conceived and structured selection-training backgrounds appear to produce significantly greater productivity, both upon program completion and thereafter.

- Program A graduates provide performance worth about $18.00/hour, as opposed to the average performance of Program B graduates valued at about $7.00/hour at graduation. The difference does not diminish with several additional years' experience.

- Compared to other employees in the are, the firm's maintenance and toolroom work forces appear to be somewhat more productive, at lease in the view of internal manager-judges.

- As employee accrue job experience after graduation or hire, individual productivity is enhanced; the magnitude of this increment is about 7/10's of a standard deviation or about $4.00/hour. This is particularly the case where trainee selection and development are administered carefully.

In a more general sense, these studies suggest an approach to dealing with a thorny analytic problem: how to measure individual employee productivity. Subjective assessments were used here to obtain both relative and absolute productivity data on employee sub-groups of particular interest to the local HR planner. Two observations might be added regarding the adequacy of these subjective approaches: first, inter-judge agreement was sufficiently high on all rating tasks to provide final scale reliability estimates in the .90's, and second, when these results were "sense-checked" with a large group of manager-experts, their uniform reaction was one of approval.

The procedures used to scale sub-group productivity in this study are not proposed as replacements for traditional methods of productivity assessment, or as sure-fire solutions to all of the planner's conceptual problems. It is suggested, however, that the subjective approaches outlined here represent additional tools in the HR planner's tool kit. From a psychometric standpoint, their characteristics are generally satisfactory, they are easily and creatively adaptable to a wide variety of problem analysis situations, and most importantly, these processes are assets to communications processes.

REFERENCES

Hunter, J. E. and F. L. Schmidt, "Qualifying the Effects of Psychological Interventions on Employee Job Performance and Workforce Productivity," American Psychologist, Vol.38, (April, 1983) pp. 473-478.

SECTION 5:

FORECASTING AND TURNOVER CONTROL

This section includes papers describing applications in the areas of forecasting and turnover control. Of particular interest is the fact that the forecasting methods are beginning to appear either as microcomputer models or mainframe-microcomputer systems. This section concentrates on applications involving practical ways to obtain manpower forecasts or to project the internal work force.

The paper by Bulla and Scott describes an application to provide for effective manpower requirements forecasting by the Houston Lighting and Power Company. A microcomputer approach was used in the data manipulation relying on such tools as the LOTUS 1-2-3 spreadsheet. This system was developed to help in the management of its work force in light of changing needs for energy coupled with more assertive regulations concerning cost control.

The next paper by Bres, Niehaus, Sharkey, and Weber documents the use of flow models to assist managers in the U.S. Naval Sea Systems Command in responding to a requirement to significantly reduce the number of shipyard employees in a relatively short period of time. Two models were developed using personnel movement or transition data computed on a mainframe computer and downloaded to a microcomputer spreadsheet for analysis. A more comprehensive "flexible" flow model was also developed to balance work force flows across time periods as well as between job categories. This latter mainframe based model was developed for one of the shipyards to permit comparative analysis with the spreadsheet results. These models are being integrated into the strategic and operational planning accomplished in the management of the naval shipyards.

The paper by Hawkins combines into one model a number of techniques for controlling personnel turnover. This model is built around classical statistical quality control methods. The idea is to try to develop standards for turnover and then determine if the current level of turnover is "too high" or "too low". The value of this work is that it provides a method to graphically develop individual turnover charts along with the relationship between turnover and length-of-service or age. In this way one can combine the effects of short term changes in turnover with the longer term cumulative length-of-service factors underlying employee tenure.

MANPOWER REQUIREMENTS FORECASTING: A CASE EXAMPLE

Daniel N. Bulla* and Peter M. Scott**

  *Houston Lighting & Power Company
   611 Walker Street
   Houston, Texas 77002

  **Scott Consulting Group
    5171 Glenwood Avenue
    Raleigh, N.C. 27612

MANPOWER REQUIREMENTS FORECASTING

This paper provides an overview of the Manpower Requirements
Forecasting program developed and implemented at Houston Lighting & Power
Company. It begins with an overview of why there is an increasing emphasis
on manpower planning, it then describes the criteria for an effective
manpower requirements forecasting process, and concludes with a description
of the program specifically developed at Houston Lighting & Power Company.

MANPOWER PLANNING

Manpower planning can best be described as the process for ensuring
that the human resource requirements of an organization are identified and
that plans are established for satisfying those requirements. There are two
primary components. The first,manpower requirements forecasting, deals with
what an organization's needs for manpower will be and when that manpower
will be needed. The second, which involves evaluation of these forecasts,
is the how it will meet those needs. The needs can be met by recruiting or
hiring, contracting, making temporary hires, retraining personnel,
transferring personnel, or through attrition programs, either normal or
forced.

This diagram (reference Figure 1) details the manpower planning
process. The manpower requirements forecast is shown within the area
enclosed by dotted lines, and the balance of the manpower planning process
is shown in the rest of the diagram.

It is important to note that there has been an increasing emphasis on
manpower requirements forecasting in recent years. Five years ago, this
emphasis occurred because many companies, particularly in nuclear power and
areas such as data processing. Compounding this was relatively high
turnover, as many employees moved to other utility companies or into other
industries.

More recently, the emphasis on manpower requirements forecasting has

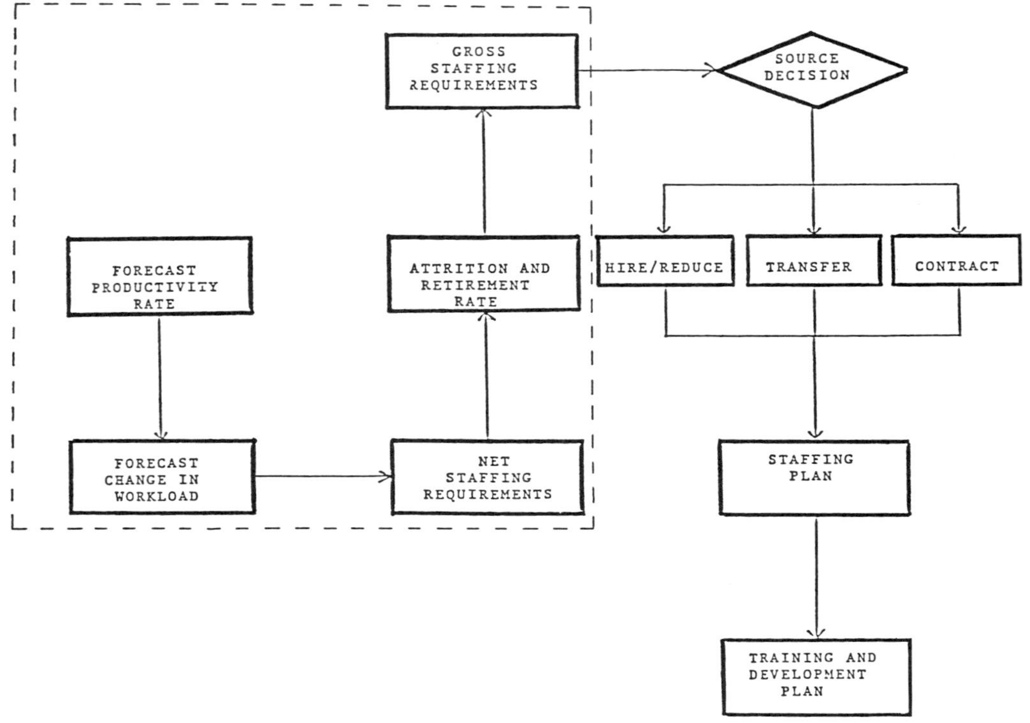

Figure 1: Manpower Planning Schematic

stemmed from an entirely different set of reasons -- all of them associated with the need to improve resource productivity. First, the utility industry has experienced a significant decline in the growth and demand for energy. Thus, the expansion of facilities has slowed and, in many areas, customer growth has been declining. Second, regulatory commissions have been more assertive in requiring utilities to control costs. Third, for the most part, the work force in the utility industry has become much more stable and turnover has lessened. At the same time, utilities have experienced a significant change in company activities. For example, there is an increasing emphasis on marketing and customer service functions and a declining emphasis on new construction. Obviously, this creates a dilemma for utility executives who are faced with declining needs for personnel in one area and increasing needs for personnel in another, particularly when this is factored by the traditional utility practice of no layoffs.

In summary, managers in all industries, not just the utility industry,are faced with decisions relative to staffing that require accurate estimates of the types and numbers of personnel they will need to achieve their business objectives. And, as would be expected, management has responded with the implementation of formal programs for obtaining these estimates of manpower requirements.

Manpower Requirements Forecasting: A Correct Approach

What is needed is a balanced and thorough methodology for preparing the manpower requirements forecast. There are four primary benefits of an accurate requirements forecast. These are:

o Providing the data to support other elements of human

resource management, such as recruiting, compensation,
performance evaluation, and training.

o   Providing the lead time necessary to develop reasonable plans
    for meeting the personnel requirements of an organization

o   Reflecting line management's perception of the future
    operating environment

o   Promoting the productive use of manpower and providing a
    reasonable process for justifying the need for additions or
    reductions to staffing

The key factors a manpower requirements forecasting methodology should
address include:

o   A multi-year forecast of the primary personnel skill
    groupings of an organization.

o   Making changes in workload and changes in productivity very visible.

o   Incorporating attrition and retirements into projections.

o   Providing a forecast of all human resources -- both company employees
    and contractors.

o   Integration with other corporate programs such as budgeting and
    planning to ensure that the forecast is consistent with
    corporate resources and plans.

Manpower Requirements Forecasting: The Process

Figure 2 describes the basic logic process associated with a manpower
requirements forecast. This process is what any manager goes through when
deciding how many of what type of personnel he needs. Take for example a
manger's thinking process for deciding how many maintenance personnel are
needed. The first step is to define the primary factors that influence work
load. For a maintenance technician this would be number of work orders,
condition of the plant, or major outages.

Then he would project the volume or the magnitude of change in workload
over a period of time. In this example, he would forecast the number of
work orders to be processed each year, the amount of maintenance that the
plant requires, and how many outage weeks are expected. Then he would
factor in the impact of the change in workload on the gross manpower
requirements. The next step would then be to consider whether or not there
will be any changes in productivity. That is, will his work force be more
productive or less productive? If it will be more productive, he can handle
an increased workload with a lesser increase of staffing. Alternatively, if
productivity will decline,then he will need a greater number of personnel.

Once the gross personnel requirements are identified, the manager must
assess whether or not there are any other factors that would change his need
for personnel. For example, will there be shut down and the need for
personnel thus reduced or eliminated? He should also determine what the
attrition rate will be, either through retirements or other turnover.

From all this information and from this basic logic process, the
manager is determining what his forecast of personnel needs is.

The basic equation for determining staffing needs involves factoring

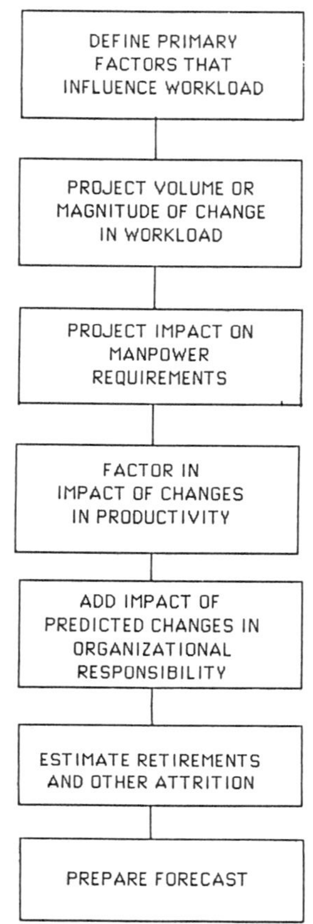

Figure 2: Manpower Requirements Forecasting: Basic Logic Process

existing staffing by changes in both workload and productivity. There are a number of factors that can influence workload, including work volume, complexity of the work, or change in assignments. Likewise, there are a number of factors that influence productivity, including changes in technology, the degree of work force experience, the degree of work force skill, or formal productivity programs. It is the line manager's task to look at these major factors for workload and productivity and to include them in his logic process for predicting his needs for personnel.

CASE EXAMPLE: HL&P

Now let's turn from the theory and look at a specific application of this process. In 1984, Houston Lighting & Power Company undertook a program to develop a manpower requirements forecasting process. It was successfully implemented in 1985 and is not about to go into its second cycle.

At the outset of the development process, HL&P management established the following seven basic design criteria:

o It had to be a management tool to aid in planning, budgeting and control.

o The forecast had to be prepared by line managers and be based upon their analysis of their own situations.

o   The forecast needed to cover a five-year time frame.

o   The preparation process had to be simple, logical and, is
    capable of being integrated with other corporate programs,
    such as planning and budgeting.

o   Productivity needed to be a factor in the determination of staff
    requirements.

o   The requirements forecast had to reflect changes in needs for
    existing responsibilities, as well as provide forecasts of needs for
    major changes in corporate programs.

o   The forecast had to cover employees and contractors and the
    categories for which forecasts would be prepared should facilitate
    overall planning and analysis.

MRF Overview

The data collection and manipulation effort required to meet these
criteria is substantial for a large, complex organization. Accordingly, the
first step in the development process was to create a computer system
capable of supporting these needs. The information systems group in HL&P
developed such a system based upon a detailed conceptual design provided by
the Organizational Development Division and Scott Consulting Group.

The manpower forecast does not forecast for individual job titles, but
rather for categories called "Skill Groups" and "Position Classifications".
Skill Groups exist to provide for the grouping of similar types of employee
classes, such as bargaining unit, management, technical and non-exempt.
Position Classifications enable groupings of similar types of job functions,
such as electrical engineer, secretary and accountant.

The actual process for preparing a forecast begins with the
distribution of an information package containing the planning assumptions
and forms and instructions necessary for completing the forecast in the
February-March time frame. The planning assumptions were provided through
the corporate planning organization and addressed areas such as expected
customer growth, sales growth, and other corporate factors which would
influence the need for personnel additions.

In the April-May time frame, the individual line managers prepared
forecasts, which were then reviewed and approved by department management.
Once the department manager was satisfied with the forecast, it was
forwarded to the Organizational Development Division,which prepared a
consolidated corporate manpower requirements forecast prepared by each
manager. Following budget approval, a final manpower requirements forecast
is advised of needs for additional staff for the next year.

MRF Preparation Detail

The primary input for the manpower requirements forecast is, as has
been discussed, the base level forecast prepared by a line manager. Figure
3 show the primary input form.

Several columns of data are requested: the first two provide a base of
known information from which to formulate projections. The remaining five
columns then constitute forecast data relating to years 1 through 5. In all
columns, notice that managers are asked to forecast for each of five basic

COST CENTER CODE: ___________   COST CENTER TITLE: _______________________________

POSITION CLASSIFICATION CODE: _______   POSITION CLASSIFICATION TITLE: ____________________

CURRENT YEAR: _______

	STAFF COMPLEMENT	(A) PRIOR YEAR	(B) CURRENT YEAR	(C) FORECAST YEAR 1	(D) FORECAST YEAR 2	(E) FORECAST YEAR 3	(F) FORECAST YEAR 4	(G) FORECAST YEAR 5
PART A	REGULAR							
	CONTRACT/OTHERS							
	TOTAL							

EXISTING WORKLOAD

	DRIVING VARIABLES	PRIMARY WORK PRODUCT/DETERMINENT						
PART B								
	COMPLEXITY							
	IMPACT ON WORKLOAD (%)							
	IMPACT ON WORKLOAD (EQUIVALENT HEADCOUNT)							

PRODUCTIVITY

PART C	TECHNOLOGY							
	EXPERIENCE/TRAINING LEVEL							
	CHANGE IN PRODUCTIVITY (%)							
	CHANGE IN PRODUCTIVITY (EQUIVALENT HEADCOUNT)							

STRATEGIC MANAGEMENT ACTION PLAN PROGRAMS

PART D								
	IMPACT ON STAFF COMPLEMENT (EQUIVALENT HEADCOUNT)							

OTHER WORKLOAD

PART E								
	IMPACT ON STAFF COMPLEMENT (EQUIVALENT HEADCOUNT)							

PART F	RETIREMENTS (EQUIVALENT HEADCOUNT)							
	ATTRITION (EQUIVALENT HEADCOUNT)							

PREPARED BY ___________ DATE ___________ PHONE # ___________

APPROVED BY ___________ DATE ___________ PHONE # ___________

Figure 3:   Manpower Requirements Forecast Worksheet

categories:

o   Resources to support existing responsibilities.

o   Productivity changes resulting from technology changes, work
    innovations, and/or improvements in the work force's
    experience level.

o   Resources required to perform strategic management action plans
    (SMAP), which in HL&P's case represent specific programs that create
    new responsibilities for an organzation that originate from senior
    management strategic planning activities.

o   Resource requirements associated with projects initiated by the
    preparer of the base level forecast.

o   Turnover resulting from retirements and attrition.

This form can be completed either manually or through the use of a
micro computer program that has been developed on Lotus 1-2-3.

After the manager has completed the base level forecast for each of the
positions in his area, they are input into the mainframe computer program
which can then produce a number of output reports. The primary outputs of
the requirements forecasting model are:

o First year recruiting needs by position classification.

o Five-year projection of manpower requirements by skill group, by
  position classification, by organization.

o Five-year projection of retirements, attrition, and gross (and net)
  additions and reductions to staff.

o A five-year hierarchical listing of organizations with major workload
  changes and organizations with major changes in productivity.

Examples of two of these forecasts are provided as Figures 4 and 5.

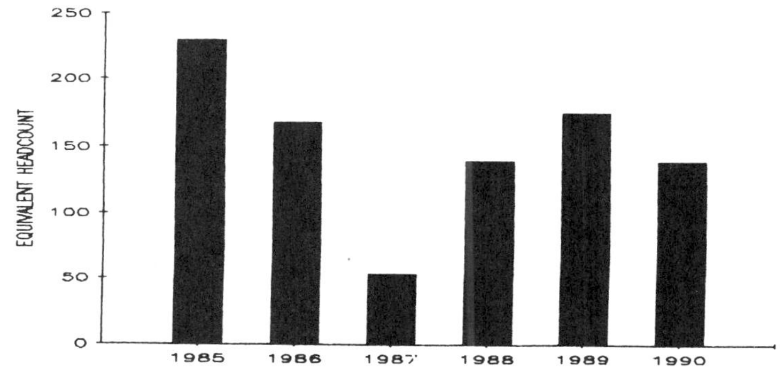

Figure 4:   Manpower Requirements Forecast: Per-year Staff Additions
            Associated with Strategic Management Action Plans

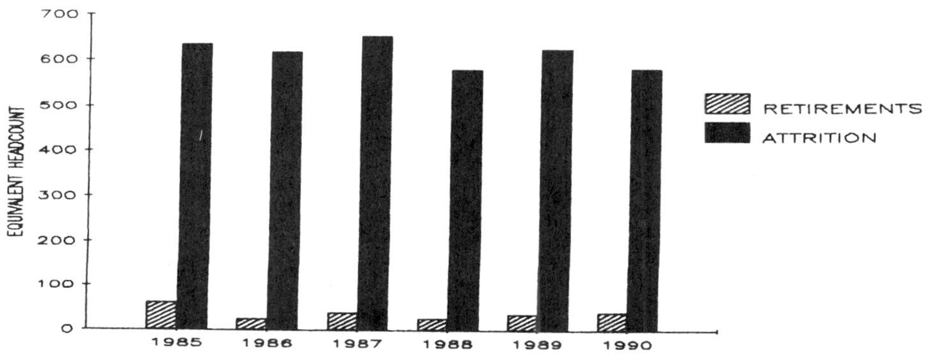

Figure 5:   Manpower Requirements Forecast: Projected   HL&P
            Employee Turnover 12/31/85 through 13/31/90

CONCLUSION

The MRF is a management tool that can be used by line managers as an
aid to planning, budgeting, and control. The points listed below indicate
how the depth of analysis and five-year time frame enhance the Corporate
planning process.

o   The existence of a single corporate-wide projection for employees
    head count directly benefits functions such as facilities planning,
    recruiting/employment, financial forecasting, budgeting, employee
    benefits, computer hardware acquisition, and training. Each
    organization will be able to develop business plans based upon a
    single set of top management approved staff projections.

o   The MRF, by virtue of its relationship with work load changes and
    productivity, provides support to the budgeting and resource
    justification process.

o   The MRF provides the company with the following capabilities
    to actively improve the management of its work force:

    -   Establishment of a baseline from which to measure and project
        the growth or decline in staffing and the attendant cost or
        savings

    -   Development of the capability to plan for the orderly staffing
        or destaffing of areas projected to sustain substantial
        increases or decreases in work load

    -   Creation of information concerning the future critical skills
        needed within the company, along with the sufficient lead time
        to support recruiting, hiring, and training/development programs.

What The MRF Has Done For Help

Implementing the MRF as resulted in the following key benefits:

o   Executive management has a quantified representation of the human
    resources required to ensure the continued efficient and effective
    running of HL&P over the intermediate term.

o   The magnitude and timing of the future needs for or surplus of,
    positions has been identified, thus making possible staffing and
    destaffing plans more in tune with aggregate management expectations.

o   The affects of productivity improvement have been made visible.

o   The magnitude of anticipated turnover in the work force has been
    quantified and presented in terms of position classifications within
    MRF base level areas.

o   The design of training programs can be improved to better
    parallel the needs of the organization.

o   Communication within functional areas and across organizational lines
    has been stimulated as a result of line managers reflecting in their
    forecasts the affects of dependent and interdependent work
    relationships.

An example of one of these forecasts as it relates to productivity is
provided as Figure 6.

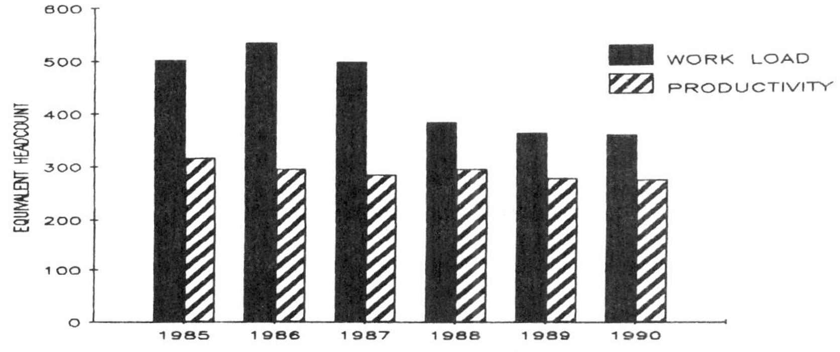

Figure 6: Manpower Requirements Forecast: Per-year effect of Changes in Work Load and Productivity

Types of Analyses Made Possible

The quantity and diversity of information collected by the MRF system makes it impractical to present an exhaustive listing of the types of analyses available to support management planning efforts. Consequently, the following points present information concerning only those analysis-related efforts thus far performed by Organizational Development using MRF output report data.

- o Span of Control Studies - identification of the projected ratio of employees per management level or combination of management levels (See Figure 7).

- o Customers per Employee Ratios - A productivity-based measurement comparing projected employee and customer counts (See Figure 8).

- o Needs/Surplus Assessment - identification of position classifications exhibiting substantial year-to-year variability (See Figure 9).

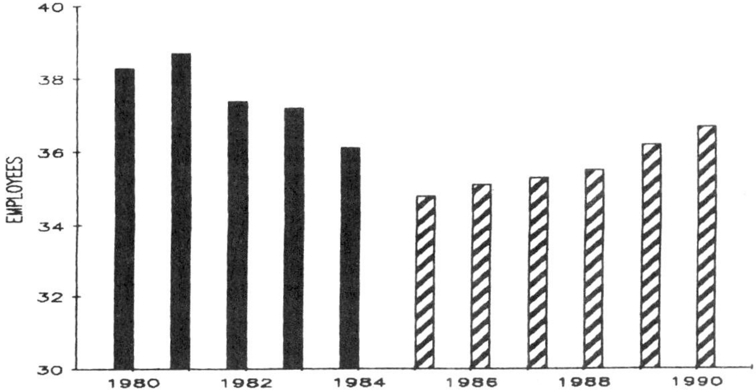

Figure 7: Manpower Requirements Forecast: Management Span of Control 1980 through 1990

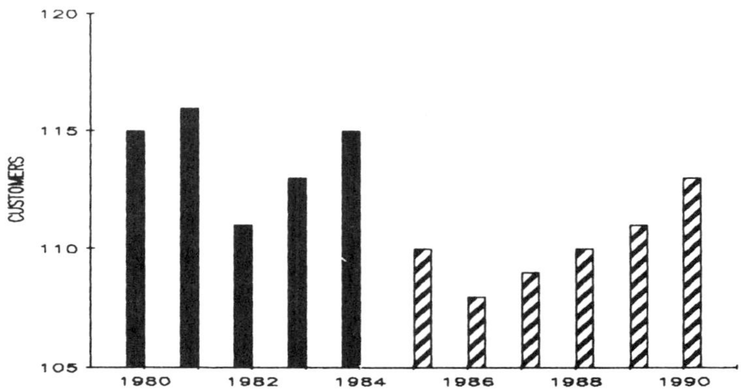

Figure 8: Manpower Requirements Forecast:Customers per Employee 1980 thru 1990

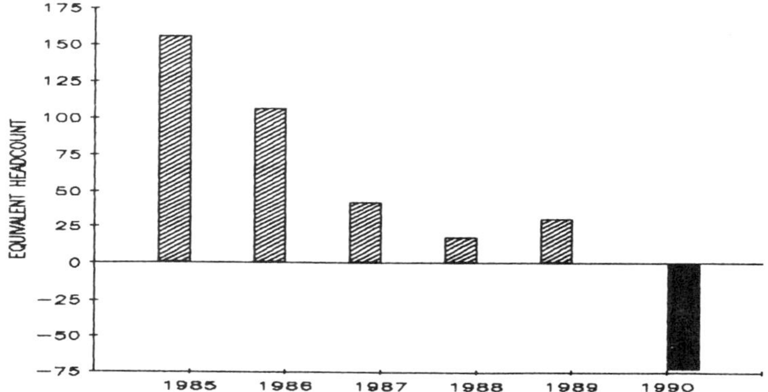

Figure 9: Manpower Requirements Forecast: Per-year Staff Changes
Associated with Other Work Load

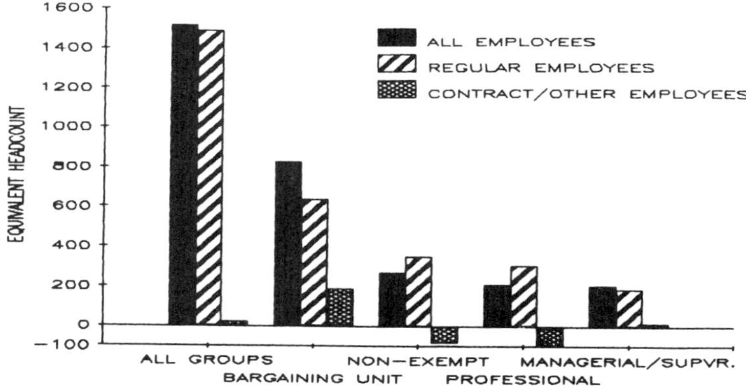

Figure 10:   Manpower Requirements Forecast: Projected Net Additions and
Reductions to Force Over the Period 12/31/85 thru 12/31/90

o   Skill Group Studies - definition of how the work force is changing
    with respect to the projected number of bargaining unit, non-exempt,
    professional, and management employees reflected in the forecast (See
    Figure 10).

The Future of The MRF

     A dynamic future is in store for the MRF. Forecast from an
applications standpoint is that the system will be used to effect the
replacement of HL&P's bottom-up labor budget process with one that utilized
a top-down approach. Moreover, all MRF computer logic will be reviewed and
refined to ensure optimum efficiency, usefulness, and integration with
related and complimentary HL&P systems.

USE OF PERSONNEL FLOW MODELS

FOR ANALYSIS OF LARGE SCALE WORK FORCE CHANGES

E. S. Bres III*, R. J. Niehaus**
F. J. Sharkey*** and C. L. Weber*

* Naval Military Personnel Command
  NMPC 1644, RM 4532 Arlington Annex
  Washington, DC 20370

** Office of the Chief of Naval Operations (OP-16H)
   Navy Department
   Washington, DC 20370

*** Naval Sea Systems Command (00R)
    Washington, DC 20362-5101

INTRODUCTION

The fundamental development of personnel flow models was completed and extensively reported in the literature in the 1970's. Developments since then include implementation of simple forms of these models on microcomputers. Specialized extensions have also been developed which permit analysis of "flexible" personnel flows in connection with promotion and upward mobility planning and with rapidly changing projected work loads. This paper discusses applications both of these recent developments in an analysis of anticipated large scale work force changes in U.S. Navy shipyards. These eight shipyards under the management of the Naval Sea Systems Command (NAVSEA) employed approximately 76,000 workers in June 1985.

A review of the technology of computer-assisted personnel flow models can be found in Niehaus (1979, 1985). The first reference (1979) is a comprehensive monograph on the design of personnel flow and external labor market models including implementation considerations. The second reference (1985) describes current and projected applications of human resource policy analysis techniques in the 1980's. A useful case study concerning the implementation of personnel flow models in the IBM Corporation can be found in Heyer (1985). Both of these papers are included in a volume (Niehaus, 1985) of papers presented in the "Organizational Human Resource Policy Analysis" sessions at the XXVI International Meeting of the Institute of Management Sciences.

The flexible flow model presented in this paper is an extension of the goal-arc distribution models originally developed by Charnes, Cooper, Lewis and Niehaus (1978) for affirmative action planning. An initial implementation of this model was completed by Charnes, Cooper, Nelson, and Niehaus (1982). The model was tested operationally by Aiken, Nelson,

Murphy, and Niehaus (1981). The basic model structure was further developed
for U.S. Navy sea-shore rotation applications by Charnes, Cooper, Golnay,
Lovgren, Mayfield, and Wolfe (1985).

This paper begins with a statement of the issues involved in required
work force reductions at the shipyards. A discussion follows describing the
models used in the initial applications. Results are then are shown from
the preliminary model runs in an operational setting. Finally, a short
review is provided of plans to continue this implementation effort in
NAVSEA.

BACKGROUND

The work described in this paper was performed to assist NAVSEA
managers in responding to a requirement to reduce the number of shipyard
employees. In order to plan for the required employee reduction, it is
necessary to be able to project the number of employees who can be expected
to leave voluntarily. It is also useful to know the number expected to
transfer from one occupation to another within a shipyard.

In the examples shown in this paper the initial work force populations
are as of June 30, 1985. Table 1 shows the relative size of the planned
reductions. Although the total reductions seem within range of losses
expected through normal attrition, Shipyards B, E and H require reductions
clearly exceeding expected losses. Further differences emerge at the
occupation level. Personnel flows for these populations were projected by
quarter, six month period, and year to the end of September 1987. This
information can be used by NAVSEA managers at headquarters and in the
individual shipyards to develop plans for hires and/or reductions by skill
categories to achieve overall reduction targets.

The first application shows how simple flow models can be quickly
implemented to respond to rapidly developing policy changes. A spreadsheet
version of a personnel flow model was first developed on a microcomputer
(IBM PC/XT), using commercially available spreadsheet software (LOTUS 1-2-
3). Personnel transition rates developed on a mainframe computer
information system were downloaded to the microcomputer via
telecommunications software and then entered into the spreadsheet. A second
stage analysis extended the number of job categories and refined preliminary
results.

TABLE 1

PROJECTED SHIPYARD WORK FORCE REDUCTIONS
(Cumulative Percent From June 1985 Actual)
Preliminary

	SEP 85	DEC 85	MAR 86	JUN 86	SEP 86	SEP 87
Shipyard A	-1.1	-1.7	-1.9	-2.1	-2.3	-2.3
Shipyard B	0	-15.5	-18.6	-21.6	-24.6	-26.4
Shipyard C	-1.6	-2.6	-3.3	-3.9	-4.6	-6.1
Shipyard D	-3.0	-4.9	-5.1	-5.4	-5.7	-4.5
Shipyard E	-6.8	-8.2	-7.4	-6.7	-6.0	-19.1
Shipyard F	0.3	-1.5	-6.7	-11.8	-17.0	-17.5
Shipyard G	1.4	-1.9	-1.1	-0.3	0.5	2.4
Shipyard H	-10.2	-10.9	-13.7	-16.6	-19.4	-34.6
Total	-1.7	-4.5	-5.9	-7.4	-6.2	-12.7

Two types of projections are possible with the spreadsheet flow model. The first type is a simple flow model with normal attrition. This projection assumes that the work force is allowed to "run down" by normal attrition with no replacement. Movements between job categories are assumed to continue at the normal rates. The second type of projection includes work force goals for each occupational category for each of the five planning periods. Projected hires and reductions are calculated to exactly meet the goals for each occupational category at the end of each time period. Individual models are developed for each of the shipyards so that management decisions can be made where any personnel actions might need to be effected. Although these models were developed to respond to aggregate reductions specified at the corporate NAVSEA level, they can also be used to develop manpower requirements tied to internal shipyard planning consistent with overall NAVSEA ship overhaul scheduling.

Another prototype study was completed using a flexible flow model to balance work force levels and flows across time periods as well as between job categories. The planning periods were also modified to use time periods of unequal length to allow the integration of short and long term planning in the same model. In this case, as with the spreadsheet models, quarters are used for the most immediate time periods. Later time periods were of six month and year length. The flexible flow model results were developed for one of the shipyards to permit comparative analysis with the spreadsheet results.

The study is also being done to provide additional requirements information for the update and improvement of the Computer-Assisted Manpower Information System (CAMAS). This Navy-wide system, dating from the early 1970's, is being migrated to an IBM 3081 computer in two stages. The first stage is to establish a baseline system which will incorporate interactive batch processing. In this case the user will be able to interactively prepare menu screens which specify needed modeling and reporting outputs. Processing will be in a batch mode as best determined by overall mainframe loading. In the second stage, CAMAS will be improved to permit interactive processing were possible as well as using advanced information retrieval methods such as relational data base software.

The next section of this paper will discuss the development of the input data used in the models, including the way that the job categories were developed. Following a general discussion of the methodologies used, results for each of the model types will be provided. The actual data have been masked because of the nature of the management decisions involved.

MODEL INPUT DATA

The flow models use data available from operational information systems, internal reports, or simple estimates. The data that are needed include: initial job category populations, personnel movement or transition rates, manpower requirements, and total manpower ceilings. The analysis used the Department of the Navy's Computer-Assisted Manpower Analysis System (CAMAS) to produce the initial job category population data and personnel transition rates. CAMAS draws upon the Navy's Personnel

Automated Data System (PADS) for the basic personnel inventory data. An existing historical data base of over ten years of PADS data allows some smoothing of transition data developed for use in the models. A more detailed description of the input data characteristics is provided below.

Job Categories

A standardized Navy job category aggregation scheme is used for

                1   ENGINEERING AND SCIENCE TECHNICIANS
                2   SCIENTISTS AND ENGINEERS
                3   OTHER PROFESSIONALS
                4   MANAGEMENT AND ADMINISTRATION
                5   OTHER TECHNICIANS
                6   CLERICAL EMPLOYEES
                7   OTHER GS EMPLOYEES
                8   BLUE-COLLAR WORKERS
                9   OPERATIONS AND SERVICE WORKERS

Figure 1: Nine DONOL Major Occupation Groups (1-Digit DONOL Codes)

analyses and reports developed from CAMAS and related information systems.
This job category aggregation scheme uses the Department of Navy Occupation
Level (DONOL) codes. In the interests of time, the initial models were
developed at the highest level of DONOL occupational aggregation as shown in
Figure 1. Career or grade level distinctions were not addressed in order to
keep the outputs focused for the highest management levels in NAVSEA.

The initial model results were reviewed by NAVSEA top management and
staff. These NAVSEA executives felt that additional detail was needed to
highlight the blue-collar work force, of particular concern in the
management of shipyards. In order to provide this additional detail but
preserve a one page summary report, a combination of DONOL occupation level
groupings was used. The white collar jobs were defined at the one-digit
DONOL code level while the blue collar jobs were defined in greater detail
at the two-digit DONOL code level. This produced 18 job categories as shown
in Figure 2. (Future standardized CAMAS programs will permit
this type of job category combination from a menu screen.) As the shipyards
have no employees in the Aircraft Mechanic category, this category was
eliminated from the report.

Transition Rates

All of the projections in this paper are based a cross-sectional or
"snapshot" approach (Markov-like models), as distinguished from the more
complex longitudinal or "cohort" approaches and entity simulation methods.
The projections assume that attrition and personnel flows between categories

                1   ENGINEERING AND SCIENCE TECHNICIANS
                2   SCIENTISTS AND ENGINEERS
                3   OTHER PROFESSIONALS
                4   MANAGEMENT AND ADMINISTRATION
                5   OTHER TECHNICIANS
                6   CLERICAL EMPLOYEES
                7   OTHER GS EMPLOYEES
                8   ELECTRICAL MECHANICS
                9   ELECTRICIANS
               10   MACHINE TOOL OPERATORS
               11   METAL PROCESSORS
               12   METAL MECHANICS
               13   AIRCRAFT MECHANICS
               14   PIPEFITTERS
               15   WOODWORKERS
               16   PAINTERS
               17   MISCELLANEOUS CRAFT
               18   OPERATIONS AND SERVICE WORKERS

Figure 2. Eighteen Occupational Groups for Shipyard Projections
          (compiled from 2-digit DONOL codes)

```
      EMPLOYEE              JOB CATEGORY
      NUMBER            TIME 1            TIME 2
--------------------------------------------------------------

       1438            ENGINEER          ENGINEER
       1524            TECHNICIAN
       2133            TECHNICIAN        ENGINEER
       2619                              TECHNICIAN
--------------------------------------------------------------
```

Figure 3. Transition Data File

will continue at rates estimated from historical behavior. Using the
eighteen categories indicated above, projections of personnel transition
rates were developed for the preceding three years.

An example of the development of the transition rate data base is
useful for those not familiar with the methodology. Figure 3 shows the type
of information needed to develop the transition data. Each employee's job
category is given for Time 1 and Time 2. Each change in employee category
from Time 1 to Time 2 is added to a count of changes between specific
categories. The resulting counts of personnel flows constitute the
transition data, which are then divided by the number of employees beginning
Time 1 in each category to yield the observed transition rates. (In CAMAS,
separate files are kept for each time period and the transition rates are
developed by a specially designed menu driven computer program.)

In Figure 3 it can be seen that Employee No. 1438 was an engineer in
both time periods. On the other hand, Employee No. 1524 was a technician in
period 1 but was not in the organization in period 2. Also, employee No.
2133 was promoted from technician to engineer between the two time periods.
Finally, employee No. 2619 was hired during period 1. This kind of data can
then be used to create a matrix such as provided in Figures 4 and 5. Figure
4 contains the actual counts. The transition rates in Figure 5 are obtained
by dividing the movement data by the starting numbers. For example, 320/400
or 80% of the technicians remained technicians, 20/400 or 5% were promoted
to engineer and 60/400 or 15% left the organization.

By reading across the rows of Figures 4 and 5 one can see how a given
job category changed from the start of the period. By reading down, one can
see how a job category was built up over the time period. For projection
purposes only the interior or internal movements are used, since one can
assume the remainder to have left the organization.

```
      JOB         NUMBER        MOVEMENT TO
      CATEGORY    YR 1      TECHNICIAN   ENGINEER    LOSSES
      --------------------------------------------------------

TECHNICIAN  400      320          20          60

ENGINEER    200        6         180          14

            HIRES     94           5

NUMBER YR 2          420         205

      --------------------------------------------------------
```

Figure 4. Personnel Movement Statistics

	MOVEMENT TO		
FROM	TECHNICIAN	ENGINEER	LOSSES
TECHNICIAN	.80	.05	.15
ENGINEER	.03	.90	.07

Figure 5. Personnel Transition Rates

Each transition matrix used in the shipyard study is a weighted average of the data from the last three years. For example, the April-June transition matrix used in the projections is computed from the data for that quarter in 1983, 1984, and 1985. Data for these three years were given weights of 1, 2 and 3, respectively for the weighted average. That is, the final transition matrix was a composite of data using the 1983 data multiplied by one-sixth, the 1984 data multiplied by one-third, and the 1985 data multiplied by one-half. Data from the most recent period were thus given the most weight in this average.

Initial Population Data

The initial population for each job category was obtained from CAMAS transition data files. These figures were then proportionately adjusted by the official on-board totals used for manpower ceiling control purposes. This minor adjustment insured that the sum of the data by job category exactly equalled the official control totals.

Manpower Requirements and Ceiling Data

Manpower requirements at the occupation level were not available for this study. These data were estimated by proportionally adjusting the initial population figures by the official manpower ceilings for the planning periods, obtained from NAVSEA planning documents. Since this adjustment was performed within the LOTUS 1-2-3 spreadsheet, any planned change in the ceiling numbers can be rapidly evaluated.

MODEL RESULTS

The transition matrices for each shipyard were downloaded onto a microcomputer (IBM PC/XT) and manually combined with the other input data into a LOTUS 1-2-3 spreadsheet. Each spreadsheet contains two different flow models based on the following assumptions: (1) natural attrition with no hiring, drawing down the work force over time; (2) a drawdown based on reductions or hires as necessary to meet management targets as set by NAVSEA. The two models use the same set of transition matrices, which only has to be transferred once for each spreadsheet. Data for one of the shipyards were also subsequently used in the test of the flexible flow model on a mainframe computer.

Simple Flow Models Without Replacement

This set of projections was based on estimated transition rates alone, with no hiring or reductions. The purpose of these projections was to show how the work force would evolve without management intervention. To illustrate this process, we can follow one row on Figure 6, which shows the results for a representative shipyard. We select the row for scientists and engineers. The entry on that row in the first column of numbers shows that, as of June 30, 1985, there were 270 scientists and engineers actually on board. Starting from this number, we then wish to project the number of scientists and engineers on board on September 30, 1985.

OCCUPATIONAL PROJECTIONS (NO HIRING)

SHIPYARD B

	ACTUAL JUN 85	SEP 85	PROJECTED DEC 85	ON-BOARD MAR 86	SEP 86	SEP 87
ENG & SCI TECH	386	370	370	370	343	315
SCI & ENG	270	249	243	233	208	174
OTHER PROF	25	23	21	21	18	15
MGR & ADMIN	280	268	265	261	242	217
OTHER TECH	209	202	192	187	177	154
CLERICAL	344	294	272	236	190	129
OTHER GS	7	5	5	3	2	1
ELEC MECH	328	310	306	290	263	231
ELECTRICIANS	549	500	481	459	408	342
MACH TOOL OP	420	410	401	382	363	324
METAL PROCESS	469	434	424	411	381	339
METAL MECH	774	723	693	668	611	539
PIPEFITTING	681	627	590	559	516	450
WOODWORKERS	201	189	184	179	167	150
PAINTERS	162	153	143	132	123	106
MISC CRAFT	951	897	836	758	695	600
OP & SVC WKRS	576	542	527	488	451	396
TOTAL	6632	6197	5953	5636	5161	4482

EXPERIMENTAL REPORT

Figure 6: Example of Occupational Projections (No-Hiring)

Examination of the transition rates derived from the June-September quarters for 1982, 1983, and 1984 (weighted 1,2 and 3, respectively) indicates that there were three possible internal sources of scientists and engineers during that quarter (i.e., nonzero transition rates): transfers from engineering and science technicians, those remaining in the scientist and engineer category from the previous period, and transfers from other GS employees. The transition rates and initial on-boards for the quarter are given in Figure 7.

Applying the transition rates to the initial on-boards, one of the science and engineering technicians on board at the beginning of the quarter enters the scientists and engineers category during the quarter, 248 of the scientists and engineers on board at the beginning of the quarter are still there at the end and no other GS employee enters the scientists and engineers category. The total for scientists and engineers in the new quarter is then 249. The populations are then projected forward one period at a time in the same fashion.

Simple Flow Models with Goals

The previous example shows that reliance on attrition alone to reduce work force size leads to occupation imbalance. Due to loss behavior that differs between occupations, attrition without replacement leads to an

SOURCE:	RATE	INITIAL ON-BOARDS	PROJECTED FLOW
SCI & ENG TECH	.0031	386	1
SCIENTISTS AND ENGINEERS	.9183	270	248
OTHER GS EMPLOYEES	.0214	7	0
TOTAL			249

Figure 7. Sources for Flows into Scientists and Engineers

```
            OCCUPATIONAL PROJECTIONS(ON-BOARD TARGETS)

                         SHIPYARD B

                ACTUAL        INCREASE          INCREASE           INCREASE           INCREASE            INCREASE
              JUN 85 SEP 85  (EXCESS) DEC 85   (EXCESS) MAR 86    (EXCESS) SEP 86    (EXCESS) SEP 87     (EXCESS)

ENG & SCI TECH  386    386      16     326       -61     314        -13     291        -3     284          13
SCI & ENG       270    270      21     228       -36     220          2     204         8     199          29
OTHER PROF       25     25       2      21        -2      20          0      19         1      18           2
MGR & ADMIN     280    280      12     236       -41     228         -5     211        -2     206          15
OTHER TECH      209    209       7     176       -23     170         -3     158        -6     154          11
CLERICAL        344    344      50     290       -28     280         29     259        35     253          80
OTHER GS          7      7       2       6         0       6          2       5         1       5           2
ELEC MECH       328    328      18     277       -47     267          4     247         5     241          23
ELECTRICIANS    549    549      49     464       -63     447          4     414        16     404          57
MACH TOOL OP    420    420      10     355       -56     342          3     317        -8     309          24
METAL PROCESS   469    469      35     396       -62     382         -1     354        -1     345          30
METAL MECH      774    773      50     654       -87     630          0     584         8     570          55
PIPEFITTING     681    680      53     575       -65     554          9     513         1     501          54
WOODWORKERS     201    201      12     170       -26     164         -1     152        -2     148          12
PAINTERS        162    162       9     137       -14     132          5     122        -1     119          14
MISC CRAFT      951    950      53     803       -83     774         46     717         9     700          83
OP & SVC WKRS   576    575      33     486       -74     469         19     434        -1     424          42

TOTAL          6632   6628            5600               5400               5000               4880

             TOTAL INCREASES  432                 0              123                 84                    546
             TOTAL (EXCESS)     0              -768              -23                -24

                                                              EXPERIMENTAL REPORT
```

Figure 8: Example of Occupational Projections (On-Board Targets)

excess of employees in some occupations and a shortage in others. A second
set of projections were made to also include hires and reductions needed to
meet manpower requirements or goals.

This second set of projections used the same transition matrices as the
prior case, but included management-determined goals at each stage of the
process. The results provide the number of projected hires or reductions
necessary to meet the goals. Figure 8 shows the model output for the test
shipyard.

The model output can again be illustrated by following the
corresponding line for scientists and engineers. As before, there were 270
employees actually on board in this category in June 1985. The goal for
September 1985 is the same as the June 1985 on-boards, 270. As seen in the
prior example, attrition alone would reduce the number on board to 249. The
present example shows that 21 new employees would have to be hired in this
category. This number is given in the increase (excess) column. Figure 8
shows that all goals are met. In this case, the required 21 scientists and
engineers are hired.

During the September to December 1985 period the transition
calculations indicate that there would a reduction in the scientist and
engineer population from 270 to 264. Since the management goal for
scientists and engineers for December 1985 is 228, a further reduction of 36
is required, as shown in Figure 8.

Further examination indicates that additional hiring will be required in
later time periods to meet scientist and engineer goals. Since this pattern
of alternate hiring and reduction occurs frequently, the modeling approach
was next extended to include the possibility of smoothing the work force
variations over time.

Flexible Flow Models

The simple flow model with goals shows the projected hires and
reductions needed to meet the management goals exactly. A more complex

164

model was next examined to allow variations from the goals to smooth work
force flows between time periods. This model also allows flexible flows
between job categories to reduce the requirements for hires and reductions.
The model uses the same inputs (initial on-boards, management-determined
goals, and personnel transition rates) as the simple flow model with goals.
Additional parameters are included to define the flexibility allowed.

The output of this model provides a one page report for each time
period. An example of one page of the model output for the test shipyard is
shown as Figure 9. The left side of the report shows the initial on-boards.
The manpower requirements or goals, the projected final on-boards, and the
deviation from the goals are shown on the right side. The intervening
columns indicate the personnel actions which relate the initial on-boards to
the final on-boards: hires, reductions, transfers in, transfers out, and
other losses (attrition). Transfers in and transfers out are further
disaggregated into expected transfers and flexible transfers. Expected
transfers are the flows between job categories that would be expected
without management intervention. Flexible transfers are the changes from
the historical pattern that management chooses to improve work force balance
without resorting to hires or reductions.

Unlike the previous model, this flexible flow model indicates
essentially no hiring in the first time period and a final on-board total
that is significantly below the sum of the goals (the end strength control
total). The reason for this is that the goals in the next time periods are
markedly lower. Hires in the first period would result in more reductions
in later periods. The model projects declining on-boards that are above
goals for December 1985 and March 1986. The projected on-boards are then at
the end strength requirements until September 1987. These results suggest
that the intermediate control totals might be adjusted to meet longer term
end strength control totals through a mixture of attrition and reductions
that results in less turbulence than indicated by the spreadsheet model
results.

FURTHER NAVSEA APPLICATIONS

There has already been a complete update of the model results to
reflect both the work force populations at the shipyards as of September
1985 and changes in the shipyard overhaul schedules. While the trends
remain the same, individual shipyard loadings are already different from
those in effect at the time the results shown in this paper were developed.
Thus, the results should only be considered as illustrative of ways to use
the personnel flow model technology.

The results from the personnel flow models were of use to NAVSEA in
assessing the impacts of the large reductions required of the shipyards.
The reports were used by NAVSEA headquarters to get a look ahead
capability. The model results were also provided to the individual shipyard
commanders to begin a dialogue on more extensive use. Considering the trends
in the Federal budget, it is anticipated that the problem of personnel
reductions will continue to be an issue for the next few years. A quarterly
tracking system has been instituted to review the accuracy of the
projections and to provide a rolling projection to account for changing
shipyard work loads.

Preliminary discussions have been held with individual shipyard
planning staffs to determine the usefulness of the models to their efforts.
It appears that the individual shipyard planners particularly prefer the
spreadsheet models. They prefer to have personnel on-board when they are
needed to minimize overhaul costs. On the other hand, the personnel staffs
tend to like the flexible flow models since personnel turbulence is kept to

DEPARTMENT OF THE NAVY
PROJECTED PERSONNEL ACTIONS FOR PERIOD 1
NAVSEA:
SHIPYARD B

MAJOR OCCUPATION AND CODE	LEV	INITIAL ON-BOARD	INCREASE	EXCESS	TRANSFERS IN			TRANSFERS OUT			OTHER LOSSES	FINAL ON-BOARD	GOAL	DEVIATION FROM GOAL
					EXP	FLEX	ACT	EXP	FLEX	ACT				
1 FNG & SCI TECH	1	386	0	0	9	0	9	3	2	5	22	368	386	-18
2 SCI & ENG	1	270	0	0	1	0	1	0	2	2	21	248	270	-22
3 OTHER PROF	1	25	0	0	0	0	0	0	1	1	1	23	25	-2
4 MGR & ADMIN	1	280	0	0	6	4	10	2	3	5	17	268	280	-12
5 OTHER TECH	1	209	0	0	8	-2	6	3	2	5	13	197	209	-12
6 CLERICAL	1	344	0	0	0	10	10	14	-10	4	38	312	344	-32
7 OTHER GS	1	7	1	0	0	0	0	0	0	0	1	7	7	0
8 ELEC MECH	1	328	0	0	0	2	2	0	2	2	17	311	328	-17
9 ELECTRICIANS	1	549	0	0	1	1	2	13	1	14	38	499	549	-50
10 MACH TOOL OP	1	420	0	0	5	3	8	5	1	6	12	410	420	-10
11 METAL PROCESS	1	469	0	0	2	1	3	0	0	0	36	436	469	-33
12 METAL MECH	1	774	0	0	6	4	10	4	1	5	54	725	773	-48
14 PIPEFITTING	1	681	0	0	1	1	2	5	3	8	49	626	680	-54
15 WOODWORKERS	1	201	0	0	4	1	5	0	1	1	15	190	201	-11
16 PAINTERS	1	162	0	0	1	1	2	0	2	2	10	152	162	-10
17 MISC CRAFT	1	951	0	0	17	0	17	5	2	7	66	895	950	-55
18 OP & SVC WKRS	1	576	0	0	19	-9	10	26	4	30	25	531	575	-44
TOTAL		6632	1	0	80	17	97	80	17	97	435	6198	6628	-430

EXPERIMENTAL REPORT

Figure 9: Example of Flexible Flow Model Output

a lower level and career planning and training can be included in the plans.

An area where further work is planned is in the development of better estimates of manpower requirements data. At the local level it is felt to would be useful to feed the manpower requirements data directly from the operational plans. Also more detail by occupation was desired at the local level. (These concerns were similar to those found in other Navy personnel modeling studies (see Niehaus (1979, Chp 5)).

NAVSEA shipyard management has decided to concentrate model development efforts in the near term at the headquarters level. Particular attention will be paid to the development of the manpower requirements data consistent with shipyard loading as determined by the ship overhaul schedule. The continued use of the models is to be paralleled by a study of the best ways to bring together existing management practices with a more comprehensive implementation. The individual shipyards will continue to be apprised of model results as they are used to develop the overall corporate plan. In the longer term, efforts will be made to extend the model technology to the local level. In summary, it is planned to continue to use the models as a tracking and evaluation vehicle. Briefings and training for a wider group of NAVSEA personnel are planned as the technology gains acceptance. With the continued strong support of NAVSEA's top management, it is anticipated that the flow modeling technology will eventually be integrated into the strategic and operational planning accomplished in the management of the naval shipyards.

REFERENCES

Aiken, D.D., D. Murphy, A. Nelson, and R.J. Niehaus "A Planning Model for Federal Equal Opportunity Recruitment Program (FEORP) Strategy Development: OASN (M&RA) Research Report No. 40 (Washington, DC: Office of the Assistant Secretary of the Navy (Manpower and Reserve Affairs), 1981).

Charnes, A., W.W. Cooper, B. Golany, V. Lovegran, W.T. Mayfield, and M. Wolfe "A Goal Programming Model for the Management of the U.S. Navy's Sea-Shore Rotation Program" in R.J. Niehaus, Ed. Human Resource Policy Analysis: Organizational Applications, (New York: Prager, 1985). pp. 145-172.

Charnes, A., W.W. Cooper, K.A. Lewis, and R.J. Niehaus, A Multi-Level Coherence Model for EEO Planning",in A. Charnes, W.W. Cooper, and R.J. Niehaus, eds., Management Science Approaches to Manpower Planning and Organization Design, (New York: Elsevier North Holland, 1978).

Charnes, A., W.W. Cooper, A. Nelson, and R.J. Niehaus. "Model Extension and Computation in Goal-Arc Network Approaches for EEO Planning", INFOR, 20, No. 4, November 1982, pp. 315-335.

Heyer, N.O. "Managing Human Resources in a High Technology Enterprise" in R.J. Niehaus, Ed., Human Resource Policy Analysis: Organizational Applications (New York: Prager, 1985).

Niehaus, R.J. Computer-Assisted Human Resource Planning, (New York: Wiley Interscience, 1979).

Niehaus, R.J. Human Resource Policy Analysis: Organizational Applications (New York: Prager, 1985).

NEW TECHNOLOGY FOR CONTROLLING TURNOVER

Michael D. Hawkins

Graduate School of Business Administration
Department of Management Science
University of Washington
Seattle, WA 98195

INTRODUCTION

This paper suggest some improvements in the technology for controlling
personnel turnover. Systems for controlling turnover are potentially very
useful because, as it is widely recognized, turnover can be very costly to
an organization. For example, Frantzreb (1979) cites a number of studies
calculating the cost to an organization of the loss of a manager or
professional to range from $6,000 to $40,000. Deutsch (1982) even
speculates that part of the success of the Japanese production system in
recent years may, in part, be due to lower rates of turnover in that
country. Not all turnover is undesirable. Some turnover has desirable
consequences, not only from an organizational but individual perspective as
well. Control then, means effective management of turnover.

This review concludes that improvements in the technology for
controlling turnover are needed. According to one classic definition of
control (Koontz and O'Donnell, 1976, p. 639),

> "Controlling implies measurement of accomplishment of events
> against the standard of plans and the correction of deviations to
> assure attainment of objectives according to plans."

Comparing the elements of this definition to current human resource
practice and the literature on turnover control, it is apparent there is one
critical element of control, development of standards, on which the turnover
literature and current practice have little to offer that is practical and
empirically valid. Indeed, some suggestions in the literature can, if
followed, give erroneous signals on the need for corrective action on the
part of management when turnover rates change. It is the conclusion of this
author that the state-of-the-art in turnover control is quite deficient.

This research looks at three literatures and proposes a turnover model
which appears to be of practical utility. The first literature is that of
industrial psychology. Reliance is on recent reviews and articles dealing
specifically with turnover control. The second is the management science
literature having to do with forecasting turnover. The third literature is
about a type of control theory that has been applied quite successfully in
industry: Statistical Quality Control (SQC). Historically there seems to

have been little connection between the SQC literature and the two other
turnover literatures. In addition to the literature review, the author also
consulted some unpublished studies of the turnover phenomenon from his
research and consulting, from research conducted by his students at the
University of Washington, and from communications between the author and
fellow human resource planners.

This paper will go through the above definition of control and present
each component of the proposed model. At various steps in the building of
the proposed model for turnover control a choice was made in selecting a
component part of the model from a number of alternative parts that were
suggested by one or more of the literature. This was done by applying two
criteria: (1) the prospective component of the model had to have them
empirically validated in a corporate setting, and (2) it must be
demonstrably easy to implement. (A longer version of this paper (Hawkins,
1986) describes each component in more technical and mathematical detail
along with some of the alternative components that were available and why
they were not selected.)

MEASUREMENT OF TURNOVER

The first activity mentioned in the definition of control is
measurement of the event being controlled. Theoretically, there are two
classes of measures for turnover: attribute and variable. Human resource
managers nearly always use attribute measures. That is, turnover occurs
when a person actually leaves the company. It is a binary event; an
individual either has or has not left the organization.

Mobley (182, chap. 6) describes a number of conceptual models that view
turnover as an entire process rather than a single event. Leaving is just
the final element in s whole array of events, decisions, and activities such
as experiencing job dissatisfaction, searching for alternative jobs, and
then deciding to leave. This, of course, suggests that turnover could be
measured along a single dimension or continuum of such events. A control
system using such a variable measure of turnover would wave a red flag of
warning before people actually left. Attribute systems can fly red flags
only after people have begun to leave. Unfortunately all of the needed
elements for a variable measure of turnover have not been empirically
validated and some others appeared to be quite difficult to implement.

There are quite a number of attribute measures of turnover. The often
cited study by Gaudet (1960), for example, presents 25 of them. Since only
three of these methods lend themselves especially well to forecasting, and
since (as we shall see later) forecasting is essential to control, most of
these measures were eliminated from further consideration.

DEVELOPING A PLAN

The next activity mentioned in the definition of control is the
development of a plan containing standards for turnover. Useful plans
typically contain a set of forecasts on how we think critical _controllable_
variables should behave under different scenarios of the behavior of
uncontrollable variables.

A great deal of success in developing techniques for predicting
turnover has been attained by statisticians and operations researchers. We
shall now look at some of their results.

FORECASTING TURNOVER

In a relatively recent review on empirically tested techniques for

forecasting turnover, Bartholomew and Forbes (1979, chap. 2-3) state that
analysis and forecasting of turnover ought to be based on:

> "... <u>homogeneous</u> groups of individuals. By this we mean groups of
> people who are similar with respect to all known factors which
> affect propensity to leave. This is a counsel of perfection which
> can never be attained in practice but the important thing is to
> ensure that there is no major source of heterogeneity."

Two of the major demographic attributes of employees that are strongly
related to their propensity to leave are length-of-service and age. If we
do not include retirements, employees with low lengths-of-service will
usually leave much more rapidly than those with high lengths of service.

Figure 1 depicts a common form of this relationship. The vertical axis
measures the turnover rate of a "cohort" over a period of time. A cohort is
simply a group of people in the same (or similar) occupation(s) who enter an
organization at about the same time. Some examples of cohorts are all the
new tellers a bank recruited during the first quarter of 1984 or all the
MBAs an oil company hired from the class of 1985.

In the figure the turnover rate id defined to be the number in the
cohort who leave during a given period of time divided by the number
originally in the cohort. If we plotted the number of people actually
leaving the cohort instead of the proportion leaving, we would get what is
known as a cumulative length-of-service distribution (CLS). It's shape
would be identical to that of Figure 1 but the units on the vertical axis
would be in terms of numbers rather than proportions.

According to Bartholomew and Forbes (p. 45) the most remarkable thing
about CLS curves is that they nearly always "have the same basic shape" and
this holds true across "all kinds of occupations and also across national
boundaries." The shape can be characterized by a high degree of skewness at
the low lengths-of-service indicating that most employees stay only a short
time in an organization and only a few stay for a long period. CLS curves
usually have a mode near the origin. If a mode is not noticed it may mean
that the units of length of service are "too coarse to reveal it."

The units of tenure in a CLS curve may differ from one kind of employee
group to another. Curves for unskilled factory workers, for example, may
best be drawn in terms of weeks, while for engineers, years may be more
appropriate.

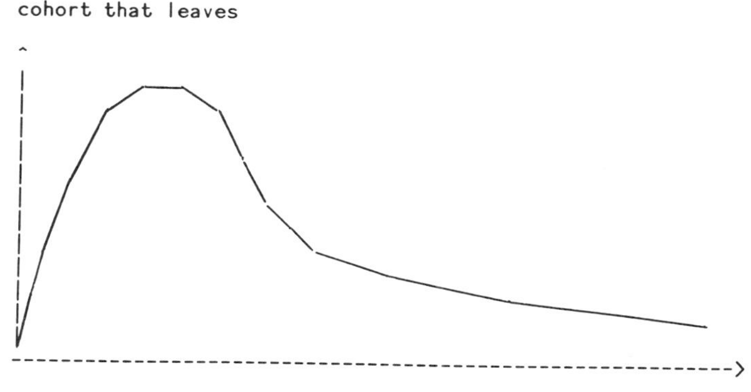

Figure 1: Turnover Pattern of Cohorts

From the shape of the CLS curve we can see why a single turnover rate
for an organization or group of employees can be a misleading index. Let us
suppose that the turnover behavior of all cohorts employed by a given
company follows curves like that in Figure 1 and the organization's rate of
growth increases. It must fuel this growth by increasing its recruitment
rates. Recruits will, of course, be composed mostly of people with low
tenure who leave at a high rate. Therefore,growth will increase the
relative mix of the less experienced, higher turnover employees and thereby
increase the total turnover rate of the organization.

Conversely, if an organization attempts to contract and decides to do
it via a hiring freeze and natural attrition, it will find past rates of
overall turnover to be poor predictors of future turnover. This is because
as recruitment ceases there will be relatively fewer and fewer of the high
turnover groups present, relatively more of the low turnover groups present,
and the overall turnover rate can drop dramatically.

Also, two organizations with identical cohort turnover patterns can
have different total rates of turnover depending on the experience base of
their cohorts. (See Bartholomew and Forbes, pp. 14-16 for examples.)

It would appear that if we want to be able to distinguish turnover that
we can control from that we cannot, then we will need to measure turnover of
key employee groups in terms of their length-of-service or a variable
related to length-of-service.

Turnover behavior of cohorts can be forecasted by fitting curves to
early cohort retention behavior and extrapolating future retention by
extending the curve. Cohort analysis is longitudinal analysis and
Bartholomew and Forbes state that it is the most "natural" way to analyze
turnover.

In contrast, with cross-sectional or "census" analysis of turnover we
look only at the most recent loss/retention patterns of cohorts. For
example, we might examine only the loss patterns of employees, who during
one of the last four years, had between 1 and 2 years of service. In such
an analysis we would be looking at only those four cohorts who most recently
had between 1 and 2 years of service rather than all cohorts who had ever
experienced it.

In comparing cohort and census analysis of turnover control to special
groups such as "fast track" MBAs whose early careers may be of special
interest. Census analysis uses data from a much shorter historical time
period than does cohort analysis. Most human resource executives the author
has dealt with trust shorter histories much more than longer ones when it
comes to using them as a bases for forecasting.

Also, for any occupational group and grade, say senior chemical
engineers, we will have a multitude of cohorts represented. Monitoring
cohorts then, means following many times the number of groups we would need
to follow with census analysis.

Census forecasting techniques turn out to be quite accurate. For
example, if we use length-of-service or age specific turnover rates in a
census analysis we can often get a forecast of total turnover for the next
year that is within plus or minus 2-5% of actual turnover. This level of
accuracy was reported in two studies documented in the literature (Bright,
1976; Price, 1978), and confirmed in communications the author has had with
human resource planning practitioners, in his consulting work and in
unpublished research conducted by his students at the University of
Washington. Since census techniques are so accurate, there is little to be

gained by using cohort techniques for control purposes and we will proceed
further only with the census technique. See, however, Personnel Technology,
Inc., (1981, pp. 18-20) for a description of a cohort based control system.

Another advantage of using the census method is that we can, if it is
desirable, use employee _age_ instead of length-of-service loss rates to
obtain accurate forecasts. Employee ages are usually highly correlated with
their lengths-of-service. According to reviews by Bartholomew and Forbes
(1979), and Mobley (1982), younger employees tend to leave (except for
retirements) at a much higher rate than older employees.

As noted earlier in this paper, there are many ways that turnover can
be measured. For forecasting purposes, however, Bartholomew and Forbes
indicate that only three of them have proven to be very useful. The first
was defined earlier to be the proportion of an initial cohort that leaves
each period of time. The other two measures, are "transition rates" and
"central rates". The transition rate measure of turnover, chosen for the
control model, is the number of leavers during a time period (say year) in
an employee group divided by the total number in the group at the beginning
of the period. This transition rate parameter can be used directly for
forecasting. If it is multiplied by the number of people in an employee
group at the start of a new year, it yields a prediction of the number who
will leave the group during the year. After adding in recruits and internal
transfers, we have a forecast of the numbers who will be in the group at the
beginning of the next year.

It is important to note here that the transition rate measure of
turnover differs from the most often used measure, called the "central
rate". In this latter measure, numbers of people leaving are divided by the
average number in a group during a period rather than by the numbers at the
beginning of a period. The transition rate was chosen because it is the
easiest rate to calculate. (Ease of calculation has been discovered to be
an important consideration in the practice of statistical quality control.)
Also, the formulas for the turnover transition rate, its expected value, and
its standard error, match exactly the formulas used for a common statistical
quality control process. Forbes (1970, p. 100) presents the best (in a
statistical sense) formula for combining t years of turnover data into an
estimate of the true loss rate, which can in turn, be sued for forecasting
purposes. An important thing to note about Forbes formulation is that it is
not a simple average of past rates.

PRACTICAL CONSIDERATIONS IN FORECASTING TURNOVER

Turning from the Bartholomew and Forbes (1979) review it is useful to
consider some practical considerations in forecasting turnover. As a
starting point one should combine years or months of service, or years of
age into bands when measuring and forecasting turnover. It has been found
to be particularly useful to group the years of service in 0-4, 5-9, 10-14,
examining the number of people on board the most recent year for which data
is available. This grouping works out quite well since turnover rates
between years within the groups usually do not vary by much.

Figure 2 depicts typical patterns of length-of-service specific
turnover transition rates for an employee group as presented by Bartholomew
and Forbes (1979). The patterned areas in the more experienced service
group reflect the author's findings of total turnover when retirements are
included. Note that the shape of the curve (exclusive of retirements) is
similar to that of the cohort curve of Figure 1.

For hourly employees, it would probably be wise to use length-of-
service bands defined in terms of months or quarters instead of years.

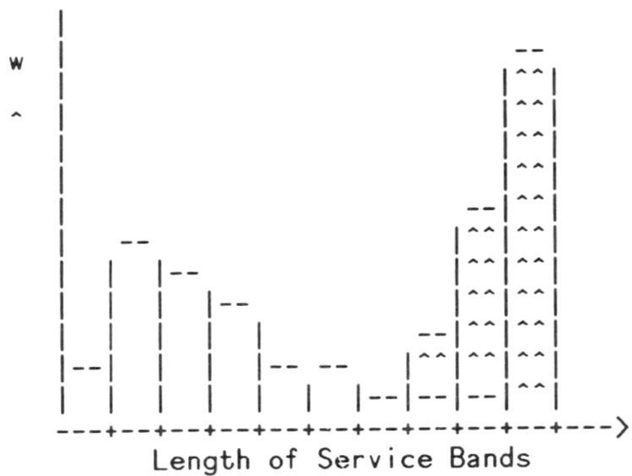

Length of Service Bands

Figure 2: Length-of-Service Transition Rates (Retirements Included)

(See, for example, Gustafson, 1980.) Some preliminary data analysis is usually required for each type of employee group to determine the most appropriate time units.

For turnover control, it is useful to break up the length-of-service band 0-4 into two or more separate bands to ensure capturing the early mode in the turnover distribution. Also, one should look at the turnover rates of the more experienced bands to see if any rates are so close that they can be grouped together. This will likely be the case if retirements are not counted as losses. If retirements are to be monitored then the larger length-of-service bands probably cannot be grouped.

For age specific rates, most human resource forecasters seem to use 20-24, 25-29, ..., 55-59, 60-64, and 65+ (e.g., Bright, 1976). There may not be any statistical basis for this grouping. It is most likely used because many of the age bands represent certain rights of passage to most of us. Most retirement still occurs by 65 even with the prohibition of mandatory retirement before age 70. Individuals over the age of 40 are protected against discrimination by various state and Federal laws, and many notions about career paths are connected with reaching the ages 30, 40, 50, etc. As with the length-of-service bands described above, there is typically little variation of turnover within years in each age band. Figure 3, based on the author's forecasting work, depicts a typical pattern of turnover transition rates by age bands where retirements are included. Note the similarly to earlier figures.

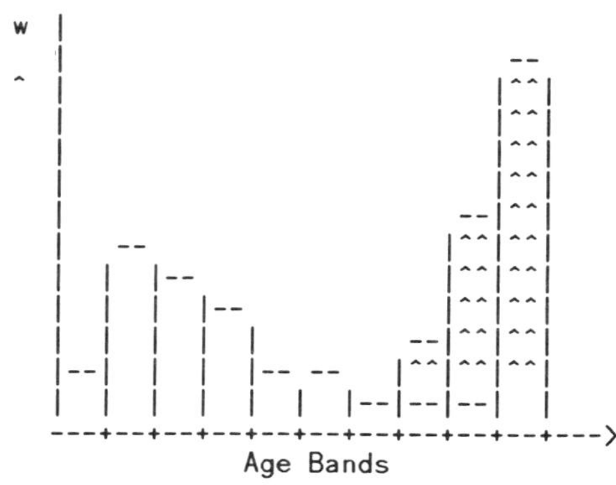

Age Bands

Figure 3: Age-Specific Turnover Transition Rates (Retirements Included)

For control purposes it will be necessary to calculate age or length-of-service transition rates for specific employee groups that have some operational meaning. For example, we might want to control the loss rates of a key occupational group such as "engineer". We would thus monitor the loss transition rates of, say, engineers ages 20-24, 25-29, ..., 60-64, and 65+. Or, we might want to monitor the turnover rates of an EEO protected group with less than 1, 1-4, 5-9, 10-19, and 20+ years of service. Borrowing from a list in Mobley (1982, p. 41) we could define useful groups in terms of position, department, supervisor, shift, location, units, division, function, recruitment source, race, sex, ethnic group, level and type of education, compensation, job history, performance rating and potential rating. A description of how length-of-service or age-specific loss rates can be calculated from data commonly maintained on Human Resource Information Systems can be found in Hawkins (1985).

DEVISING STANDARDS

Returning to our definition of control we next see that our turnover plan must contain "standards" for the activity being measured. There are several kinds of standards which are relevant to turnover. The first has to do with whether or not a measured turnover rate is too high or too low. The second is, even if a rate is too high or too low, to what extend does it matter to the organization? On the question of whether or not a rate is too high or low, the literature is often silent (e.g., Frantzreb, 1977a).

Much of the literature suggests that we seek out benchmark rates of turnover in terms of the total turnover rate of the organization or of specific parts of it (e.g., Price, 1977, pp. 44-45). Price lists central turnover rates by various occupations and industries. Up to date turnover statistics using the central separation rate by industry, region, and number of employees in the organization are published by the Bureau of National Affairs and the U.S. Department of Labor's Bureau of Labor Statistics. These numbers are often used by personnel professionals as benchmarks by which to compare their own organization's turnover rates. In a recent article Laser (1980) even suggests a rule of thumb that an organization should take corrective action if its total turnover rate is 10 to 15% higher than other organizations in the same geographical area or industry.

The problem with using total loss rates as benchmarks or standards in a turnover control system, as we have already seen, is that the total rates for an occupational group in an organization can vary dramatically from year to year even though the underlying turnover propensity of individuals in these groups does not change. Comparing your total turnover rate with that of an industry or competitor benchmark may suggest that you have a serious control problem, when, in reality the high rate you may be experiencing is due to demographic factors outside of your control.

COST STANDARDS

There is a second "standards" question to answer in addition to whether or not a turnover rate is too high or low: Does it matter if a particular rate is too high or too low? This is an are in which the literature provides a number of useful tools.

Articles using human resource accounting techniques to determine the cost of turnover are familiar to most human resource planners. Some recent ones are Cascio (1982), Fitz-Enz (1984), Frantzreb (1979), Gustafson (1980), and Hall (1981). While there are generally recognized weaknesses in each methodology, the techniques have been applied usefully in a number of corporations.

The review by Mobley (1982) points out that there are both positive and
negative consequences of turnover. The negative consequences are well known
and include the out of pocket and opportunity costs involved in separation
pay and in recruiting and training replacements. The positive consequences
include such things as the displacement of poor performers. Mobley (1982,
p. 30) points out, however, that while progress has been made in determining
the dollar cost of turnover, there has been little in the way of quantifying
the benefits of turnover. "From a management perspective, what is needed is
a mechanism for evaluating the net utility to the organization of turnover
-- that is, a means of integrating the positive and negative costs and
consequences of turnover for individuals at differing levels of position,
performance, and potential." A good first step, however, for human resource
managers rates for high and low performing employees.

CORRECTING DEVIATIONS

Once a turnover rate has been compared to standards and found to be too
high or too low and also worth investigating, the final step in the control
process is to correct the deviation. This is an area where the industrial
psychology literature on turnover has a number of useful ideas to offer the
human resource planner. Psychologists usually examine turnover from the
individual's rather than the organization's point of view and devise and
test theories as to why individuals leave organ-izations. Even though
Mobley (1982, p. 77) says that much of this literature is theoretical and
without as much empirical evidence as might be desired, the literature is
important because corrective action pre-supposes some cause and effect
relationship between our actions and subsequent turnover.

Examples of corrective actions include changes to the recruitment
process, adoption of weighted application blanks, hiring OD consultants to
facilitate a climate of various units in the organization, modifying wages-
salaries-benefits, improving job content, and providing incentives to
supervisors for lowering turnover. Many of the corrections suggested by the
literature are expensive to implement, which reinforces the need for methods
to determine which changes have the highest priority for implementation.

Mobley's (1982) book includes a short chapter with diagnostic questions
to ask for turnover problems associated with 1) recruitment, selection,and
early socialization, 2) job content, 3) compensation practices, 4) career
planning and development, and 5) alternative work schedules. These
questions can be used to focus in on the most appropriate corrections to
make. Frantzreb (1977b) and Peskin (1980, chap. 10) also suggest practical
action steps the human resource planner can take and how a control system
might be organized. Price (1977) and Mobley (1982) also provide lists of
causal and correlational factors related to turnover.

In summary, some of the tools we require for controlling turnover are
available. What is missing, however, are standards for how much turnover is
too-high/too-low and standards by which to measure the benefits of turnover.
Let us now turn to the topic of statistical quality control to find some
ways to develop these standards.

STATISTICAL QUALITY CONTROL

The techniques of Statistical Quality Control (SQC) were originally
developed in the context of manufacturing and assembly operations. In
recent years they have also been successfully applies to the measurement and
control of the quality of services as well. SQC techniques were exported
from the U.S. Japan in the early 1950s by such statisticians as W. Edwards
Deming and the revolutionary increase in the quality of Japanese
manufactured goods in recent decades has been attributed in large part to

the acceptance and implementation of SQC techniques in that country.

Using turnover as a measure of quality is quite appealing. A great deal of money is spent by the human resource management departments of most companies to recruit, select, orient, motivate and compensate employees. How good is the human resource system that does this? What kind of benefits are being realized from the substantial investment put into the human resource system? In other words, what is the quality of the output realized from the human resource system in terms of high performing employees who remain with the organization?

In order to apply SQC to turnover control, we must adopt the fundamental viewpoint of SQC. Paraphrasing Grant and Leavenworth (1980, p. 1),

> "The measured non-programmatic turnover of employees in a free
> society is always subject to a certain amount of variation as
> result of chance. Some stable `system of causes' is inherent in
> any company. Variation within this stable pattern is inevitable.
> The reasons for variation outside this stable pattern may be
> discovered and corrected."

Employees have many individual differences, some of which will affect their likelihood of staying on or leaving a company. In many cases there is simply nothing the organization can do, or nothing it may want to do, to affect some of these decisions. Trying to reduce personnel turnover when it is merely operating within its stable pattern of variation is likely to have no, or possibly detrimental, results. One can "tinker" too much with a complex system if it is operating in its normal manner, and if we "push a problem down" here, another problem is likely to "pop up" elsewhere. There are certain problems that arise which can be corrected and which show up in changes to measured turnover. SQC then, is a tool for telling us when it is most useful to intervene in a system and when it is not.

THE "P" CHART OF SQC

The quality of a manufactured item or service, was with turnover is sometimes measured as a continuous variable and sometimes as an attribute variable. Quality is measured on an attribute basis when a product or service either conforms to standards or it does not, or the conformance is in terms of a countable number of defects. An inspector in a furniture factory, for example, may judge the result of a painting operation on a chair to be either acceptable or not acceptable.

There are several kinds of attribute measure control charts but the one that best fits the turnover situation is called a "p" chart. The variable p in SQC is simply the proportion of a sample of services or manufactured items chosen at random from all services offered or products produced that is rejected after being inspected. This is directly analogous to the turnover transition rate variable which is simply the proportion of a sample of employees who are "rejected" in the sense that they leave a company (perhaps on their own initiative). This basic attribute definition of turnover is all we need from a statistical point of view to be sure that we can apply the p chart technique to controlling turnover.

To use the p chart technique for controlling turnover, we must take a random or 100% sample of a group of employees at a point in time and determine the proportion in which leaves organization during a subsequent period of time. This proportion is then plotted on a p chart. The horizontal axis of the chart measures units of time, and the vertical axis the proportion of the group which has left. A sample chart is depicted in Figure 4.

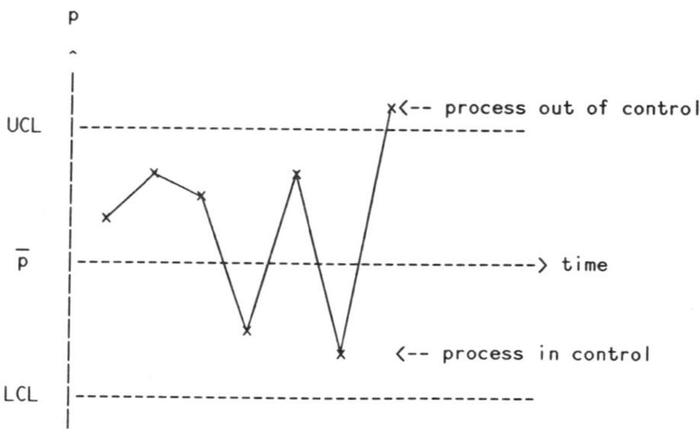

Figure 4: A Typical "p" Chart

There are three horizontal lines on a p chart. The middle or center line is the underlying historical average value of the quality measured, p. In essence p is also a forecast of future values of turnover.

The other two lines on the chart are the Upper and Lower control limits (UCL and LCL respectively). As long as the p values stay within the control limits, the process is assumed to be "in control" and no corrective action need to be taken. However, anytime a p value falls outside one of the limits, the process is assumed to be "out of control". (Another useful indicator that a process is out of control is an "extreme run" of observations on the same side of the center line.)

The term "out of control" simply means that the underlying process has somehow changed from previous levels, as predicted by the center line. When the process goes out of control, a trouble-shooting process is initialized, a cause sought for the change and appropriate corrections made. In some manufacturing processes this means that an entire plant must be shut down until the problem has been located and fixed.

The distance between the center line and the control limits is determined by trading off two kinds of risks involved in control. The first risk is assuming that the process is out of control when indeed it is not. This risk arises because it is theoretically possible for a given random sample of employees to exhibit turnover rates anywhere between 1 and 1.0 once in a long while. If the control limits are placed too close together, the more likely it is that the process will appear out of control when it is not. Any trouble shooting that results is simply "windmill chasing"; looking for problems that do not exist with the distinct possibility of creating more problems.

If control limits in a p chart are "too far" apart, there is a risk that even moderate changes in the underlying process will not appear as outliers on the chart. Statisticians will recognize the two risks described here as the classic Type I and II errors.

The Upper and Lower control limits on the chart are derived using the formula for the standard error of p. This formula depends not only on the value of p but also inversely on the size of the employee group being monitored. For very large groups, the distance between the limits can be relatively small, but for small groups the distance must be relatively large. Thus the practice of using a fixed standard, say p plus or minus 5% for all groups, may give misleading indications for the need to correct turnover.

By now the reader will understand that the tools of SQC will not tell
him/her precisely what turnover ought to be. Only whether or not the
underlying propensity to leave has likely changed. Nevertheless SQC can be
a valuable tool for pointing out approximately when and where a turnover
problem is occurring. It is a red flag, and a prioritizing tool.

Earlier in this paper we noted the difficulties of determining the
dollar benefits of turnover. Similarly, in the manufacturing setting it is
sometimes difficult to determine the exact costs and benefits of
inferior/superior quality production or service. The use of control charts
has in many cases become more or less a substitute for a determination of
those cost. That is, the charts do what cost data do: prioritize the
operating manager's trouble shooting time.

THE "W" CHART

Figure 5 is provided as a way of graphically depicting turnover based p
charts along with the relationship between turnover and length-of-service or
age as per Figures 2 and 3. Figure 5, although somewhat complex, depicts
both relationships in a "w" chart. The horizontal axis of each individual
control chart in the figure is, of course, time. The horizontal axis of the
"w" chart as a whole is in units of length-of-service or age. This chart
not only depicts when an employee group's turnover is out of control but it
also reinforces the necessity of looking at age or service-specific turnover
rates.

Such a chart could be constructed for key employees groups, say
engineers. Historical data on past rates of turnover would be gathered and
the control limits for the chart constructed. Then current patterns would
be plotted on the chart. No action would be taken with regard to employee
groups exhibiting control.

However, when an out of control situation is encountered, diagnostics
such as those suggested by Mobley (1982) would be applied to the employee
group at the appropriate service band, and appropriate corrective action

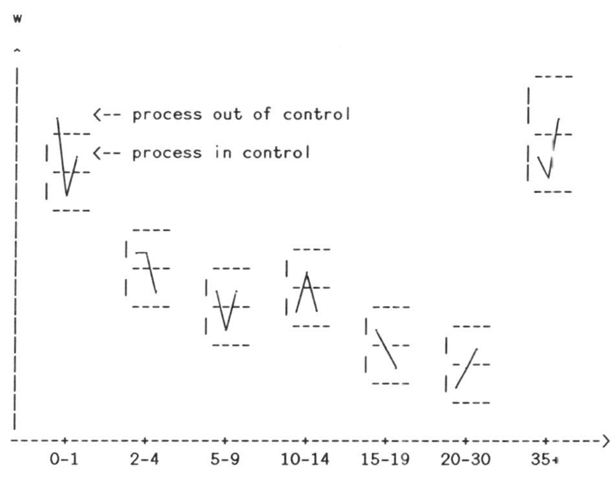

Figure 5: The "w" Chart for Turnover Control of an Employee Group

taken. The age or service band in which control is lacking may help the
diagnosis. For example, lack of control at the 10-14 year service band is
not likely to be due to poor recruitment or selection processes.

The "w" chart may have potential as an important feedback device.
Indeed, in manufacturing settings, when a p chart is the first feedback
provided to production employees on their work, the quality of that work
often improves dramatically. The p values begin to cluster around the
center line and rarely cross the control limits. (This signals the need to
recalculate the limits using the data samples taken after the clustering
began.) For turnover control, the "w" chart could be used as a feedback
mechanism to line managers whose activities affect turnover and to staff
personnel responsible for recruitment, selection, training and development,
etc.

On the surface the proposed control technology appears as if it would
involve the monitoring of hundreds of employee groups. However, such a
large scale effort would probably not be necessary. First of all, if any
group exhibited control for long periods of time, monitoring should stop, or
be done only once in a long while. Second, in cases where control is
lacking and corrective action usually fruitless, it may be best to live with
the excessive high/low turnover. As Grant and Leavenworth (p. 244) say "For
control limits to be respected, there needs to be evidence that it is
possible to stay within the control limits most of the time."

In summary, this paper examined the literature and some current
practices on forecasting and controlling turnover. It was argued that the
current technology for turnover control can suggest the need to take
corrective action in response to changes in turnover rates when in fact, the
changes were due to growth, contraction, or demographic characteristics of
various employee groups. A "w" chart integrating some of the most accurate
turnover forecasting techniques with the "p" chart of statistical quality
control was suggested as a means of developing appropriate control standards
and for providing useful feedback to management on the need for corrective
action.

The next step in this research will be to examine specific employee
groups in a corporate context. "W" charts will be constructed for growing,
static, and contracting employee groups using different definitions for
employee groups in order to determine the best grouping procedure. This
differences in reasons for leaving (as obtained from exit interviews) by
out-of-control and in-control groups will be measured to assess the
controllability of the turnover observed.

REFERENCES

Bartholomew, David J., and Andrew F. Forbes, Statistical Techniques for
    Manpower Planning, (New York, NY: John Wiley and Sons, 1979.)

Bright, William E., "How One Company Manages Its Human Resources," Harvard
    Business Review, (January - February, 1976), pp. 81-93.

Cascio, Wayne F., Costing Human Resources: The Financial Impact of Behavior
    in Organizations, (Kent Publishing Co., 1982).

Deutsch, Arnold, "How Employee Retention Strategies Can Aid Productivity I,"
    The Journal of Business Strategy, Vol. 2, No. 4 (Spring, 1982), pp. 106-
    109.

Fitz-Enz, Jac, How to Measure Human Resource Management, (McGraw-Hill,
    1984).

Forbes, A.F., "Markov Chain Models for Manpower Systems," in D.J. Bartholomew and A.R. Smith, eds., Manpower and Management Science, (London, U.K.: The English Universities Press, Ltd., 1970), pp. 93-113.

Frantzreb, Richard B., "Measuring Labor Turnover," Manpower Planning, Vol. 1, No. 8 (January, 1977a), pp. 1-6.

__________, "Controlling Turnover," Manpower Planning, Vol. 1, No. 12 (May 1977b), pp. 1-6.

__________, "The Costs of Turnover," Manpower Planning, Vol. 3, No. 5 (February, 1979), pp. 1-8.

Gaudet, Frederick J., Labor Turnover: Calculation and Cost, (New York, NY: American Management Assoc., AMA Research Study 39, 1960).

Grant, Eugene L., and Richard S. Leavenworth, Statistical Quality Control, (New York, NY: McGraw-Hill Book Co., 5th edition, 1980).

Gustafson, H.W., "Force-Loss Cost Analysis, 1980, in William H. Mobley, Employee Turnover: Causes, Consequences, and Control, (Reading, MA: Addison-Wesley Publishing Co., 1982) pp. 139-185.

Hall, T. "How to Estimate Employee Turnover Costs," Personnel, (July-August 1981), pp. 43-52.

Hawkins, Michael D., "Building a Data Base for Human Resource Planning Flow Models," paper presented at the Annual Conference of the Human Resource Planning Society, San Diego, California, March 5, 1985.

__________, "Supplying the Missing Links in Turnover Control," Working paper, (Department of Management Sciences, University of Washington, Seattle, 1986).

Koontz, Harold and Cyril O'Donnel, Management, (New York, NY: McGraw-Hill Book Co., 6th edition, 1976).

Laser, Stephen A., "Dealing with the Problem of Employee Turnover," Human Resource Management, (Winter, 1980), pp. 17-21.

Mobley, William H., Employee Turnover: Causes, Consequences and Control, (Reading, MA: Addison-Wesley Publishing Co., 1982).

Personnel Technology, Inc., PAL. Cohort Turnover Analysis Instruction Manual, (Seattle, Washington, 1981).

Peskin, Dean B., The Doomsday Job: The Behavioral Anatomy of Turnover, (New York, NY: Amacom, 1973).

Price, James L., The Study of Turnover, (Ames, Iowa: The Iowa State University Press, 1977).

Price, W.L., "Measuring Labor Turnover for Manpower Modeling," in A. Charnes, W.W. Cooper, and R.J. Niehaus, eds., Management Science Approaches to Manpower Planning and Organization Design, Volume 8 of TIMS Studies in the Management Sciences (New York, NY: North Holland Publishing Co., 1978) pp. 61-74.

SECTION 6

WORK FORCE DYNAMICS AND COMPENSATION POLICY

In this section the technologies for forecasting and turnover control
are extended to include models for human resource supply-demand as
comprehensive systems. All the efforts have strong computer-assisted
components using or planning to use microcomputers were appropriate. The
models were aimed at compensation and retention issues in terms of the
effects of broad strategic policy issues affecting the staffing and
retention of the organizations involved.

Quigley and Henshaw work underway at Lockheed Missiles and Space
Company. Their work force movement model provides compensation planners
with a precise, yet flexible system for determining the actual costs of
merit fund (or any salary action) distributions over time. The
microcomputer based model provides corporate decision makers with an
effective guide for planning annual salary actions. It accounts for the
interaction of terminations, hiring, promotions and merit fund decisions in
one spreadsheet. Sensitivity analyses can be performed to simulate any
number of factors affecting work force dynamics.

A comprehensive supply-demand model system is described by Atwater,
Bres, Cecil, Nelson, Niehaus, and Rosasco. This work involved the
evaluation of the impacts of proposed legislative changes of the Federal
retirement system on the retention of Department of the Navy civilian
employees. The probable impacts were of high level concern since the Navy
employs over 325,000 civil servants many of whom are in high technology
jobs. The graphical displays in the paper show the impacts of three highly
complex (two Senate and one House) proposals as they relate to the current
Civil Service Retirement System. The influences of uncertain and cyclical
labor markets, various retirement options in other employment sectors, and
the tastes and preferences of the Navy work force are important factors in
this analysis..

Lacy describes another comprehensive compensation based modeling
effort work encompassing the over one million civil service employees of the
Department of Defense. The paper provides a descriptive account of the
demographics and of the recent historical retention statistics of the DoD
work force. The issue of erosion of Federal pay and how that might affect
retention is the overriding concern of the models that were developed and
tested. The statistical findings uphold the hypothesis that DoD civilians
are more likely to quit Federal service as the potential value of lifetime
compensation in the government falls relative to private sector earnings.

A MODEL TO SIMULATE THE EFFECTS OF WORK FORCE DYNAMICS

ON COMPENSATION POLICY

Michael O. Quigley and Terrrance J. Henshaw

Lockheed Missiles and Space Company
Dept. 27-31, Bldg. 560
Sunnyvale, CA 94088

INTRODUCTION

Industry's traditional approach to allocating and managing compensation costs is to set aside a specific amount of money for merit pay. The size of this fund is often expressed as a percent of overall compensation. The fund is usually based on inflation, profits, labor market competition and related financial factors. Merit funds are distributed as salary increases among eligible employees based on performance appraisals, special accomplishments, and other factors indicative of meritorious performance.

During any given year, a company's total cost for the distribution of funds is usually some factor less than the total amount of funds set aside under the merit compensation program. Work force dynamics account for significant savings in the actual cost of a merit program. Attrition and internal movement of personnel affect the total pay out of any across the board compensation action. As employees leave the company for other positions, the share of the merit fund is not "used". That is, terminated rate structure since they do not remain in the work force at the end of the merit fund year. Newly hired employees do not take part in the merit compensation fund distribution and consequently, their salaries do not reflect increases due to the distribution of the merit fund program.

The authors have developed a work force movement model which provides compensation planners with a precise, yet flexible system for determining the actual costs of merit fund (or any salary action) distributions over a fixed time. This model provides annual salary actions. It accounts for the interaction of terminations, hiring, promotions and merit fund decisions in one micro computer spreadsheet. Through this model, sensitivity analyses can be performed to simulate any number of factors affecting work force dynamics.

Computer based work force modeling in support of management decision making in the compensation area is of critical importance to industry. Profitability is measured at the margins. Precise control in compensation administration can provide savings of one, two and three percent of payroll. This benefit is measured in two ways. First, an effective model gives

planners the capability to access the real cost of a merit fund
distribution. This model provides an effective estimate of the costs as
percent of payroll at the end of any merit distribution cycle, e.g., one
year. Second, the difference between the actual cost of a merit fund and
the initial merit fund can be used as a savings to the company or as an
opportunity to increase the initial merit distribution. Distributing
additional funds among worthy employees can create greater incentives for
productivity and reduce personnel losses to competitors.

The model was developed at Lockheed Missiles and Space Company (LMSC)
in Sunnyvale, California. LMSC is a major contractor in the highly
competitive aerospace/defense industry. In this environment, compensation
managers must balance Defense Department initiatives to limit salary growth
with fierce competition for highly skilled engineers and scientists. LMSC
employs 20,000 salaried personnel. Management of the merit compensation
aspect of the company's payroll demands the capability to model or simulate
the outcome of merit compensation decisions long before the actual
distribution of funds to employees.

STATEMENT OF THE PROBLEM

A major compensation problem confronting a large high technology
oriented company like Lockheed Missiles and Space Company is managing the
growth of compensation costs for its 20,000 salaried employees. The need to
manage this growth is based on several factors: 1) controls and constraints
imposed by the customer (the federal government), 2) competition with other
defense contractors, and 3) company profitability. Compensation limitations
must be balanced against employee compensation requirements and pressures
created by labor market competition. In addition, the company's merit
program is based on the premise that annual pay increases will motivate good
performance - reductions in merit funds could have a negative effect on
performance. A computer based model which maximizes the benefits of a
limited merit fund can significantly enhance a company's ability to reward
its employees. The model described in this paper provides the tool
necessary to balance the conflicts inherent with this dilemma. The popular
spreadsheet software package LOTUS 123 was used on an IBM PC to design this
model.

BACKGROUND

Salary costs are directly affected by internal work force dynamics. In
a completely stable work force, (i.e., no hiring, no terminations and no
promotions/demotions) salary growth will be exactly equal to the amount
funds provided for merit compensation plus base pay. However, no work force
is completely stable, and consequently, the actual growth of salary costs
are tied to the pattern of people movement in and out of the work force.

Additions to the work force, new hires, generally earn less than
tenured employees. Consequently, the average salary goes down as new
employees are brought into a company. Over 60 percent of new hires at a
high technology company like LMSC are recent college graduates. These
employees enter the work force at a rate of pay substantially lower than
experienced, tenured employees. New entrants to the work force receive
salaries 30 to 40 percent less than tenured employees. Consequently, an
influx of new hire will reduce a company's average compensation costs.

Terminations also affect average salary. Older employees retire at
fairly high rates of pay. A high number of such terminations will lower a
company's average salary rate. Conversely, employees in their first three
years with a company account for 50 to 60 percent of voluntary terminations.
These employees tend to receive lower rates of pay in comparison with

retirees. The interaction of high salaries for retirees and low salaries
for other voluntary terminations has an offsetting effect on average salary.
A precise estimation of hiring and termination rates can provide a useful
estimate of average salary. Estimating the interactive effects of hiring
and terminations on average salary provides the basis for cost estimating in
this model. The model described in this paper uses age as the primary
predictor of salary. An analysis of work force demographics found a
correlation coefficient between age and salary level of .54. Company's do
not (nor can they) pay people on the basis of age, but for a number of
reasons, age is the one variable which most consistently predicts a person's
salary. As people mature, they acquire higher levels of education, more
experience, greater responsibilities, and frequent opportunities to receive
merit and general wage increases. In addition to providing an efficient
predictor of salary, age is very useful in designing a work force model. It
is one variable which all employee's possess prior to and during their
tenure with a company. Experience and educational achievement are variables
which are not as readily measurable in a mathematical model. Thus, age was
used as the major independent variable.

Salary level may be described as a maturity curve through which a work
force moves in a probabilistic pattern. The average salary for any given
future period of time can be predicted through a model which accounts for
internal and external movement of people through the work force. The
movement pattern for salary, terminations, and hiring is consistent and
predictable over time. At LMSC, the age and salary distributions for new
hires, tenured employees and terminated employees were studied over three
years. The results showed a very steady pattern. In a large work force
like LMSC this pattern is fairly smooth and consistent since aberrations
balance out. This information provides a very solid base for establishing
the marginal probabilities for creating a salaried work force movement
model.

APPLICATION

The model was designed to provide a global estimate of future
compensation costs. The focus was not on month-to-month fluctuations in the
average rate but on the rate at a future point in time (one year). The
objective was to simulate the interactive effects of terminations,
acquisitions and work force maturation on the organization's compensation
costs.

The development effort relied on mainframe analytical tools to derive
the necessary empirical distributions and to determine the starting state of
the work force. The results of this analysis were entered into a microcomputer based spreadsheet for development of the mode. Development in a
stand alone environment was selected to reduce costs, to enhance portability,
to be easy to use, and to gain the flexibility needed to manipulate input
variables in the model. Additionally, real-time access to work force data
was not required since the transitional probability distributions were based
on multi-year historical patterns. Work force analysis was conducted using
SAS (Statistical Analysis System) and LOTUS 1-2-3 was used for model
development.

The model is a single hierarchy Markov type process that transitions
the work force from a starting state to a point one year later. This
requires an estimation of system flows by extracting projected terminations
from the system, maturing, or aging, those that remain, and adding
recruitment for replacement and growth to the system. Growth or contraction
of the work force, projected turnover, and the size of the merit adjustment
fund are the manipulated system variables. Since the primary objective was
to project a composite average salary at a future point, the accuracy of

this figure was the predominate evaluation criterion.

System Starting State

The beginning state of the system, Time t, is obtained from current data in the personnel master file. A frequency distribution and average salary for two year age groups from 22 to 62 form the projection base. A weighted average salary is computed from this data. Table 1 shows the work force distribution at the start of the first projection period.

Terminations

Estimating terminations from the system required a two step process. First, an estimate of the probable number of quits was required by the mode. This data was derived from a turnover analysis based on length-of-service. A table of projected terminations at varying levels of work force growth is output from the terminations model to the compensation model.

Total terminations are spread across the work force based on an empirically derived age distribution. This distribution is based on a three year historical pattern. The distribution is updated annually to incorporate changes in observed patterns over time. Figure 1 and Table 1 show the projected distribution of terminations that will occur before Time t+1. Terminations are immediately extracted from the beginning population since the model provides a point estimate of future salary costs and the intermediate system transitions are not affected by terminations.

The projected number of terminations derived from the turnover model are generally treated as fixed. Although it is possible to manipulate this variable the turnover phenomenon proves, in practice, to be largely independent of policy initiatives designed to affect the magnitude of its occurrence. The termination projection is altered only when trends indicate a significant variance from expected levels.

Table 1:   Projected and Observed Values of System Characteristics

| | TIME t | SYSTEM CHANGES | | | | TIME t+1 | | |
| AGE | % | HIRES % | | TERMS % | | POPULATION % | | AVG. SALARY | |
		PROJ	OBS	PROJ	OBS	PROJ	OBS	PROJ	OBS
22-23	3.27	22.44	21.26	2.80	2.26	4.84	3.22	453.23	469.84
24-25	5.47	11.77	14.79	5.75	7.15	5.51	5.88	493.23	492.32
26-27	5.77	8.80	10.39	7.02	10.89	6.06	6.24	538.28	536.41
28-29	4.75	7.92	6.95	5.28	7.39	5.61	5.51	572.46	567.35
30-31	4.13	6.14	6.32	5.15	5.52	4.65	4.70	599.85	591.19
32-33	3.69	5.61	4.24	3.96	4.67	4.13	3.84	624.17	617.87
34-35	3.80	4.86	4.52	4.00	3.50	3.90	4.03	652.58	644.38
36-37	4.38	3.84	4.28	3.96	3.66	4.06	3.92	679.46	669.41
38-39	3.71	4.00	3.88	2.98	3.42	4.08	4.20	707.09	683.30
40-41	4.52	3.72	3.76	2.85	2.80	4.13	4.12	720.66	725.71
42-43	4.43	3.73	3.52	2.43	2.02	4.48	4.60	746.95	729.78
44-45	4.78	2.99	2.80	2.98	1.71	4.48	4.60	762.81	753.16
46-47	5.43	2.76	2.96	2.77	2.64	4.89	5.01	769.13	765.98
48-49	5.64	2.50	2.00	2.89	1.79	5.25	5.20	792.23	785.12
50-51	6.03	1.99	1.72	2.63	1.87	5.45	5.48	808.39	805.87
52-53	6.48	1.70	1.68	2.72	1.87	5.79	6.04	812.71	807.00
54-55	5.86	1.38	1.24	4.85	4.36	5.59	5.88	806.99	810.13
56-57	4.67	1.22	1.16	4.38	3.65	4.69	4.62	809.05	812.99
58-59	4.18	.85	.92	4.85	4.98	3.87	4.03	813.75	808.23
60-61	3.94	.65	.80	5.96	4.74	3.45	3.49	794.82	803.72
62+	5.07	1.14	.84	19.79	19.13	5.10	5.35	782.98	787.24
TOTAL	100.00	100.00	100.00	100.00	100.00	100.00	100.00	699.07	699.60

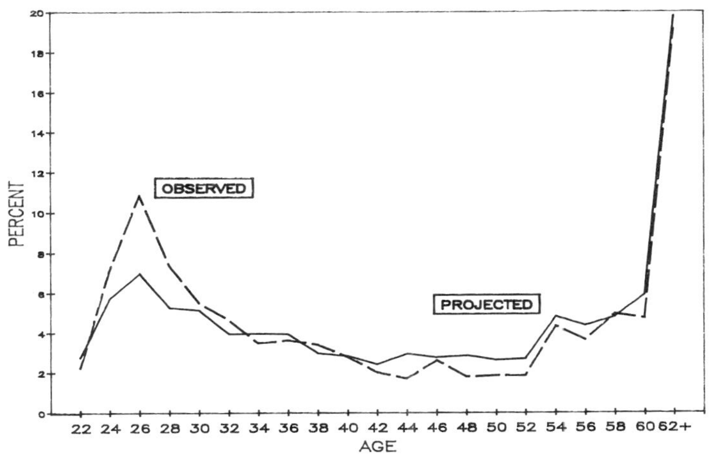

Figure 1: Distribution of Terminations by Age

Maturation

The age, or maturing, of the work force accounts for all changes in compensation resulting from increased experience. This would account for promotional increases because the system is heavily influenced by a time-in-grade orientation. In the one year projection horizon, all employees will age one year. A uniform distribution of ages was assumed and half of each two year age group was moved to the next higher group. An analysis of the

current population indicated that the model could withstand this assumption. The intra-group age distribution generally did not exceed a 55% - 45% split in any one category. Only employees in the work force at the start of the period are aged. During the first year, new hires generally do not receive merit compensation benefits.

Acquisitions

Adding personnel to the system to replace terminations and to satisfy growth requirements is the final system input. The number of recruits is the sum of terminations and net work force growth. As with terminations,a three year moving historical pattern is used to distribute projected hiring over the age groups. This distribution is shown in Table 1 and Figure 2. Although new hires have a maturation function, this group is not aged in the model. It is assumed that no maturation related compensation changes will occur during the projection period for a new hire (i.e., during the first year). This aspect of the model, while reflecting reality, overstates the projected size of the first age group. The normal flows between the other age groups, based on the assumption of a uniform intra-group age distribution, results in only minor distortions in the remaining age groups.

Projected The Future Average Salary

The derivation of the age distribution at Time t+1 occurs when the combined effects of termination, maturation, and accession flows have been processed through the system. This distribution, in combination with the average salary for each age group, is used to compile a new weighted average salary for the work force. The average salary for each age group is projected through a two step process. For the first three age groups, the

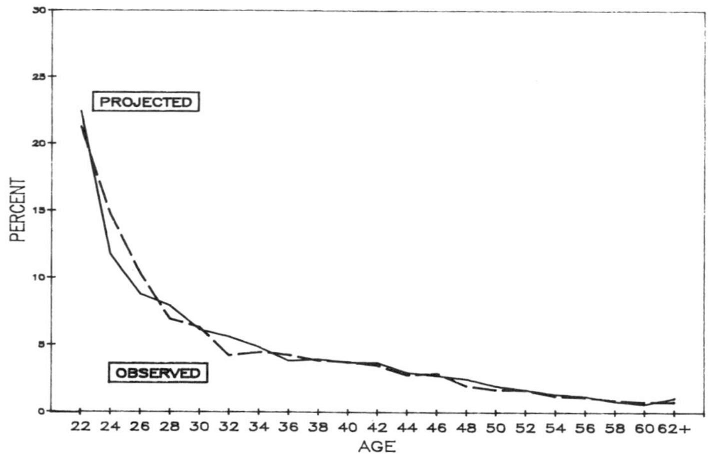

Figure 2: Distribution of Hires by Age

average salary at Time t is inflated by a percentage of the available
adjustment fund. This partial inflation of the rate reflects the different
market conditions that govern the hiring of new college graduates as opposed
to more experienced labor. In all other age groups the Time t rate is
inflated by the size of the merit fund expressed as a percent of the total
Time t payroll. New hires in these groups are assumed to enter the system
at the new average salary of each respective group. A weighted average
salary is calculated using the Time t+1 age distribution. Total projected
weekly compensation costs and the rate of change from the beginning of the
period can then be calculated.

<u>Model Testing</u>

After initial development the model was tested using data from a prior
twelve month period. Actual data on net increase in the work force, total
terminations, and the size of the merit adjustment fund were input to the
model. The simulation algorithm produced results accurate to within two
tenths of one percent of the actual weekly compensation costs at the end of
the period.

<u>Sensitivity Analysis</u>

The utility of the compensation growth model as a decision making tool
is enhanced by the ability to alter certain system variables. It is rarely
known with certainty, for example, the extent to which the work force will
grow or contract during a given period. By manipulating this variable,
entering terminations as a function of growth and injecting varying amounts
of salary adjustment funds into the system, the effects of multiple
scenarios and policy responses can be determined. This capability is
essential to informed decision making. The model does not make the
decision, it simply provides an additional information input to support what
is often a intuitive decision based on sound management judgment.

Most models rely on the past as an indicator of the future. It may
become apparent from the analysis that compensation goals cannot be attained
if system flows occur based on historical patterns. Meeting what are often
competing objectives (e.g., controlling salary growth versus a market based
salary structure) may require a fundamental shift in the work force mix if

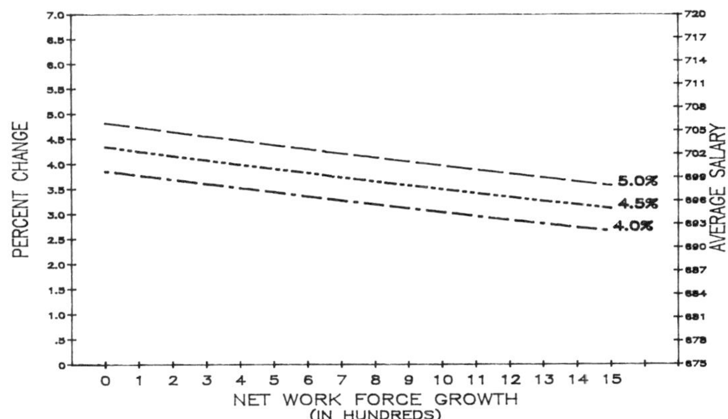

Figure 3: Change in Average Salary Growth by Work Force Growth
(1984-1985 Fund Year)

the firm is to maintain a flexible compensation program while assuring a
cost competitive position. It may be necessary, for example, to shift
hiring to less experienced and therefore less costly sources of labor. Such
revelations are equally as important as those that show the impact of
multiple parameters on a status-quo system.

RESULTS

In operation, the modeling process begins with an estimate of personnel
requirements over the projection period. This figure is derived from a
separate internal forecasting process. The growth estimate becomes a
baseline and is considered the most probable outcome for the year. Lower
and Upper growth estimates are also simulated. The size of the salary
adjustment fund is entered as a percent of the Time t weekly payroll. By
simultaneously varying work force growth and size of the adjustment fund an
impact matrix from varying policy alternatives is generated. This
information is easily presented in graphical form as shown in Figure 3. The
essence of the decision is to find the optimal relationship between growth
in the work force, total compensation costs, and the external labor market.
If constraints, such as a corporate imposed growth limit, are present the
decision is one of determining the maximum allocation of funds that can be
injected into the system while still meeting management control criteria. In
this company the model was used to negotiate a growth limit with the
corporate based on projected work force changes.

During the projection period, changes in the system are monitored
against projected outcomes. If growth is occurring at either a faster or
slower rate than expected, appropriate modifications in the input variable
can provide timely information which policy revisions are considered. This
ability to adjust rapidly to changing conditions is an essential
characteristic of a sound decision support tool.

Validation

The first full year to which the model was applied occurred between
August of 1984 and July of 1985. The reliability of the model was validated
by substituting actual work force growth, terminations and expended
adjustment funds into the mode. For comparison purposes, the period ending
age group distributions of terminations, hires, and the total work force
were extracted from the personnel master file. Table 1 and Figures 1, 2,

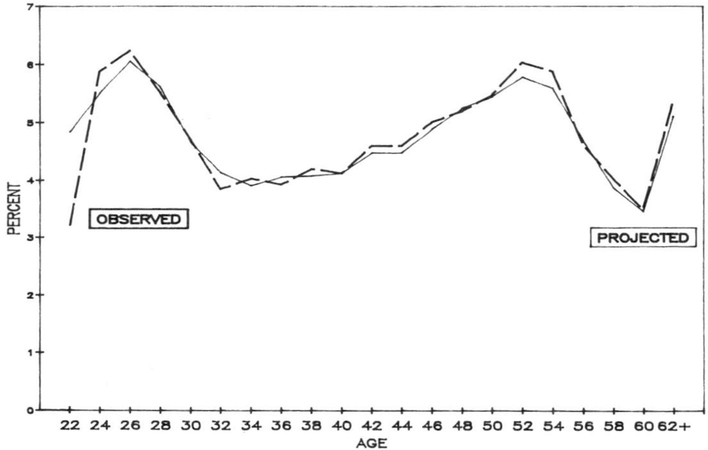

Figure 4:   Work Force Distribution by Age

and 4 compare the projected and observed values for these distributions.
Actual system flows during the projections period were effectively simulated
by the empirically derived historical distributions. The projected
distributions were not, however, perfectly estimated. For example, the
decision not to age the new hire population caused a distortion in the
projected ending age distribution. The effect, as shown in Figure 4, is
evident primarily in the first age group. Of a mean absolute projection
error of 5.1% for the age group distribution, 46% occurs in the first age
group. The resulting contribution to higher reliability, however, warrants
this imprecision.

The projected and observed average salaries for each age group is shown
in Figure 5 and Table 1. The projection error by age group ranged from less
than 0.2% to 3.5%. The mean absolute projection error was $7.51 or 1.1%.
The model projected an average weekly salary of $699.07 (The average salary
for LMSC is not presented in this paper for proprietary reasons). The
actual salary at the end of the period was $699.60. This represents an
accuracy of 99.92%. On the marginal change in average salary, the model was
accurate to 97.8%.

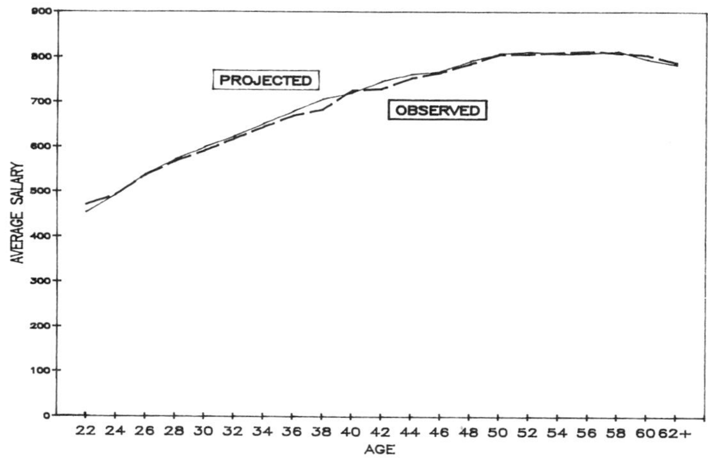

Figure 5:   Average Salary by Age

During the one year validation period, the model was used by management
to make fund allocations. Monitoring of the system and manipulation of the
model gave management valuable information to support revisions to the merit
program. The model was used to determine the extent to which additional
funds could be injected into the system. The results to date indicate that
the model provides a viable tool for compensation policy analysis.

FUTURE DIRECTIONS

In practice, the model has shown a high degree of reliability in
emulating the dynamics of the work force. Two test of the system have
produced errors of less than two tenths of one percent when actual post
facto transactions are entered into the model. In any planning activity,
the results are only as effective as the accuracy of the data input to the
model. The use of sensitivity analysis to determine the impact of a given
fund allocation under varying assumptions of work force growth is a useful
way of handling the problem of inadequate planning data. This approach,
however, requires management to guess as to the most probable scenario when
making important policy decisions. To increase the usefulness and viability
of the compensation growth model future enhancements might include:

A. The improvement of other planning processes that materially affect
    the model's performance. The most significant of these processes
    is demand forecasting. The nature of the defense business makes
    forecasting the need for personnel difficult at best. Efforts that
    rely on line management judgment have proven to be valuable tools
    in the planning process. Models to project turnover and internal
    movements of people will also improve system inputs.

B. Expand the model to single year age categories. While it appears
    that the marginal improvement in the accuracy of the model would be
    small, this change will allow for improvement in the projection of
    average salary by age. Certain assumptions that are made relative
    to compensation and age could be better incorporated into a single
    year age group model.

C. Improve the integration of the compensation model with external
    labor market data. Decisions on compensation policy must be
    sensitive to competitive pressures operating outside of the firm.
    This information in conjunction with model outputs may indicate
    that structural modifications in normal work force dynamics will be
    required to meet management objectives.

D. Incorporate the model into other business processes. There are
    several areas where accurate information on the future cost of
    labor could improve results. Forward pricing negotiations and
    contract cost estimating, for example, are an ongoing activity in
    the defense business. Data on future compensation costs derived
    from probable changes in the structure of the work force could be
    used to set objectives for negotiation outcomes.

The value of models as strategic planning tools should not be
overlooked. The purpose of strategic thinking is to judge the future impact
of current decisions. Models that accurately simulate the effects of policy
alternatives can serve as a valuable decision support resource. In human
resources, their application can have clear and substantial cost
consequences with clear bottom line implications. In conjunction with sound
management judgment, models can enhance the overall effectiveness of human
resource planning processes.

CONCLUSIONS

This paper describes a framework for developing a work force flow model
to simulate the cost consequences of compensation policy. The model
provides a useful tool to support the decision making process. It allows
management to see the impact of alternative scenarios given projected or
planned changes in the work force. Sensitivity to the constraints and
opportunities emanating from the changing character of the work force
provides management with a better understanding of the reward system. This
in improved control of the cost consequences of a merit program. This model
has proven very accurate during a one year test. Continued testing and
refinements will be made in subsequent applications. The authors plan to
generalize this model to include other aspects of human resource planning.

DECISION INFORMATION SUPPORT FOR A COMPREHENSIVE

RETIREMENT SYSTEM CONVERSION

D.M. Atwater*, E.S. Bres III**, L.S. Cecil***,
J.A. Nelson*, R.J. Niehaus****, and E. Rosasco***

  * DMA, Inc.
    13750 Raywood Dr.
    Los Angeles, CA 90049

 ** Naval Military Personnel Command
    NMPC 1644, RM 4532 Arlington Annex
    Washington, DC 20370

*** U.S. Navy Office of Civilian Personnel
    Management (OCPM 013)
    800 N. Quincy St.
    Arlington, VA 22202-1998

**** Office of the Chief of Naval Operations (OP-16H)
     Navy Department
     Washington, DC 20370

INTRODUCTION

There are a number of simultaneous events which are increasing the
awareness of the Federal work force toward private sector opportunities.
Among these are: Congressional review of the Civil Service Retirement System
(CSRS), the development of a new portable retirement system linked with
Social Security, a compensation system which lags private sector
comparability, and the rapid growth of new technology. (In order to assist
the reader, a glossary of terms is provided as Table 1.)

The Federal retirement program, a major component of the compensation
system, is designed to promote and reward career service. Significant
changes to the Federal retirement program are being considered by Congress.
These proposed changes include reducing current CSRS benefits and designing
a new three tier retirement system (Social Security, defined benefit plan,
and a thrift plan) for employees hired since January 1984. This paper will
discuss the development and use of large scale modeling systems to evaluate
the impacts of the proposed three tier retirement system on Navy's civilian
work force. These impacts are of high level concern since the Navy employs
over 325,000 civil servants, many of whom are in high technology jobs.

This paper will address three research issues. The key issue is the
impact of the proposed new retirement system on the retention of Navy
civilian employees. The influences of uncertain and cyclical labor markets
and the tastes and preferences of the Navy work force are key factors in

TABLE 1

GLOSSARY OF TERMS

Annual Cost of Leaving Model	ACOL
Civil Service Retirement System	CSRS
Consumer Price Index	CPI
Cost of Living Allowance	COLA
Current Population Survey	CPS
Gross National Product	GNP
Individual Retirement Account	IRA
Navy's Availability Dynamics Model	NAVDYN
Navy's Civilian Decision Support System	CIVDSS
Navy's Civilian Occupational Planning Estimate System	COPES
Navy's Computer Assisted Manpower Analysis System	CAMAS
Navy's Retirement Calculation Model	RETCALC

this analysis. The second issue is the linkage of micro and mainframe computers in the overall decision modeling process. The third issue reviews the relationship of these studies to the planned development of more comprehensive human resource supply-demand planning systems to provide continuing long term information support.

The use of large-scale human resource supply-demand modeling systems for corporate planning is a recent phenomenon. For example, see Niehaus (1985) for a collection of papers discussing emerging applications of such systems for human resource policy analysis. In addition to the work reported in this paper, there have been extensive efforts, particularly in the area of military personnel retention. For example, see Fernandez, Gotz and Bell (1985), who provide a management review of the Annual Cost of Leaving (ACOL) regression models and suggest improvements to include the behavioral characteristics of the members who choose military service. This latter model (also see Gotz and McCall (1984)) departs from the ACOL approach by using a dynamic programming model to make projections of the retention of U.S. Air Force officers. Further, Arnold, Black and Warner (1985) have developed an ACOL II model concerned with the long term retention of Department of Defense civilians.

The work reported in this paper has its roots in the combination of internal personnel planning methods developed by the U.S. Navy (Charnes, Cooper, and Niehaus (1972), Niehaus (1979)) with external labor market models originating in the American Telephone and Telegraph Company (Atwater and Sheridan (1980)). The result of this work has been named the Civilian Occupational Planning Estimate System (COPES). An earlier paper by Atwater, Bres, and Niehaus (1985) provided a programmatic description of the external labor market portions of this system. That paper includes a prototype application of one of the models needed for analysis of the impact of proposed Federal civilian retirement policies on the Navy's civilian work force.

MANAGEMENT ISSUES

One of the key management issues in assessing retirement options is determining the impact on employee turnover. Fundamentally, this involves the individuals choice of whether he is better off staying in the organization, retiring, or pursuing another job opportunity in the labor market. Other management issues include cost control, resource allocation, and productivity. The dynamic nature of these issues makes assessment of retirement options difficult.

Models and forecasting systems are useful analytical tools that can

assist management in quantifying the impact of alternative retirement
options. The feasibility of developing these models include the: (1)
availability of personnel data, (2) software to support the analysis, (3)
ability to define the issues, and (4) timing and cost to produce the
required analysis. Both quantitative and nonquantitative analysis are
necessary to address the management issues involved in assessing retirement
options.

APPROACH

Two approaches are addressed in this paper. One at the employee level
and one at the corporate level. These approaches are then merged in
developing the results presented in the case study.   A microcomputer system
using data base management software (dBase III) provides the means to
quantify and capture key decision making values at the individual
participant levels. The results are use to identify the "flex" points in
the stay/leave decision for different employee groups and to calibrate the
mainframe computer modeling system for simulating and forecasting overall
retention decisions under alternative retirement options. The employee level
model has been named the Retirement Calculation (RETCALC) model. The
RETCALC model is a subsystem of COPES. The corporate level retention model
has been named the Navy Availability Dynamics (NAVDYN) model. The
RETCALC/NAVDYN models consist of two separate but interrelated components as
shown in Figure 1.   Both subsystems will be extended to allow on-line
interactive use.

The RETCALC model compares an individual's retirement annuity under the
current CSRS, an alternative CSRS, and a new multiple part retirement
program. The alternative CSRS and the new multiple part retirement program
have flexible elements that allow the comparison of monetary benefits under
different retirement scenarios. The flexible elements in the alternative
CSRS option elements include: accrual rates, minimum retirement age limits,
penalty amounts for early retirement, and contribution rate elements. The
new multiple part retirement program consists of a defined benefit plan
(employer contribution only), Social Security, and a thrift plan. The
multiple part program includes flexible minimum retirement age limits,
penalty levels for early retirement, flexible accrual rates, employee and
employer contribution rates to the thrift plan, and thrift plan growth
elements. The annuity amounts are computed by age and length of service.
Multiple reports are printed and files are retained so that comparisons of an
individual's contributions and benefits under alternative retirement
programs can be graphed and analyzed.

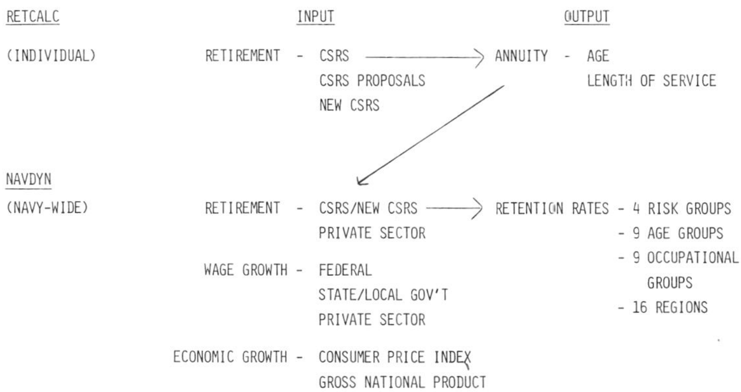

Figure 1: RETCALC/NAYDYN Models

The NAVDYN model is a labor supply model which identifies choices for employee groups and determines the impact of retirement program changes in terms of external loss rates. NAVDYN compare outside job opportunities to employee's current job opportunities. This model approaches the problem of choice between job opportunities from a monetary perspective. Unlike other models, it also incorporates both non-monetary choices and uncertainty about the future. A key factor in the identification of the "best" job opportunity is compensation. In this paper, compensation includes both salary and benefits. Other factors include non-monetary characteristics of jobs, such as work environment, personal (non-task) considerations, and technology. All these factors are dynamic in nature. Compensation levels and relative job opportunities change over time. (See the earlier papers by Atwater, et.al. (1980), (1982), (1984) for a discussion of how non-monetary characteristics can be included in the models.)

NAVDYN uses employee salary and annuity comparisons developed by the RETCALC model as the data base for determining the stay/leave behavior for nine major occupational groups. NAVDYN compares Navy salary and retirement annuity data to both other government and private sector salary and retirement opportunities. This comparison also includes economic factors such as the Consumer Price Index and the Gross National Product. The model uses estimated salaries for Navy, other government, and the private sector for each occupational group by region to separate

employees into four risk groups. The risk groups range from the most susceptible to least likely to leave Navy civilian service. External loss rates are then projected for each risk group.

The RETCALC/NAVDYN models identify those employee groups most susceptible to leave in the aggregate and broken down by occupational group, region and length of service. In addition, the models address the retention issue for future career civil servants without a CSRS contribution lock. The CSRS contribution lock is the effect of the unavailability of cumulative Government contributions until retirement eligibility. This contribution lock has historically penalized mid and late career civil servants who leave the Federal sector by only refunding the employees' contributions. The CSRS contribution lock is a disincentive for civilian employees to seek alternative opportunities in the private sector.

The RETCALC/NAVDYN models also address the issue of portable retirement benefits. Unlike the current retirement system, the new retirement system will be portable since Social Security is transferrable to the private sector and the thrift plan can be converted to an individual retirement account (IRA) or certain private sector retirement systems. The proposed new retirement program will increase the civilian work forces sensitivity to relative changes in private and public sector employment conditions.

MODEL INPUT DATA

Two extensive data bases were constructed to develop, validate, and use the RETCALC/NAVDYN models. The RETCALC models data base includes 175 individual cases. The data for each case includes an individual's age, length of service, and career salary pattern. These cases represent the current demographics of the Navy's civilian work force. The RETCALC output consists of an evaluation of four different retirement programs for each case consistent with the types of programs under review by Congress. Thus, a total of 700 different combinations were used to calibrate the coefficients used in the overall NAVDYN modeling analysis.

The data base for the NAVDYN consists of several very large data files

covering both the internal Navy work force and the external labor markets
throughout the United States. The internal Navy work force data were
developed using the Computer-Assisted Manpower Analyses System (CAMAS). Two
cohort files were constructed by occupation, career level group, and length-
of-service for the sixteen regional areas in which the Navy employs
civilians. These files consist of data for a beginning cohort and its
remainder at the end of each subsequent year. The first file which covers
1975-1983, includes an initial population of 247,953 Navy civilian employees
and contains approximately 1.4 million records. The second file covering
1980-1984, has an initial population of 296,372 employees and contains
approximately 0.8 million records. The results from the 1975-83 file were
used to test and validate the NAVDYN model. The 1980-1984 file was used to
develop the results for actual policy analysis.

The public data files used in NAVDYN were extracted from the March
Current Population Surveys (CPS) for 1976-1984. This period is consistent
with periods covered on the Navy files. In aggregate, over one million
records of household data containing special survey occupation and wage
variables are included. In addition, published Gross National Product (GNP)
and Consumer Price Index (CPI) data were used. GNP and CPI projections were
made after reviewing a number of published national forecasts.

VALIDATION AND TESTING

The RETCALC/NAVDYN models were developed under a short time frame with
frequent changes in response to Congressional deliberations on both the CSRS
and new retirement systems. Consequently, there was limited development and
testing time. The development effort yielded models which could sufficiently
differentiate between retirement program alternatives to assist in the
analysis of legislative options. It was possible to replicate previous loss
patterns using the base case. Technical improvements are desirable if the
RETCALC/NAVDYN models are used for situations requiring accuracy normally
needed for operational decision making.

Numerous validation runs were made to analyze retention behavior. The
NAVDYN model was tested by comparing actual losses from the 1975-1983 Navy
cohort file with model results for the same period. The results are
encouraging for persons between twenty and sixty years of age. The initial
modeling approach for the youngest and oldest age groups is being
reexamined. Future analysis will use separate models for these age groups.

Another type of preliminary study was a sensitivity check of the
principal modeling variables grouped into benefit related and wage related
subsets. All of these variables are intended to measure the willingness of
an individual to leave the employment system. The benefit related variables
include: cumulative contributions to the current retirement program, benefit
loss due to exiting the current retirement program, and available second
pensions in alternative job opportunities.   The wage related variables
include the change in government wages relative to other wage opportunities
in the private sector. The most sensitive factor is the lost benefit from
exiting the current retirement program. To our knowledge, this fact is
significant new information not explicitly known before.   In the future
compensation analysts should pay more attention to the current pension
increase foregone (after becoming eligible for full vesting) when an
employee decides to leave his present job.

A separate analysis was done to calculate the effect of a large relative
private sector wage increase over the life span of employment. Figure 2
shows the impact of a ten percent relative private sector wage advantage for
different age groups. Increased employee losses resulting from this relative
wage difference are most significant at the early and late career stages.

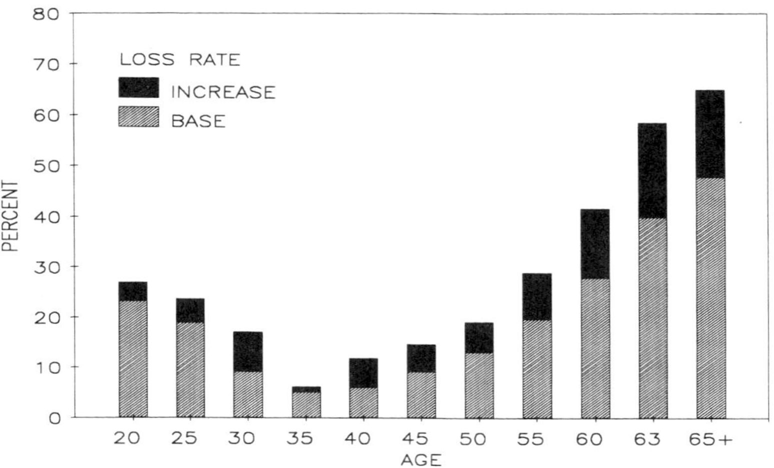

Figure 2:   Impact of 10% Private Wage Increase: External Loss
Increase Over Base Case

RESULTS

A number of retirement scenarios were examined using the RETCALC/NAVDYN
models to determine the impact on Navy's civilian work force. Federal employees hired prior to January 1984 are covered by the Civil Service Retirement
System (CSRS).   Federal employees hired since January 1984 are covered by an
interim retirement program which includes Social Security. Congress is designing a permanent retirement system for these post 1983 employees which will
include Social Security, a defined benefit plan, and a thrift plan. This
paper presents the analysis of the design options for this new retirement
system as proposed by the Senate Government Affairs Committee and the House
Post Office and Civil Service Committee. These design options for the new
retirement system are significantly different than current CSRS provisions.

The Navy data base for the final analyses was the 1980-1984 civilian
personnel cohort file. After calibration with data from the 1980-1984 file,
the model was used to project behavior of a base population of personnel on
board as of December 31, 1983. Although this base population includes
employees under the current CSRS, these employees were projected under the
proposed new retirement programs because they reflect the full composition
of the Navy civilian work force. Use of this full work force population is
one of the few approaches that can compare alternative retirement programs
covering employees hired after January 1984 in all phases of their careers.

The current CSRS and Congressional proposals for a new retirement
system are summarized in Figure 3.   The current system and proposed
alternatives are labeled as follows:

    CSRS - Civil Service Retirement System (current system)
    SENATE A - Senate Option A (proposed new system)
    SENATE B - Senate Option B   "
    HOUSE - House Proposal   "

The NAVDYN model produced a number of loss reports for each of the four
alternatives. These reports included projected losses by year across an
eight year period from 1985-1992 for: (a) total population (b) length of
service groups, (c) major occupation groups, and (d) selected geographic
regions.

| | | SENATE PROPOSAL | | |
	CURRENT CSRS	OPTION A	OPTION B	HOUSE PROPOSAL
Social Security	Medicare Coverage Only	Add-on Plan	Add-on Plan	Add-on Plan
Basic Pension Plan	Defined Benefit Plan	Defined Benefit Plan	Defined Benefit Plan	Defined Benefit Plan
	5 Year Vesting	5 Year Vesting	5 Year Vesting	5 Year Vesting
	Accrual Base	Accrual Base	Accrual Base	Accrual Base
	● High 3 Year Average Salary	● High 5 Year Average Salary	● High 5 Year Average Salary	● High 3 Year Average Salary
	Accrual Rate	Accrual Rate	Accrual Rate	Accrual Rate
	● 1-5 Yrs, 1.5% ● 5-10 Yrs, 1.75% ● 10+ Yrs, 2.0%	● 1-15 Yrs, .9% ● 15+ Yrs, 1.1%	● 1-15 Yrs, .9% ● 15+ Yrs, 1.1%	● 1.0% All Years
	7% Employee Contribution	No Employee Contribution	Employee Contribution Formula of 7.0% – OASDI Contribution	Employee Contribution Formula of 7.0% – OASDI Contribution
			● 1.3% to Social Security Wage Base ● 7.0% Our Wage Base	● Flat 1.3% Contribution Regardless of Wage Base
	Normal Retirement	Normal Retirement	Normal Retirement	Normal Retirement
	● 55 with 30 yrs ● 60 with 20 yrs ● 62 with 5 yrs	● 62 with 5 yrs	● 55 with 30 yrs ● 62 with 5 yrs	● 55 with 30 yrs ● 60 with 20 yrs ● 62 with 5 yrs
	No Voluntary Early Retirement	Voluntary Early Retirement	Voluntary Early Retirement	No Voluntary Early Retirement
		● 55 with 30 yrs, 2% penalty up to 62 ● 55 with 10 yrs, 5% penalty up to 62	● 55 with 10 yrs, 5% penalty up to age 62	
	COLA, Full CPI	COLA	COLA	COLA, Full CPI
		● 55-61, No CPI ● 62-66, CPI – 2% ● 67+, Full CPI	● 55-61, CPI – 2% ● 62+, Full CPI	
Capital Accumulation Plan	None	Tax Deferred Savings Plan	Tax Deferred Savings Plan	Savings Plan
		Employee Contribution Up to 10%	Employee Contribution Up to 10%	Employee Contribution up to 10%
		Employer Matches Employee Contribution up to 5%	Employer Matches Employee Contribution up to 6%	Employer Matches Employee Contribution up to 6%
		● 1-5% matched 100% ● 6-10% not matched	● 1% matched 100% ● 2-3% matched 50% ● 4-6% matched 25% ● 7-10% not matched	● 1-6% matched 100% ● 7-10% not matched
Voluntary Transitional Provisions	None	Employees credit in current CSRS is frozen and employee begins credit in new system.	Same	Employees in current CSRS may not join new system. Employees may join savings plan without employer matching.

Figure 3: Comparison of Senate and House Retirement Proposals

Figure 4 shows the aggregate loss by year under the alternative
retirement programs. These results show that the two Senate alternatives
produce larger projected losses in the initial years with subsequently
smaller losses in the later years of the eight year period which is
projected. The age and length of service penalties increase early period
losses because retirement eligible employees leave rather than accept new
age eligibility standards. Another reason for these loss rates is that the
employer matching of employee thrift plan contributions are vested on a
graduated basis. The employee becomes entitled to the employer's matching
contributions at a rate of 20% per year during the first five years reaching
100% after 5 years. The impact of the Senate retirement proposals rapidly

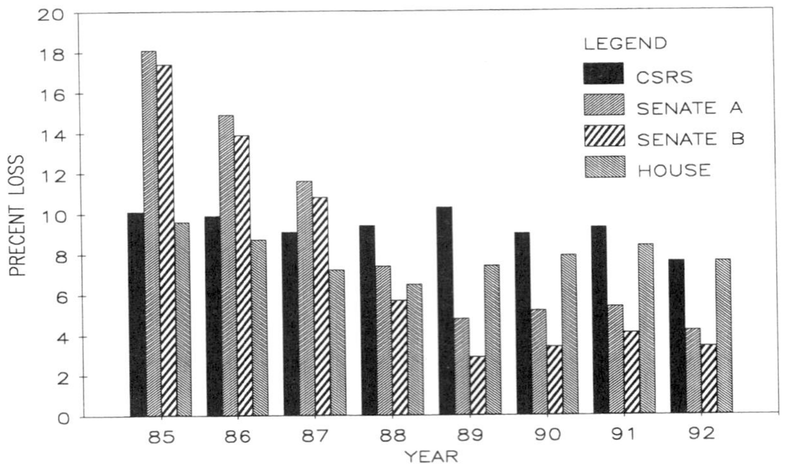

Figure 4:   Projected External Loss Rates (1985-1992)

drains the retirement eligible pool as external opportunities for
alternative private sector employment and leisure become relatively more
attractive.

The House proposal appears to offer considerably higher benefits
accruals to covered employees than the Senate options. This proposal
excludes age and length of service penalties. The tastes and preferences of
individuals for the program increase as it is fully installed. The net
projected effect of the House proposal as shown on Figure 4 is a slightly
increased retention rate over the CSRS base case.

A single year (1986) was selected for exposition of the length of
service projections shown in Figure 5. In this case the early year of the
projection was used so that a relatively large number of the retirement
eligibles would still be in place. The pattern is as expected on Figure 5
with the greatest number of losses indicated at the early career and
retirement eligible stages. The Senate proposals, less generous than the
House proposal, produce higher losses over the entire career life cycle.   A

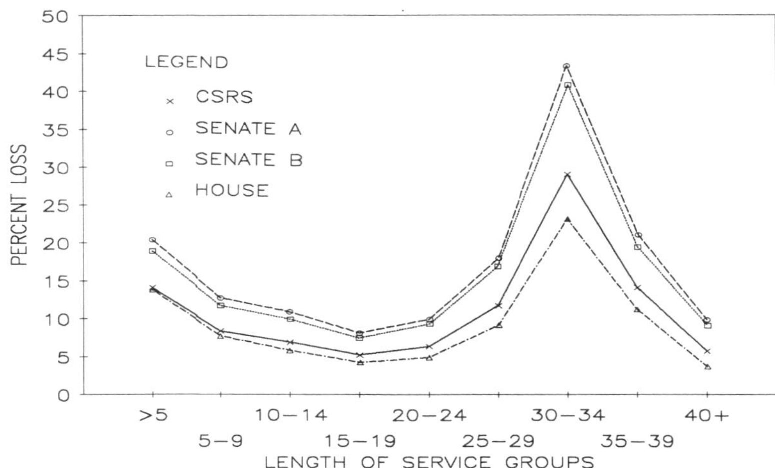

Figure 5:   Projected External Loss Rates by Length of Service - 1986

long term cost benefit to the Government of less generous plans is that fewer people who start employment will stay long enough to collect a pension other than Social Security and the vesting in the thrift plans.

Projections by major occupation group can also be produced. While not shown, the projected pattern of losses over time follows the same trends shown on Figure 4 with higher losses for some alternatives in the earlier years than in subsequent years. There are fewer losses projected for the professional and skilled occupations than for occupations with fewer entry requirements. The less generous retirement plans again produce higher losses throughout. In these cases the overall losses for less skilled personnel are higher. However, the projected additional losses for the highly skilled personnel is particularly troublesome to the Navy since these people where more much more difficult to recruit.

Table 2 compares loss data for three different regions: Region 1 (Southern California - Arizona); Region 9 (Greater Washington D.C.); and Region 10 (Tidewater Virginia). The differences in the external loss rates reflect the characteristics of the age and length of service of the Navy civilian work force in the region. The same pattern of losses associated with each of the retirement program alternatives persists across the regions.

The projected loss results under these alternatives retirement programs appear to be consistent since larger losses are projected for the less

TABLE 2

EXTERNAL LOSS RATES BY REGION

YEAR/SCENARIO	SO. CA/ARIZONA	WASHINGTON DC	NORFOLK VA
1985			
CSRS	0.101	0.094	0.162
SENATE A	0.182	0.165	0.292
SENATE B	0.175	0.159	0.280
HOUSE	0.096	0.091	0.153
1986			
CSRS	0.099	0.091	0.158
SENATE A	0.149	0.136	0.240
SENATE B	0.139	0.127	0.222
HOUSE	0.086	0.081	0.138
1987			
CSRS	0.091	0.083	0.146
SENATE A	0.116	0.107	0.185
SENATE B	0.108	0.099	0.173
HOUSE	0.072	0.067	0.114
1988			
CSRS	0.094	0.085	0.152
SENATE A	0.073	0.067	0.117
SENATE B	0.056	0.051	0.090
HOUSE	0.065	0.060	0.104
1989			
CSRS	0.103	0.094	0.164
SENATE A	0.048	0.042	0.077
SENATE B	0.028	0.024	0.046
HOUSE	0.074	0.067	0.119
1990			
CSRS	0.089	0.083	0.142
SENATE A	0.051	0.045	0.083
SENATE B	0.033	0.029	0.054
HOUSE	0.079	0.071	0.127
1991			
CSRS	0.092	0.086	0.076
SENATE A	0.054	0.048	0.006
SENATE B	0.041	0.035	0.066
HOUSE	0.084	0.077	0.134
1992			
CSRS	0.075	0.071	0.000
SENATE A	0.041	0.038	0.000
SENATE B	0.033	0.029	0.054
HOUSE	0.076	0.068	0.111

generous plans. The study shows that Navy civilians react as one might
expect when one changes economic benefits. Higher losses to other job and
leisure opportunities are projected when pay and retirement benefits are
reduced as suggested by the Senate options. Better retention is projected
for the House proposal where the benefits are somewhat comparable to the
current CSRS. The results show that it may be possible to develop a new
alternative retirement system that would produce similar losses to the
current CSRS at a lower cost to the Government.

It is emphasized again that the base population for this study provides
a representative rather than an actual situation relating to the Navy work
force. Of the 308,400 Navy U.S. citizen full time employees on-board on
December 31, 1984, approximately 273,100 or 89 percent were still covered by
the old CSRS. This means that the full impact on the Navy of any of the new
retirement system proposals will not occur for some time to come. The level
of retirement benefits appears to have a direct effect on the stay/leave
decision across a career, even in the early stages. Thus, such effects
should not be ignored in human resource supply/demand planning.

COPES METHODOLOGY

a. <u>Computer Systems Support Requirements</u>

In addition to retirement analysis, the RETCALC/NAVDYN models yielded
considerable information for designing the support capabilities. These
design issues include better user assess and fundamental improvements in
modeling technology. The COPES development program has been modified to
incorporate the added knowledge obtained in the course of this study.

The strategy for computer hardware/software support for COPES appears
essentially correct. The plan is to accomplish incremental development
using fully configured micro computers linked to a large mainframe computer.
In our case we are using IBM PC/AT workstations linked to an IBM 3081
computer. On both the microcomputers and mainframe, standard commercially
available packages are used for all processing. We are currently developing
COPES microcomputer applications using dBase III, LOTUS 1-2-3, STATA, and
CHARTMASTER as data base, spreadsheet, statistical, and graphics packages.
On the mainframe, we are using SAS to manipulate the internal work force
data files obtained from the Navy's CAMAS and external work force data files
obtained from public sources such as the Department of Labor and the U.S.
Census Bureau.

b. <u>Copes Extension</u>

The retirement program is just one component of the compensation
analysis capability of COPES. Technical improvements, beyond stand alone
features, are desirable for more comprehensive supply/demand studies related
to operational decision making. Specifically, planned development efforts
will combine the regression models of the type used in NAVDYN with goal
programming based flow models similar to those currently available in CAMAS.
The nonlinear nature of the flows which are found when work load
requirements are built into the problem requires a system of models
combining the strengths of the NAVDYN with the strengths of personnel flow
models using Markov-like structures. It should be possible to construct
such a new integrated supply/demand model with the knowledge gained in
through the NAVDYN studies.

The regression models currently used in NAVDYN can be improved.
Desirable new features include: (a) variable horizon retention (loss)
capabilities; (b) explicit determination of the Federal labor markets

external to the Navy; (c) explicit evaluation of special skill/ regional
wage capabilities, and (d) longer term projections.

The variable horizon retention (loss) modeling capabilities would be
designed to reflect future expectations of employees at different points in
their careers. Models of the type currently used in NAVDYN have a limited
horizon of 7-9 years. Models of the type used in the annual cost of leaving
(ACOL II) studies (See Arnold, Black and Warner (1985)) generally have a
horizon covering an entire 30-40 year career. It is felt that civilian
personnel retention studies should employ models with a horizon which
dynamically changes, extending further into the future as one moves into
his/her career. In this case one could use a NAVDYN type model for the
earlier career stages and a combination NAVDYN/ACOL type model for the mid
and later stage analysis.

The planned development of special skill/ regional wage capabilities
involves moving from the broad categories of occupational skills to more
specialized skills which also reflect regional wage characteristics. This
effort must address the issues of (a) small number problems, (b) limited
historical information, (c) specification biases, and (d) market dynamics
which are discontinuous.

The planned COPES studies of the influence of Federal labor markets
require consideration of the effects of qualification requirements for
Federal jobs into the analysis. For many jobs above the initial levels, the
qualification requirements or the need to have gained Federal status
effectively restrict eligibles to those already in the Federal work force.
Because of the initial work involving the relationship of different work
force populations to the Navy work force, this task is seen as a
modification of existing capabilities rather than a separate new effort.

Finally it is planned to use the improved COPES capabilities to make
longer term projections of the work force. This involves extending the
projections to ten to twelve years in the future rather than the five to
seven years as is done currently. Such longer term projections have more
statistical uncertainty but provide guidance as to the general direction of
trends that take a longer time to develop.

SUMMARY AND CONCLUSIONS

This paper presents new external labor force models that assess the
impact of retirement changes on Navy's civilian work force. The
RETCALC/NAVDYN models indicate the new retirement system for employees hired
since January 1984 will effect civilian retention rates. Civilian employees
will become more responsive to other job opportunities due to changes in the
relative wage advantage and the portability of retirement benefits. This
impact will become more pronounced as a larger percentage of the work force
becomes covered under the new retirement system. The RETCALC/NAVDYN models
are part of the management tools being developed to analyze and plan more
effectively for future work force changes.

REFERENCES

Arnold, J.E., M. Black, and J.T. Warner, "Retention cf DOD Civilians," DOD
    Contract No. MDA903-83-C-0376 (Arlington, VA: Systems Research and
    Applications (SRA) Corp.,1985).

Atwater, D.M., E.S. Bres III, R.J. Niehaus, and J.A. Sheridan, "Integration
    of Technological Change into Human Resources Supply-Demand Models", in G.O.

Mensch and R.J. Niehaus, Eds. Work, Organizations and Technological Change, (New York: Plenum, 1982)

Atwater, D.M., E.S. Bres III and R.J. Niehaus, "Human Resources Supply-Demand Policy Analysis Models", in R.J. Niehaus, Ed. Human Resource Policy Analysis: Organizational Applications, (New York: Prager, 1985) pp. 92-120.

Bres, E.S., R.J. Niehaus, F.J. Sharky, and C.L. Weber, "Use of Personnel Flow Models for Analysis of Large Scale Work Force Changes", Presented at 1985 Human Resource Planning Society Research Symposium, University of Pennsylvania, Dec 4-6, 1985.

Atwater, D.M. and J.A. Sheridan, "Assessing the Availability of Non-Workers for Jobs", Human Resource Planning, Vol. 3, No 4, 1980, pp. 211-218.

Charnes, A., W.W. Cooper, and R.J. Niehaus, Studies in Manpower Planning, (Washington, DC: U.S. Navy Office of Civilian Manpower Management, 1972), NTIS No. A066952.

Fernandez, R.L., G.A. Gotz and R.M. Bell, "The Dynamic Retention Model", Report No. N-2141-MIL (Santa Monica, CA: Rand Corporation, 1985).

Gotz, G.A. and J.J. McCall "A Dynamic Retention Model for Air Force Officers", Report No. R-3028-AF (Santa Monica, CA: Rand Corporation, 1984).

Niehaus, R.J. Computer-Assisted Human Resource Planning, (New York: Wiley Interscience, 1979).

Niehaus, R.J. Human Resource Policy Analysis: Organizational Applications (New York: Prager, 1985).

ANALYZING THE LINK BETWEEN COMPENSATION AND THE QUIT DECISIONS

OF CIVIL SERVICE EMPLOYEES

Larry W. Lacy

Office of Secretary of Defense (FM&P)
Pentagon, Room 3D265
Washington, D.C. 20301

INTRODUCTION

Federal civilian managers must compete in the same labor markets as do
private employers. Federal managers, however, have far less freedom than do
their counterparts in the for-profit sector in offering the compensation
necessary to attract and retain qualified workers. Detailed civil service
guidelines stipulate the grade, or rank, that any person can receive for the
training and experience required for any particular job. Similarly, each
grade is limited to a fairly narrow salary range. Where someone falls
within this range depends on his years of experience and, for supervisors
under "merit pay," his performance. As a consequence, even the most
talented inexperienced person must start at the bottom before climbing the
ladder to higher paying jobs in the career Federal service. For experienced
workers, rewards for outstanding achievement are, with a few exceptions, a
small percentage of regular salary.

Congress and the President determine how binding these pay constraints
are for Federal managers, all of whom want the best qualified workers
possible. Political decision makers in recent years have tended to respond
more to the immediate imperative of controlling Federal spending than to the
longer term considerations of the competitiveness of Federal pay. This
emphasis upon controlling costs may be due, in part, to the lack of
information on the tradeoffs between budget savings and the quality and
stability of the civilian work force.

Human resource managers in the Department of Defense (DoD), the largest
employer of civil servants, have a major stake in compensation decisions.
They also have a responsibility to inform the Congress and the President of
the work force consequences of pay policy. In September 1983, the Office of
the Secretary of Defense began funding research into the link between
Federal civilian pay and the ability of DoD to retain its experienced
workers. Other projects have been aimed at assessing the quality of newly
hired civilians, but this paper will discuss only the question of the
connection between compensation and worker retention. After discussing the
scale of the task facing DoD human resource managers, the procedures for
setting Federal pay levels, nonfinancial influences on turnover, and annual
separation rates from the DoD labor force, we will review the first 15

months of DoD-sponsored research into civilian retention. This research
builds upon previous research into turnover among Federal employees. This
work includes Long (1982), Borjas (1982), and Utgoff (1983).

THE DEPARTMENT OF DEFENSE AS AN EMPLOYER

The great size of the DoD civilian payroll is highlighted by the
statistic that about one percent of all U.S. civilian workers are employed
in this single Federal department. DoD also accounts for 37 percent of
total executive branch employment. DoD maintains a work force that differs
somewhat in composition from that of the private sector as a whole. About
one in three DoD civilians is a woman, compared to two in five in the
private sector, and more than one in five is a minority group member, a
higher fraction than in the remainder of the economy. The average age of
DoD civilians is 41. The average for the private sector is 35. Fewer in
DoD are at the extremes of worker age, under 25 or over 65, than among non-
government workers. Over nine-tenths are high school graduates and one-
fifth have earned a college degree. This indicates that the DoD civilian
labor force is somewhat better educated as a whole than are private sector
workers, one-fifth of whom did not complete high school.

For the 1985 fiscal year, DoD budgeted $30.3 billion for employing
civilians. (This does not include any civilian pension costs which are
financed by the Federal-wide Civil Service Retirement System.) Civilian
costs took up about 11 percent of the total DoD budget, compared to about 18
percent in the 1975 fiscal year. This declining share is attributable to
two factors -- a drop in constant dollar civilian expenditures of about 6
percent and rapid growth in spending for weapons.

These payroll dollars purchase the services of people from a wide range
of occupations. About two-thirds of DoD civilians are considered to be
white collar and receive salaries set according to the "General Schedule."
The remaining blue collar or Wage Board workers are paid hourly wages based
on prevailing rates in their local area. Table 1 provides the percentages
of blue and white collar workers fitting into Dod's board occupational
groups.

TABLE 1

OCCUPATIONAL GROUP DISTRIBUTION

OF DEPARTMENT OF DEFENSE CIVILIAN EMPLOYEES

Total	100%
White Collar Workers	68%
Professional	13%
Administrative	18%
Technical	12%
Clerical	22%
Other	3%
Blue Collar Workers:	32%
Metal trades	5%
Mechanics and repairmen	10%
Production	10%
Other	6%

DETERMINATION OF CIVIL SERVICE PAY LEVELS

Since 1969, the Bureau of Labor Statistics (BLS) has surveyed private establishments to determine what adjustments are needed to make Federal white collar pay comparable to that in the private sector for equivalent jobs. The National Survey of Professional, Administrative, Technical, and Clerical (PATC) Pay collects salary information from approximately 3,300 establishments drawn from the 44,000 within the scope of the survey. Included within the PATC survey are 107 jobs in 24 occupations. BLS staff interview personnel specialists in each establishment to determine how many employees do work that matches Federal job descriptions. Results are weighted, using the probability criteria employed in the sample selection, to obtain estimates of the numbers with comparable jobs in the survey universe. This process usually means that job matches from smaller firms are weighted more heavily than from larger businesses. (BLS and OPM plan to expand the scope of the PATC survey ways likely to reduce the size of estimated Federal-private wage gap.)

The Office of Personnel Management (OPM) uses the weighted PATC results to estimate private sector salaries for each covered job by grade level. Averages from the various jobs are combined into a single salary for each grade. The percentage difference between this salary and the Federal pay level constitutes the comparability increase that will be recommended to the President for that grade level. In most years, the figures for the various grades are combined into a single comparability adjustment recommendation for the entire General Schedule. The President can accept this figure or submit an alternative percentage to Congress. The legislative branch can, in turn, accept the President's plan or devise another.

An alternative pay setting approach is to compare what people with similar characteristics, such as level of education and years of experience receive in the Federal and private sectors. Considerable debate centers on which method of estimating pay comparability is better.

In 1975, General Schedule employees' salaries for the first time rose by less than the comparability adjustment derived frcm the PATC survey. After catching up in 1976, the General Schedule fell behind again in 1978 and by 1985 Federal white collar pay had dropped 19 percent behind the PATC survey estimates of private sector pay. Figure 1 displays the erosion of white collar pay.

For blue collar manpower, local, rather than national, wages provide the basis for calculating the adjustments needed to bring Federal pay up to

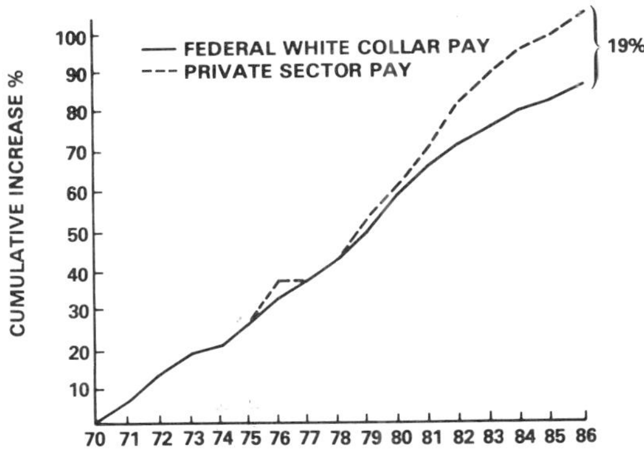

Figure 1: Erosion of Federal Pay

private sector levels. In most cases, a Standard Metropolitan Statistical
Area forms the core of the 135 wage survey areas.

Since the 1979 fiscal year, blue collar workers have also been subject
to nationwide pay caps. This left them by 1985, on average, 11 percent
behind the estimated private hourly rates prevailing locally.

One retirement plan covers virtually all civil servants hired before
1984. Widely recognized as one of the most generous pension programs, the
Civil Service Retirement System (CSRS) permits retirement with full benefits
as early as age 55 with 30 years of service. The various features of the
CSRS combine to exert a marked effect on retention. The greatly reduced
payments to employees retiring before full eligibility and the generous
payments thereafter produce a common career pattern. Many join the Federal
government young, remain until age 55, and retire soon thereafter.

Only Federal workers hired since the start of 1984 are required to have
Social Security coverage. Congress has exempted these new employees from
participation in the CSRS, but has yet to choose a plan for them that would
supplement Social Security. The legislative debate over Federal retirement
benefits has extended to modifications in the CSRS itself, in particular
raising the age for retirement benefits. This discussion has proceeded,
just as have deliberations over annual pay adjustments, without information
on the work force consequences of compensations policies.

SEPARATION RATES FROM FEDERAL GOVERNMENT

Many factors other than comparative compensation levels determine the
number of people who leave the Federal government for private sector jobs or
quit the active labor force altogether. The importance of financial
considerations cannot be assessed without disentangling them other
influences on separation rates. Later sections will discuss how this was
done with statistical techniques. What follows here is a brief discussion
of these nonfinancial factors which include:

(1) the employee's taste for government service,

(2) the employee's age,

(3) the employee's sex,

(4) the availability of non-Federal jobs, and

(5) the size of the Federal government.

Many other variables may also be important in separation decisions, but
these five play a particularly pervasive role.

Taste for Federal Employment

The U.S. Government offers distinctive, if not unique, employment
conditions. Most apparent is the scale of the Civil Service work force.
Few large corporations have as many employees as a mid-size Federal agency
and none as many as Defense. Combined with the element of size, which
affects separation rates in ways discussed below, are the pervasive role of
detailed bureaucratic procedures, considerable employment security but no
chance for very high salaries, and an opportunity for public service.

Reacting to this distinctiveness, new employees assess how well they
like the Federal government as a place to work. Those who are unhappy will

tend to leave. Over time, this self-selection process leaves those with a
stronger attachment to Federal service. These stayers will be less
responsive to changes in their compensation, compared to a group in which
self-selection had not been working, in deciding whether to complete their
Federal careers.

<u>Age</u>

Public and private retirement rates obviously rise sharply after
employees reach 55 to 65, depending on the employer. Job mobility
conversely tends to drop with age in both sectors. In part, this is because
older workers have acquired information about job alternatives and are more
likely to have made choices they find satisfactory. With increased
experience, the older worker also acquires job-specific skills likely to be
more valuable to his current employer than to other organizations. This
"human capital" factor may be particularly important for many civil servants
whose experience in public administration would have limited relevance to
for-profit sectors jobs. In addition, workers typically acquire families
and associated responsibilities after a few years of employment. This may
leave many less willing to take the risks that often go with changing jobs.

<u>Sex</u>

Women's labor force participation has become increasingly like that of
men. The addition of large numbers of women to the national work force has,
in fact, been a major source of output growth in recent years when worker
productivity has been largely stagnant. Many young women, however, still
leave their jobs to rear children. Some return after the children are all
in school, whereas others choose not to work again outside their homes.

<u>Availability of Non-Federal Jobs</u>

Many civil servants might be quite willing to take higher paying non-
Federal positions if the opportunity presented itself. Non-Federal salaries
could, however, be rising relative to civil service earnings even when few
are being hired. This could happen, for instance, if blue collar unions
push private sector salaries up beyond market-clearing levels. Another
possibility is that, as in the recent past, non-Federal workers may do
better in keeping up with inflation during a recession. Federal employees
might then be looking at their own decreased real wages as well as the
ground they lost to their non-Federal counterparts, but have little chance
to find a non-civil service job.

<u>Size of the Federal Government</u>

The number of job openings in an organization is directly related to
its size. A worker for a big employer is more likely to find a better
position by an internal transfer than is a person in a small business.
Federal employees can move within their immediate organization, to other
parts of their agency, or to other departments without quitting Federal
service. This large difference in scale makes unqualified quit rate
comparisons between sectors very misleading.

Actual quit rates for DoD civilians exhibit no discernible trend for
the last eight years. As shown in Table 2, about 2 percent of blue collar
DoD civilians have voluntarily left the Federal work force each year prior
to retirement, a rate about half that of white collar workers. Retirement,
by contrast, peaked for both groups in the 1980 fiscal year. This coincided
with a technical change in how retirement benefits are calculated that gave
eligible civil servants an incentive to leave then rather than continue
working.

211

TABLE 2

VOLUNTARY QUITS AND RETIREMENTS
FROM THE DEPARTMENT OF DEFENSE
(Percent of Full-time Employees)

Fiscal Year	Voluntary Quits		Retirements	
	Blue Collar	White Collar	Blue Collar	White Collar
1977	1.9	4.4	4.5	3.1
1978	2.3	4.8	4.5	2.8
1979	2.5	4.9	5.0	3.2
1980	2.2	4.4	5.7	3.9
1981	2.4	4.7	4.3	2.7
1982	2.0	4.1	3.7	2.6
1983	2.0	4.3	3.9	3.2
1984	2.3	4.6	3.7	2.7

Source: Defense Manpower Data Center

The DoD separation data also show the expected decline in quit rates among older employees. For example, the percentage leaving, most to take non-Federal jobs, is four times as high among 25 to 29 year old employees as among those twenty years older.

Also as expected, the proportion of female DoD workers quitting, 6.2 percent, was higher, almost twice that of the 3.3 percent for men.

In spite of a paucity of data on private sector separations with which to compare the losses shown above, DoD quit rates for permanent employees are clearly low. One point of reference comes from Bureau of Labor Statistics figures for 1980 and 1981 which indicate that about 14 percent of blue and white collar workers engaged in private manufacturing voluntarily left their jobs each year (1983). Some of this divergence may reflect the lack of distinction in the BLS data between permanent and temporary employees. DoD's quit rate would be higher if it included temporary workers who are typically clerks, secretaries, and blue collar civilians hired to handle short term workload peaks in depots and shipyards. Although no target rates have been chosen as the maximum allowable, clearly at some point in the future employee losses could rise enough to handicap DoD seriously in completing its mission. The research which will be described next is intended to produce an understanding of the link between compensation and retention which will help prevent DoD from reaching that point.

THE RESEARCH MODEL

The complex econometric model described in nontechnical terms below is based on a relatively simple concept of decision-making. The DoD employee is assumed to choose whether to remain a civil servant or leave for a non-Federal job on the basis of lifetime compensation potentials in the two sectors, his taste for Federal service, and the availability of private sector jobs. How these factors influence the quit decisions of particular people is assumed to be conditioned by considerations such as the employee's occupation, sex, race, education, which Military Department is the employer, the geographic region of employment, the year of joining DoD, whether the DoD job is in an urban area, and whether the employee is a supervisor.

Similar factors are assumed to affect retirement decisions which will be investigated in research planned for the coming year.

This simple concept of quit choices requires that the Federal employee have some idea of future earnings potentials, including pensions, in both his current job and the alternatives outside the Federal government. This concept does not necessitate perfect information, a practical impossibility, but rather an informed evaluation of which job would produce the greatest lifetime returns. It is further assumed that the employee bases this evaluation on what he has observed to b the career progression of others with similar skills in similar jobs.

There is the additional assumption that dollars earned now are valued more than dollars that will be received in the future. The employee, in deciding on his future career, implicitly discounts future salary and retirement payments to their "present value." This discounting reflects both the natural preference for consumption now rather that later, which is uncertain because of the possibility of death, as well as the adjustments necessary to remove the effects of inflation.

The actual research is being conducted under a DoD contract by a consulting firm, Systems Research and Applications Corporation (SRA). For this study, SRA has developed a second generation of the Annual Cost of Leaving (ACOL) model that has been used for many years for analysis of the retention of military personnel. The ACOL model compares the financial returns that can be expected from staying in the government for varying periods with the returns expected if the employee leaves immediately to take a non-Federal job. Returns to staying consist of the government ay received until quitting plus the private sector pay received thereafter until final retirement at age 65, plus any civil service pensions received up till death. The returns to leaving are calculated in the same way but on the basis of an immediate departure. All dollar amounts are discounted to their present values at the time of the decision to stay or leave. The present values are transformed into their annuity equivalents to facilitate comparisons over varying future career lengths. A computer compares the returns to leaving and staying for all possible lengths of future Federal employment and selects the time period that produces the maximum financial advantage, or minimum disadvantage, for staying. As a hypothetical example, the computer might determine that a 40 year old civil servant with 15 years of service would maximize his earnings if he stayed 15 more years to earn full Federal retirement benefits and then took a non-Federal job.

The annuity value selected by the computer, which represents the annualized cost of leaving the Federal government, then becomes an independent, or explanatory, variable (i.e., the ACOL variable) in a multiple regression equation. If the cost is positive, the civil servant would lose financially by quitting immediately. A negative cost indicates that leaving now would increase lifetime earnings. The ACOL model predicts a person will stay if there is at least one more period of continued Federal service for which the ACOL variable is positive (abstracting from the influence of other factors).

Other independent variables in the equation represent various non-financial factors that affect quit decisions as discussed earlier in this section. The dependent variable, i.e., the behavior to be explained, is the probability that a person will quit during the next year. In general terms, the regression equation is of the following form:

P = f(ACOL, T, U, X)

P = probability of quitting Federal service

ACOL = the annualized cost of leaving

T = taste for Federal service

U = unemployment rate

X = all other factors affecting the quit decision

The computer uses values for the ACOL and other variables for thousands of DoD employees to test the strength of the relationship of each of the factors with the probability of quitting.* Variable values for each person in the study population enter into the calculations separately. By contrast, most ACOL studies of the military have used group information, e.g., the percentage of first-term enlistees who stay for a second term of service. The disaggregated approach used by SRA provides a stronger basis for estimation of the links of the explanatory variables with quit behavior. The civilian retention analysis also marks a significant advance over the military ACOL studies in how taste for government service is handled. No direct measures of this variable exist. Earlier research used a simple trend variable that took on the value of one in the first year of service, two in the second, and so forth, to control for taste and the self-selection process. SRA used complex statistical procedures to infer employment preferences from the observed behavior of both those who stayed and those who left.

The statistical analysis was conducted with a combination of cross-sectional and longitudinal information on the personal characteristics and career paths of about 20,00 people who took civilian DoD jobs between the 1974 and 1977 fiscal years. The study used personnel records through June 30, 1983, or until the employee left DoD. In order to focus on quits rather than retirements, the sample included only employees who were between the ages of 20 and 45 with less than 20 years of Federal service upon joining DoD. The analysis covered three broad occupational groups--technical workers, scientists and engineers, and administrative personnel. This excluded all blue collar workers, who will be covered in subsequent research, as will as white collar clerical staff and several occupations that fit in the residual category "other".

Estimating values of the ACOL variable for each person required comparing the future lifetime income the civil servant could expect if he remained at least one more year with what he could expect if he quit for a non-Federal job immediately. The specific salaries that DoD employees would have earned, or actually did earn, upon quitting are not known. SRA assumed that each of the 20,000 DoD workers could have expected, if he left, to earn the same as would non-Federal workers in the same occupational group with similar years of education and experience and demographic characteristics. The 1979 Current Population Survey, conducted by the Bureau of the Census, furnished the basis for estimating non-Federal earnings of technical and administrative workers. The 1978 National survey of Natural and Social Scientists, managed by the National Science Foundation, was used for the remaining employees in the study population. Potential future Federal income was projected by assuming that each person's salary growth would equal the past average rate of DoD employees with similar characteristics and years of experience in like jobs. In line with the broadening gap in earnings, future real non-Federal pay was assumed to rise beyond inflation by between 0.5 and 1.0 percent a year whereas real civil service earnings were held constant.

---

* The regression equations were specified in PROBIT form to constrain the value of the dependent variable (the probability of quitting) between zero and one.

Part of the ACOL variable consists of deferred income received after reaching retirement age. In many cases, a worker could get civil service retirement income, Social Security payments, and a non-Federal pension. The amount coming from each would depend on many factors including the length of Federal service and the benefits available with the non-Federal pension. Retirement income was projected using the formulas set by law for the Civil Service Retirement System and Social Security. A shortage of information prevented accounting for non-Federal pension income.* Worker life expectancy was set according to tables in the Statistical Abstract of the United States. (Future research will add payments from Social Security to the model.)

STATISTICAL FINDINGS

The research model described in the previous section was tested with a complex statistical technique, similar to multiple regression analysis.* Separate quit models were tested for each of three groups, technicians, administrative workers, and scientists and engineers (S/E's). The ACOL variable had the predicted negative relationship with quits, statistically significant at the one percent level, for the first two groups. The result upholds the hypothesis that DoD civilians are more likely to quit Federal service as the potential value of lifetime compensation in the government falls relative to private sector earnings.

To test the importance of long-term versus current compensation in quit decisions, the same tests were redone substituting a variable measuring only current Federal-private sector salary differences in the place of the long-term ACOL variable. The results were essentially the same. This suggests that the much easier approach of using current salary differences, rather than ACOL variable, may suffice in some cases. (An obvious exception is when the focus of the analysis is on retirement benefits).

Regardless of whether current or long-term earnings are considered, technicians were found to vary their quit rates for monetary reasons much more than do administrative workers. A possible explanation is that Federal technicians have more job opportunities in the private sector. This could be because their job experience is more relevant to non-governmental work requirement than is that of DoD administrative workers.

The statistical results indicate that S/E's do not vary their probability of leaving the Federal government in response to changes in relative earnings, either long-term or current. This result is somewhat surprising because many DoD S/E's, particularly those in laboratories, perform work very similar to that of their private sector counterparts. In addition, engineers, who made up nine-tenths of the S/E's in the analysis, were generally in great demand throughout the period studied. A possible explanation, which can be only speculative now, is that S/E's in DoD are more content with their jobs than are technical and administrative workers. DoD may be able to understand quit behavior better in the future with information from a recently begun longitudinal survey of recent civilian hires.

As another test, past quit rates were predicted using the results of the statistical regressions and compared to actual separations. The predicted rates corresponded to the actual data very closely for the nine years covered in the analysis for both technical and administrative workers. Figure 2 compares predicted and actual quite rates. The fit between the predicted and historical rates was poor for S/E's reflecting the statistical findings discussed above. (The computer program which produced he statistical findings did not calculate R2, a commonly used measure of closeness of fit between predicted and actual values.)

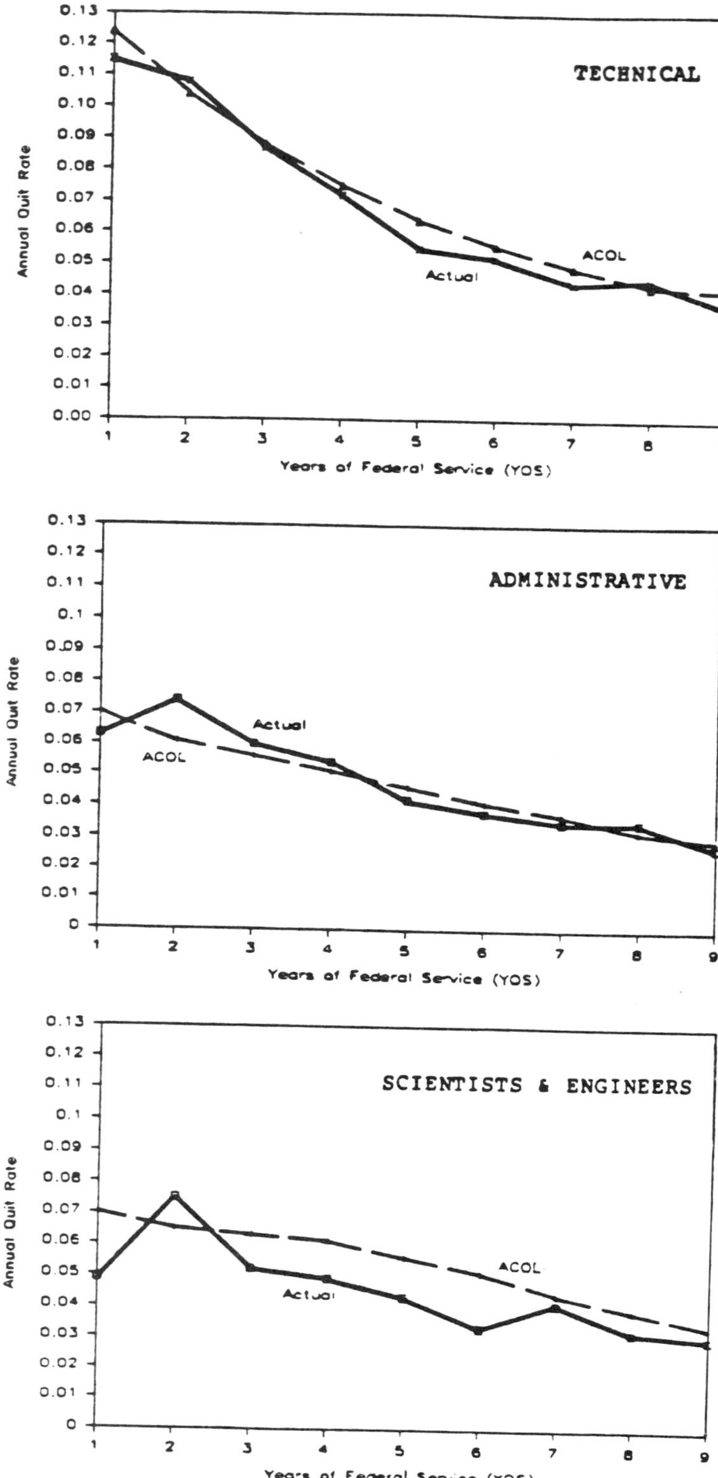

Figure 2:   Predicted and Actual Quit Rates

    As discussed in the previous section, the availability of non-Federal
jobs should affect the probability that a Federal employee will leave. In
most cases, full-time workers do not quit one job until they have found
another. The analysis used U.S. unemployment rates--measured by year,
occupation, region, race, and sex--as the index of private sector job
opportunities and produced findings consistent with this argument for
administrative workers and S/E's. The tests found no link between quit
probabilities and unemployment for DoD technicians, who had been indicated
to be the most sensitive to compensation differences. No explanation
suggests itself for this seemingly varying behavior among the three groups.
Other results from the regressions were in accord with the earlier
observation that male and older workers have lower quit rates irrespective
of income considerations. Race was not significantly linked to separations.

    The statistical results presented above may be more meaningful if used
to simulate how DoD employes would react to a pay cut relative to the
private sector. Because S/E's were not found to be responsive, the
simulation covers only technical and administrative workers. A computer

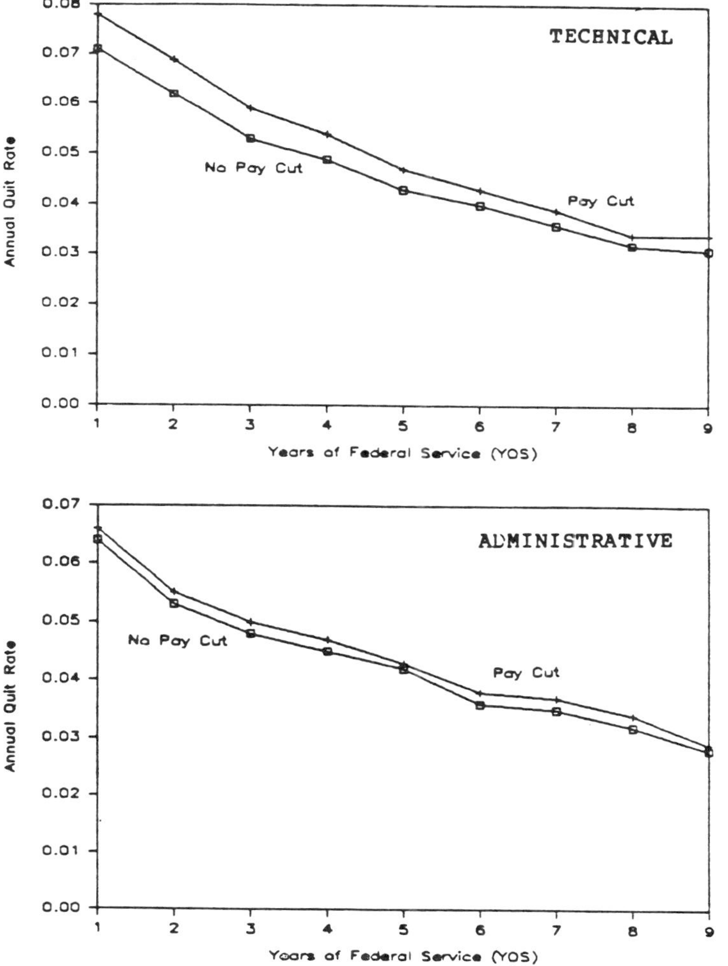

Figure 3:   Predicted Quit Effects of 10% Reduction in Real
            Federal Pay (5% cut in nominal pay, 5% inflation)

calculated how a permanent 10 percent cut in Federal compensation, half in nominal pay and half in inflation loss, would affect the value of the ACOL variable via a reduction in the expected stream of future Federal salary and retirement benefits. Projecting over a nine-year period, a count of this size would, according to the simulations, cause 3.4 percent more administrative workers and 7.8 percent more technicians to leave the government. Figure 3 presents the projection results. A 10 percent salary change may be close to the limit of the usefulness of such projections. We have no recent experience with dramatic shifts in actual Federal compensation. Therefore, the statistical findings reflect only the effects of the relatively small past variances in compensation.

APPLICABILITY TO PRIVATE SECTOR AND FUTURE RESEARCH

The research approach described here could., in principle, be applied to any large firm that sets compensation levels centrally. Analysis of how pay affects retention would seem inappropriate where bargaining between employer and individual workers determines salaries. For large firms with central pay management, accounting for self-selection based on taste for a particular employer--a crucial factor in the DoD study--would be important to the extent that large firms differ significantly in employment conditions. Finally, any statistical investigation of the link between pay and quit rates would, of course, require extensive historical information on salary histories as well as on other employee characteristics and turnover behavior.

DoD will continue to support research into the retention of its civil service workers. Future study will look at new occupations, including blue collar, and extend the analysis to workers nearing retirement eligibility. A computer simulation model, now being developed, will allow DoD to look at the possible effects of a wide range of alternative compensation policies.

REFERENCES

Borjas, George J., "Labor Turnover in the U.S. Federal Bureaucracy," Journal of Public Economics, 19, (1982), pp. 187-202.

Long, James E., "Are Government Workers Overpaid? Alternative Evidence," The Journal of Human Resources XVII, (Winter, 1982), pp. 123-131.

Systems Research and Applications Corporation, "Retention of DoD Civilians," Contract No. MDA903-83-C-0376 (April 1985).

U.S. Department of Labor, Bureau of Labor Statistics. Handbook of Labor Statistics, Bulletin 2175 (December 1983).

Utgoff, Kathleen C., "Compensation Levels and Quit Rates in the Public Sector," The Journal of Human Resources XVII, (Summer 1983), pp. 394-406.

SECTION 7:

IMPACT OF INFORMATION PROCESSING ON HUMAN RESOURCE PLANNING

     This section provides a survey of the state of information processing
support on human resource planning as of the end of 1985. The availability
of computational support particularly as an activity in the human resources
and planning departments has changed the level of acceptance of analytical
efforts.

     Verdin and Pagano provide the results of a phone survey of 81 members
of the Midwest Human Resource Planners Group. The organizations represented
in the survey were generally large, with average total sales of $4.8 billion
and over 15,000 employees. Thirty-seven percent of the sample were
manufacturing firms, 24 percent were in financial services, and the
remaining 39 percent in a variety of types of retailing and service firms.
The thrust of the study was on who uses human resource information support,
how it is being used and how its use might affect productivity and quality
of output.

     The paper by Wilson discusses the deployment of a microcomputer based
human resource management system (HRMS) as a distributed information system.
This is a case study of the use of multiple microcomputers in various
geographic locations for supporting the human resource management function.
This paper is timely as it confirms the conclusions of the Verdin and Pagano
study with a comprehensive case example.   The studies in this section show
how simple but effective applications are emerging with this shift of
technology to the functional human resource departments.

CURRENT TRENDS IN THE USE OF COMPUTER TECHNOLOGY

BY HUMAN RESOURCE MANAGERS

Jo Ann Verdin and Anthony M. Pagano

Department of Management, Box 4248
University of Illinois at Chicago
Chicago, IL 60680

INTRODUCTION

There have been a number of studies examining the characteristics of
Human Resource Information Systems (HRIS) in large corporations (Magnus &
Grossman, 1985; Mathys, LaVan & Nogal, 1984), how systems are liked to
various human resource functions (Amico, 1981; Hoff, 1983; LaPointe, 1983;
Weirmair, 1981), and factors related to the planning, implementation and
development of HRIS systems (Ceriello, 1984; Simon, 1983). In general, the
vast majority of large companies have some type of HRIS system available, at
least for basic payroll, record-keeping and administrative tasks.
Applications include compensation, benefits, EEO/AA, applicant tracking,
training and development, labor relations, turnover analysis, and human
resource planning. The focus of this research, however, has been on
characteristics of the computer system rather than who uses the information
and how its use might affect productivity and quality of output.

This study focuses on the extent human resource managers and
professionals are directly using computer systems' what applications they
have implemented, and their perceptions of changes in productivity and
quality of output. In addition, organizational characteristics were
measured as well as system characteristics such as the types of equipment
and software utilized. The following research questions were addresses:

1. Are human resource mangers using computer systems themselves for
   data retrieval and analysis? At what hierarchical levels in the
   organization does this direct, hand on usage take place?

2. What applications have been implemented by these managers? Are
   there characteristics of the organization or computer system which
   are related to the type of applications implemented?

3. How is the total number of applications implemented related to
   organizational and system characteristics?

4. How has the use of computer technology impacted these managers'
    perceptions of HR department productivity and quality of output?
    Are these perceptions of output related to organizational and
    system characteristics?

METHODOLOGY

During October, 1984 a phone survey was conducted of 81 members of the
Midwest Human Resource Planners Group using a structured schedule. The
organizations represented were generally large, with average total sales of
$4.8 billion and over 15,000 employees. fifty-eight percent of the human
resource departments reported between 11-100 people, with 20 percent having
less than 10 employees and 22 percent having more that 100. About half
utilized a decentralized structure for their human resource department,
while 37 percent were described as centralized and 14 percent as having some
combination structure. Thirty-seven percent of the sample were
manufacturing firms, 24 percent were in financial services, and 39 percent
provided consulting, retailing, energy, health care, communications, or
transportation services.

HUMAN RESOURCE MANAGEMENT UTILIZATION OF COMPUTER TECHNOLOGY

The result of a survey sponsored by _Personnel Journal_ (Magnus &
Grossman, 1985), indicated that some personnel function was automated by
99.7 percent of the 434 companies responding. This trend was also found by
Mathys, LaVan, and Nogal (1984), with over 90 percent of the 161 companies
surveyed reporting a computerized HRIS.

In this study, when respondents were asked if professional human
resource employees are directly using computer technology, 70 (89%) out of
79 respondents with personnel functions reported such utilization. Only 9
(11%) of the human resource departments were not using computer technology
at this time.

Characteristics of Nonusers

As might be expected, many of the companies not using computer
technology are relatively small, with 50% having less than 400 employees.
However, two of the firms reported over 20,000 employees. Over 55% were
either manufacturing or consulting organizations, while only one was from
the financial services industry. This pattern might reflect the widespread
use of computer technology in banks, brokerage firms, and insurance
companies. The number of human resource professionals ranged from 2 to 23.
Approximately 55 percent of the human resource departments were described as
having a centralized structure.

Characteristics of Users

The organizations using computer technology were relatively large. The
average number of employees was 16,000 while the average sales reported was
$4.2 billion. Further, the average number of people in human resource
management was 100. Over half of the respondents described the structure as
decentralized, with centralized and a combination of structures mentioned by
33 percent and 15 percent, respectively.

When asked who was actually using the computer, all management
levels were mentioned to some extent. Table 1 summarizes these results.
Respondents were asked to reply to all questions, so percentages do not add
to 100 percent. Although the majority of usage comes from the supervisors,
second level managers, and professionals, 43% of the top managers were
reported to use the computer directly. This is an indication of the prolif-

Table 1

Frequency of Levels Using System by Industry
(Frequency (Percentage))

Level	Manufacturing	Financial	Other	Overall
	N=26	N=18	N=24	N=68
Supervisors	22 (85)	13 (72)	14 (58)	49 (72)
Second Level	21 (81)	12 (67)	16 (67)	49 (72)
Top Managers	12 (46)	8 (44)	9 (38)	29 (43)
Professionals	18 (69)	14 (78)	14 (58)	46 (68)

eration of office automation and personal computer technology to all levels in the organization.

There were some differences in utilization as related to industry (See Table 1). A relatively greater percent of supervisors and second level managers directly used the computer in manufacturing firms than financial services or other industries. However, professionals used the computer systems to the greatest extent in the financial services industry. Utilization by top managers was about equal across industry groups.

APPLICATIONS

Respondents were asked how the computer system was being utilized i their department. As seen in Table 2, management and utilization of basic human resource data was mentioned overall by 72 percent of the computer users and the compensation area was indicated by 79 percent. Training and development administration was mentioned by 51 percent of the respondents, applicant tracking by 45 percent and human resource planning by 33 percent.

However, the application listed by 88 percent of the respondents was the use of the computer for special projects. Apparently computer systems which allow direct access by the manager or professional can be effectively used to answer questions as well as completing special studies and analyses. Specific areas mentioned include payroll, international relations, test validation, benefit administration, work force and job analysis, relocation analysis, organizational charts, computer assisted instruction, attitude surveys. labor relations, and productivity analysis. It is apparent that human resource professionals are using computer technology for planning and decision-making as well as record keeping and administration.

Table 2 also indicates the frequency each of the applications was mentioned by respondents from manufacturing, financial services, and other industries. Manufacturing firms primarily utilized basic HRIS systems and compensation applications while function financial services also made more use of applicant tracking and training and development systems. This could reflect the relative importance of human resource development to service industries in comparison to manufacturing firms. Human resource planning applications were mentioned by approximately one quarter of the manufacturing and financial service organizations, while half the remaining firms utilized computers in this manner.

To determine what organizational characteristics were related to the

Table 2

Frequency of Applications by Industry
(Frequency (Percentages))

Application	Manufacturing	Financial	Other	Overall
	N=26	N=18	N=24	N=68
Basic HRIS	22 (84)	12 (67)	15 (62)	49 (72)
Applicant Trk	12 (46)	11 (61)	8 (33)	31 (45)
Training	13 (50)	11 (61)	11 (45)	35 (51)
Compensation	24 (92)	13 (72)	17 (70)	54 (79)
HR Planning	7 (27)	4 (22)	12 (50)	23 (33)

implementation of each application, t-test were calculated for number of employees, sales, number of human resource employees. In this way the following hypothesis was tested for each application: There is no significant difference in the mean number of employees (sales, number of human resource employees) for organizations with an application as compared to organizations without that application. The results indicated there were significantly higher sales for companies with applicant tracking systems, although the overall number of employees and sales were not significantly different for any other application. It appears that organizational size, as measured by sales or number of employees, is generally unrelated to what specific applications are implemented.

The one factor which was significantly higher for every application was the number of human resource employees in the organization. This is similar to the result reported by Murdick and Schuster (1983) relating the number of employees in the human resource department to the number of additional human resource functions computerized. These results indicate that both the specialization and human resources available in larger departments facilitate the development of a variety of applications.

TOTAL NUMBER OF APPLICATIONS IMPLEMENTED

An index was developed which indicates the total number of the applications listed above which have been implemented. This total ranges from 1 to 5 and serves as an indirect measure of the scope of computer utilization by the companies in the study.

As above, organizational characteristics are measured by the total number of employees, sales, and the number of human resource employees. Computer system characteristics are determined by the total number of software programs used (ranging from 1 to 5 and including mainframe retrieval packages, spreadsheets, graphics, word processors, and in-house programs); the number of hierarchical levels using the system (ranging from 1 to 4 including supervisors, second level managers, top managers, and professionals); and the type of equipment available. The type of equipment was categorized as (1) mainframe, mini computer, and micro computer, (2) mainframe plus either a mini or micro, (3) mainframe only, and (4) micro only or mini plus micro. The frequency distribution of the type of equipment is shown in Table 3. This factor thus ranges from 1 for companies with the greatest variety of equipment available to 4 for companies with more limited computer capacity.

In order to determine the relationship between the number of
applications implemented and organizational and system characteristics,
correlation analysis was used. It was found that a higher number of
applications is significantly correlated to the organizational
characteristics of sales level (,29, pr < .05) and number of human resource
employees (.51, pr < .001). In addition, the number of applications was
also related to the number of managerial levels using the system (.38, pr
<.001) and the equipment available (-.55, pr < .001). In general it appears
that larger organizations with more equipment, software, and levels of
utilization will implement a greater number of applications. By careful
system design, implementation and training of all levels of users, the scope
of utilization of computer technology can be broadened.

PERCEIVED PRODUCTIVITY AND QUALITY OF OUTPUT

A few researchers have studied the perceptions of computer users on
productivity and quality of output. Quillard et al. (1983) found that in
general the 83 personal computer users interviewed felt access to the
machine had positively impacted their job performance. Changes included:
increased speed of the work and subsequent completion of more work, improved
quality of performance, and new analyses leading to better understanding of
the work.

Forty percent of the work group heads interviewed by Gutek, Bikson, and
Mankin (in press) in 55 offices representing 26 different organizations
perceived substantial increase in the productivity of their offices while 47
percent indicated some change had occurred Only 13 percent of these
respondents felt no change resulted. The quality or value added to the work
was also seen to improve a great deal by 43 percent of the respondents, while
some improvement was noted by 30 percent of the group. However, one measure
of performance, labor costs, was reported not to have changed by 51 percent
of the managers. Only 15 per-cent reported substantial reductions and 34
percent some reductions in labor costs.

The results from the 70 computer users in this study are similar. AS
summarized in Table 4, 56 percent of the respondents indicated that the
productivity of the human resource department was higher, 34 percent
indicated somewhat higher productivity, and only 10 percent saw no change.
When asked about the impact on the quality of the products and services of
the human resource department, 59 percent indicated higher quality, 34
percent somewhat higher, and 7 percent saw no change.

In order to determine the relationship of productivity and quality of
output to organizational and system characteristics, the two variables shown
in Table 4 were combined to make one scale. A score of 1 indicated both

Table 3

Frequency of Type of Equipment

Type of Equipment	Frequency	Percent
Mainframe, Mini, & Micro	16	23.5
Mainframe plus Mini or Micro	35	51.5
Mainframe only	13	19.1
Micro only or Mini plus Micro	4	5.9
Total	70	100.0

productivity and quality were perceived as higher, 2 combined higher and
somewhat higher, 3 was a middle ground of higher plus no change or both
somewhat higher, 4 represented no change and somewhat higher, and 5 indicated
no change for both factors. When correlated with the organizational and
system characteristics described in the previous section, no significant
relationships were found. In fact, the only variable correlated with the
perceived output scale was professional use of the computer, indicating that
familiarity with the system by the professionals responding to the survey was
related to perceived success.

FUTURE TRENDS

Organizational barriers regarding the use of personal computers and
terminals by managers and professionals will continue to fall over the next
few years. Hardware continues to develop incrementally, with both speed and
storage capacity increasing and the price decreasing. Features such as
voice activation and touch sensitive screens are being refined, laser disks
are being developed, and high speed, high quality laser printers are being
offered at prices under $2,000. Graphics capabilities may also become
available at competitive prices as demand for these features increases.

As users become comfortable with basic word processing, spreadsheet,
database and retrieval programs, their expectations and demands increase.
Software developers may find it necessary to include truly "user friendly"
input and output capabilities, as well as statistical analysis capabilities.
Elements of artificial intelligence programs may also be applied to the
business setting (Helferich, 1984; McGee, 1985). This application is
similar to software currently being used by physicians as a diagnostic tool.
Given a set of symptoms, these programs help determine possible causes and
treatments.

Table 4

Frequency of Perceived Impact on Output

1. How has the introduction of computer technology affected the
    productivity of the human resource department?

Impact	Frequency	Percentage
Higher	38	55.9
Somewhat Higher	23	33.8
No Change	2	10.3
Total	70	100.0

2. How has the introduction of computer technology affected the
    quality of the products and services of the human resource
    department?

Impact	Frequency	Percentage
Higher	40	58.8
Somewhat Higher	23	33.8
No Change	5	7.4
Total	70	100.0

In many organizations, a number of types of computers and peripherals
have been purchased which do not allow networking or communication among the
machines. The hardware and software is being developed and implemented
which allows data to be transferred between machines automatically, and in
some cases between programs, In addition, some systems allow several
personal computers to share data from a common disk. As a result of these
trends, users are able to utilize a mainframe when appropriate, store data
in a central location, and analyze part of the information as needed using
the micro computer. In this manner, the best combination of hardware and
software can be selected to solve a particular problem.

Human resource managers and professionals will be able to take
advantage of these trends in a number of ways. The number and
sophistication of applications will continue to increase. Decision support
systems for use in planning and forecasting are improving. In addition, the
use of computers for applicant testing, managerial training, and succession
planning will continue. Eventually, the computer may be viewed as just
another tool which provides better and faster information for use in
managing many different human resource functions.

MANAGERIAL IMPLICATIONS AND CONCLUSIONS

The results of this survey indicate that human resource managers and
professionals in large firms are using computer technology themselves. This
trend is found for all managerial levels, including over 40 percent of top
managers. Thus, it is quite realistic to design and implement an
information system which incorporates direct access and retrieval by all end
users in the human resource department. Further, as the price of computer
hardware continues to fall and the software appropriate for basic human
resource information systems, specific applications, and ad hoc retrieval
and analysis continues to improve, more small and medium sized firms will be
able to utilize this technology for human resource management.

The human resource applications implemented varied across industries,
with manufacturing emphasizing basic data management and retrieval, while
the majority of financial service companies reported applicant tracking and
training administration as well. Human resource planning was not as
frequently mentioned, although this may change as users become more
knowledgeable and software easier to use. About one third of the
respondents reported using the systems for forecasting, career or succession
planning activities.

The specific applications implemented were related only to the number
of human resource employees. It is probably unrealistic to expect
professionals in a very small department to implement a great many different
applications. System planners may find it more efficient to implement high
priority applications first and then add special applications as resources
permit. In this way the needs for specific types of firms may be met and
the managers and professionals using the system may select the appropriate
applications to meet their needs.

In addition to the specific applications mentioned, the majority of
computer users cited special projects as a beneficial way to utilize
computer technology. It is through these projects that information needed
to answer specific questions can be retrieved and special analyses required
for decision-making can be completed. It appears that the utilization of
computers for data retrieval ad hoc report writing, and spreadsheet and
statistical analysis has spread from computer experts to human resource
managers and professionals.

There was a significant relationship between the number of applications

and sales, the number of human resource employees, the number of managerial
levels using the system, and the type of equipment. In order to have the
computer used for several purposes it appears beneficial to have a
relatively large human resource staff, to encourage the use of the system at
all levels, and to provide easy access through the appropriate equipment.
Organizations providing mini and/or micro computers in addition to mainframe
systems have implemented more applications than those with less diverse or
smaller systems. This may be due to easier access by users through
terminals or micro computers, the ability to utilize a mainframe for some
applications and a smaller machine for other areas, or an overall
organizational philosophy which rewards computer usage and allocates
resources in this way. Management does to some extent have the potential to
impact the scope of computer utilization by providing both human and capital
resources and by encouraging and rewarding the direct use of this technology
by all managerial levels.

Like previous results, the respondents in this study reported higher
productivity and quality of output for human resource departments. However,
these perceptions were unrelated to both organizational and system
characteristics. This may be due to the low variance in the measure of
productivity and quality or a result of the omission of the variables which
are related to such perceptions. From the results of the study, it appears
that changing the hardware, software, and managerial levels using the system
will not affect user perceptions of output. Also, organizational size is
not related to this output measure.

But what factors may be related to perceived productivity? Individual
circumstances such as importance of computer knowledge to one's career or
job performance, willingness to learn new skills, the situation before
computers were installed or widely used, the individual's involvement in the
planning and implementation of the system, experiences with previous
systems, and the background of the human resource users may be related to
perceptions of outcomes. In addition, work group norms regarding the
computer may also impact an individuals perceptions. Further research is
needed to isolate those factors which are related to an individuals
perception of the overall impact of computer technology.

Finally, it is apparent that better measures of system impacts are
needed. Mathys, LaVan, and Nogal (1984) found only 25 percent of the firms
surveyed attempted to evaluate their human resource information systems.
Measures used included error rate, use of the system, a survey of the
system, cost, and response time. Other outcome measures which could be used
to evaluate information systems are the impact on individual decision-
making, the speed of response to ad hoc questions, the status of human
resources within the company, and the amount of savings as a result of
automation. In order to maximize outcomes, it may be necessary to select
individuals for managerial and professional positions who are willing and
able to use current systems, to develop new applications, and to continually
upgrade their computer skills.

REFERENCES

Amico, Anthony M., "Computerized Career Informations," Personnel Journal,
    Vol. 60 (August, 1981), pp. 632-633.

Ceriello, Vincent R., "Computerizing the Personnel Department: How Do You
    Pick the Right Software?" Personnel Journal, Vol. 63 (November, 1984), pp.
    53-58.

Gutek, B. A., Bikson, T. K., & Mankin, D., "Individual and Organizational
    Consequences of Computer-based Office Information Technology," In S.
    Oskamp (Ed.) Applied Social Psychology Annual, Vol. 5, (Beverly Hills, CA:
    Sage Publications, in press).

Helferich, Omar K., "Computers that Mimic Human Thought: Artificial
    Intelligence for Materials and Logistics Management," Journal of Business
    Logistics, Vol. 5, No. 2 (1984) pp. 123-127.

Hoff, Roger D., "The Impact of Cafeteria Benefits on the Human Resource
    Information System," Personnel Journal, Vol. 62 (April , 1983), pp. 282-
    283.

LaPointe, Joel R., "Human Resource Performance Indexes, "Personnel Journal,
    Vol. 62 (July, 1983), pp. 545-553.

Magee, John F., "SMR Forum: What Information Technology Has in Store for
    Managers," Sloan Management Review, Vol. 26 (Winter, 1985), pp 45-49.

Mathys, Nicholas & LaVan, Helen, "A Survey of the Human Resource Information
    Systems (HRIS) of Major Companies," Human Resource Planning, Vol. 5 (June,
    1982), pp. 83-90.

Mathys, Nicholas, LaVan, Helen, & Nogal, Garry, "Issue in Purchasing and
    Implementing HRIS Software," Personnel Administrator, Vol. 29, No. 8
    (August, 1984) pp 91-97.

Magnus, Margaret & Grossman, Mort, "Computers and the Personnel Department,"
    Personnel Journal, Vol. 64 (April, 1985) pp. 42-48.

Murdick, Robert G. & Schuter, Fred, "Computerized Information Support for
    the Human Resource Function," Human Resource Planning, Vol. 6 (March, 1983,
    pp. 25-33.

Quillard, J. A., Rockart, J. F., Wilde, E., Vernon, M., & Mock, G. A Study
    of the Corporate Use of Personnel Computers, (Center for Information
    Systems Research, Working Paper 109). Unpublished manuscript,
    Massachusetts Institute of Technology, 1983.

DEPLOYMENT OF A MICROCOMPUTER BASED HRMS AS A DISTRIBUTED INFORMATION

SYSTEM: H.R. POLICY MANAGEMENT IMPLICATIONS AND IMPACT

Richard L. Wilson

Human Resource Systems
3118 Reseda Court
Tampa, Fl 33618

INTRODUCTION

With the size, complexity, and structure of today's organizations they
need dynamic information systems. These systems are computerized, and until
recently, predominantly mainframe. With the advent of microcomputer
technology we are experiencing the proliferation of computers through the
organization to assist in the management of information. This change offers
the information, greater response time, more control over information
management, and more immediate output (Mazursky, 1984).

No function benefits more from the adoption of micro-technology than
Human Resources. With the "desk-top computer" the H.R. manager directs the
function from within the department without the added costs and delays
associated with data processing intervention. He or she has the "total
system" at his/her disposal, managing the capture, input, storage, and
output of information on employees. The only limitations are skills,
imagination, and experience (Moody, 1984).

A particularly complex and exciting dimension of the technology is its
use in the multi-size organization. Referred to as a "distributed
information system" (DIS) the organization operates the computer and human
resources software at each location where human resources has a department.
This distributed environment of the microcomputer distinguishes it from the
"traditional" definition. It is not simply a local computer system. Though
each is autonomous, they are interacting processors. Though they operate
without direct supervision of a central computer facility, central
operational policies govern their use. Most importantly, through the
communications linkage the corporate H.R. Center oversees functional
distribution of processing (Figure 1). While each location does its
respective site information management, the corporate center orchestrates
the overall operations and is the focal point for consolidating the
reporting and analysis of human resources information.

Under this concept the human resources function has total system
control. It determines the priorities for use, data capture, data storage,

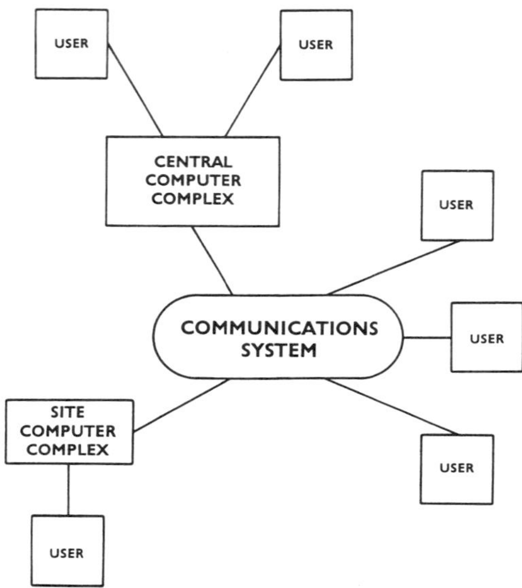

Figure 1: Concept of a Distributed Information System Network

data retrieval and reporting. There is no intervention from or cost to Data Processing or MIS. The system technology issues and the consequent human resources policy management implications are the important dimensions for examination through the case study.

THE DISTRIBUTED INFORMATION SYSTEM

The Concept

The objective of using a human resources management system is not simply to replace clerical tasks. More importantly, the system functions to provide insight into the processes of problem solving, data analysis, decision making, planning, controlling, and organizing human resources. Providing such insight is where the information system comes in.

Beyond the organized collection of computer hardware components, the information system consists of the specifically designed system and applications software, operational procedures, and information management activities (Katzan, 1984).

The structure for the case study's information system corresponds to a hierarchical arrangement (Figure 2). Moving from bottom left to the top, we have detailed and specific information at the data entry level which is aggregated and massaged at each level to yield the appropriate effect. So, the system manages more information at the top, albeit very synthesized. There is an inverse relationship of information to people. Moving down the hierarchy from the top to the bottom right, at the higher organizational level are fewer people with broad policy responsibility. At the bottom are more people -- many of them specialists.

In human resources management environment data entry is the key operator's responsibility. Specialists for each functional area of human resource's capture their own pertinent information. At the "inquiry/response" level, again the key operator retrieves information, i.e., individual employee records, or determining the number of females in a department, or an employee listing.

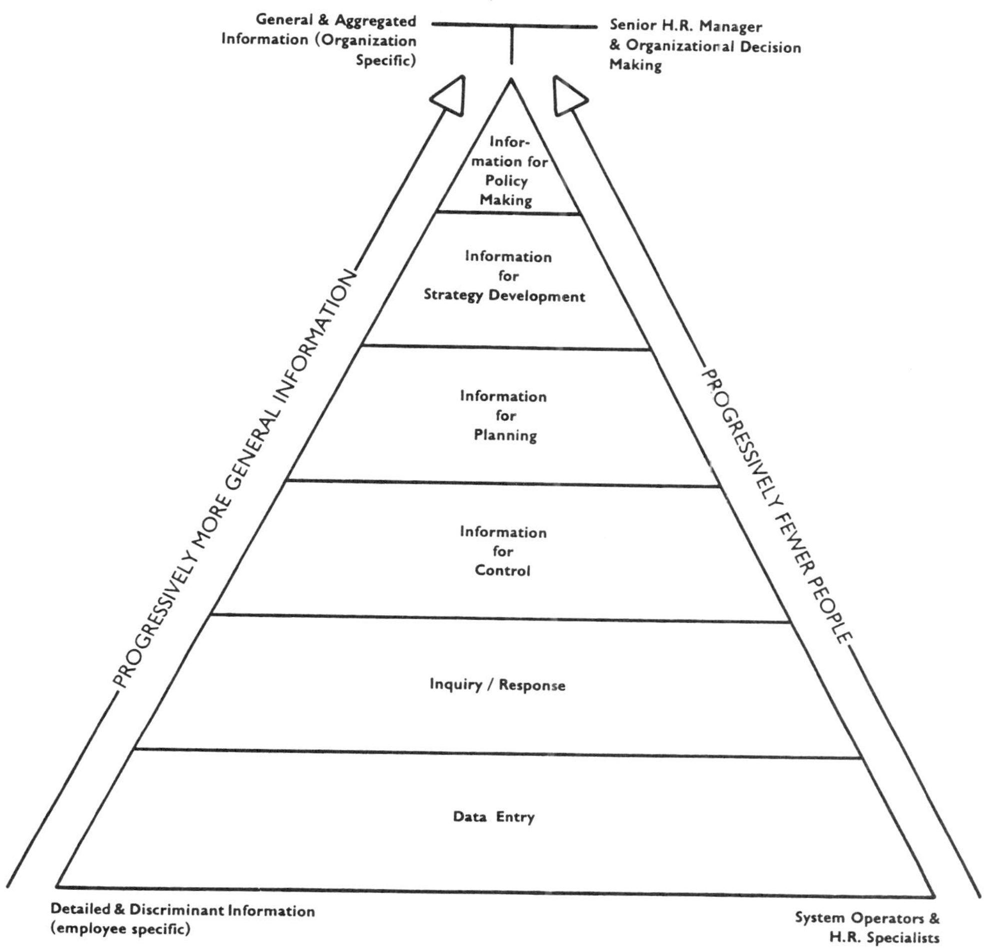

Figure 2: Information System Support Heirarchy for Human Resources

At the "information for control" level, custom reporting begins. The person is usually a particular specialist and/or the functional area staffer who conducts an analysis to determine the status of the human resource relative to a guideline. classic examples are compensation administration and turnover analysis.

The next level is "information for planning." Here the focus is broader. The information is for decision analysis like determining the cost of budgeting new hires, like a three percent cost of living increase, like the impact of a reduction in force on the organization, or like the cost of training of a group of apprentices. The people involved are the human resource (H.R.) function managers. The information is not as nearly as discriminate. The reports concern aggregations of data by specific groupings.

The "information for strategy development" level addresses the board concerns about allocation and use of resources. It provides input for scheduling and provides a general organizational perspective. The information is representative of the whole organization. The reports are

Table 1:   A Matrix Examining the Local and Global Human Resource System Uses

| | | * * * LOCATION * * * | | | |
Human Resource System Use	CORP	SITE 1	SITE 2	SITE 3	SITE 4
Source Data Capture		*	*	*	*
Transaction Processing		*	*	*	*
Data Editing		*	*	*	*
Record Updating/Maint.		*	*	*	*
Record Deletion					
Data Base Mgmt. "A"		*			*
Data Base Mgmt. "B"					
Application 1	*	*	*	*	*
Application 2	*	*			*
Application 3	*				

Data Base Mgmt. "A":	Structural changes to the basic software files and fields set up by corporate. These changes are addendi.
Data Base Mgmt. "B":	Changes made to add special fields. Mostly composites derived from existing fields for purposes of complex reporting, i.e. field "skill A" + field "skill B" = new field "skill X".
Application 1:	Reporting which is basic listings and composites of information to meet H.R. management requirements—employee directories, merit budget worksheets, etc.
Application 2:	Reporting which addresses planning issues and tests "what of" scenerios for resource allocation, i.e. seasonal hiring experiences, overtime requirement, etc.
Application 3:	Reporting which assists in policy decision making, i.e. job movement and manpower planning.

statistical, or tabular, or graphic. The senior H.R. manager drives this level of use of the information system.

At the pinnacle, there is the "information for policy making". This is again under the direction of the senior most H.R. manager. The outputs derived from the system are usually a compilation of information from outputs at all levels. Both the discrete cases and synthesized aggregates are tools to assist in the analysis before adding or changing policy.

This graphic representation can become distorted in the distributed information system environment. Clearly, the data entry activity is a responsibility at each location, though not always does information summary or aggregation take place there. As Table 1 points out, there is replication of activities from site to site. The matrix is an example of corporate human resource's segmentation of responsibility and operational control The system logic employed here is the assignment of the table's activities as requisites for successful migration of information to and from corporate.

The System Components

The nucleus of this information system is a microcomputer configured with extended memory, a peripheral external memory device for backup and data storage, and printer. The software is a market product customized to conform to the database requirements of the organization. This constitutes the structure of the corporate "host" computer. Similar configurations are at each site (Figure 3). Each location's personnel manager oversees data management (the capture, storage, and access of information). The dimensions of the system that qualifies this structure as a distributed information system (Katzan, 1979) are:

a. the data communications link, and

b. the maintenance of records of employees by location.

The organization satisfies the definition of system by supporting a well-defined set of human resources functions with the hardware/software which it deployed.

Three issues are fundamental to sustaining operation of the case study's human resources department: goal management, control, and intelligence. They have particular significance in the information system environment since they represent needs that constantly reoccur. Goal management is the process of setting, monitoring, and achieving the purpose and mission of the H.R. functions (Katzan, 1979). Control refers to the activities associated with getting work done in compliance with organizational guidelines (Katzan, 1979). Intelligence is the gathering, processing, interpreting, and communicating of the information in the decision-making process (Katzan, 1979). They are interdependent and require an integrated system which responds with ease of management and control, and which yields the various types of information at each level, as noted in Figure 2.

Objectives and Design of the DIS

The primary objective is to facilitate and support the data management functions in multiple sites. With the microcomputer based distributed information system many secondary objectives emerged as much as "side effects" as by design. These include:

1.   Developing staff to manage the systems,

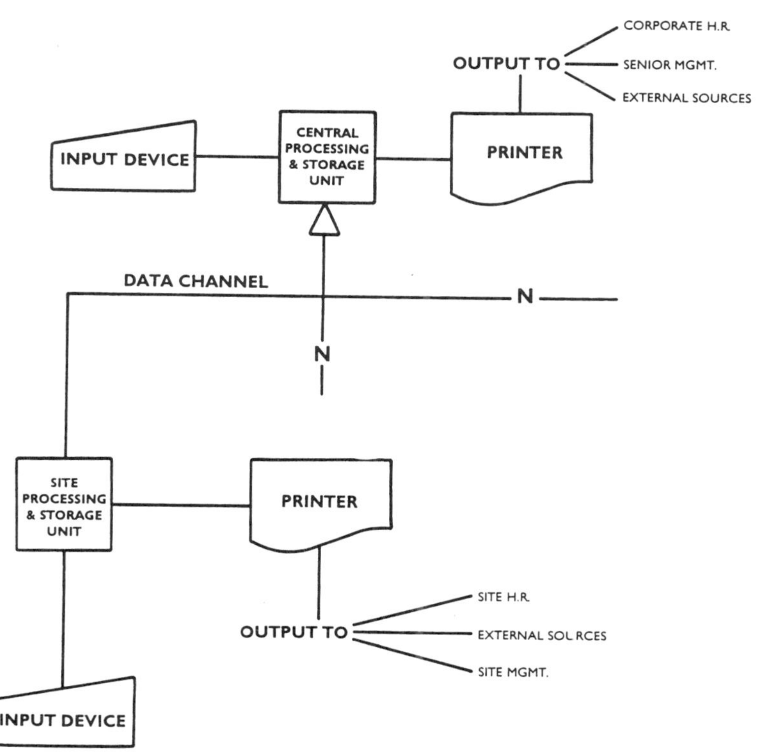

Figure 3:   Configuration for Human Resource Microcomputer
             Distributed Information System

2. Extending data processing capability beyond corporate
   human resources,

3. Creating remote support for personnel management,

4. Increasing timeliness and accuracy of reporting,

5. Being more responsible to employee information needs,

6. Managing incremental growth more cost effectively, and

7. Building a system corresponding to organizational
   patterns.

Out of these and other objectives came the specific design characteristics for the system and its software. For effective and purposeful information the human resources department took into consideration accuracy, reliability, security, responsiveness and resource sharing. The concern is that the information is correct (accurate); and that the hardware and software is not vulnerable to failure (reliable). They want to know that the information is protected from unauthorized disclosure and accidental or intentional tampering. They need to be able to satisfy a user's request in a reasonable length of time (responsiveness). And, they want an operational structure providing for the sharing of personnel, data, and facilities among the distinct computer sites.

Beyond these considerations were those for the basic system functions. The system configuration had to support the "applications". Again referring to Figure 2, human resources can perform source data entry at the lowest level of responsibility. Storage of data is through internal harddrive memory devices and an external device with "removable cartridge" memory. Software features include selection of data by specific criteria; updating to change dynamic employee information (pay, job, location); and sorting of data by name, location, etc. for information display. Other features are merging files and records to update or create a new file, indexing to insert new information in proper sequence, and deletion to remove existing records. Getting information in and managing it through the computer was half the need. The balance of the system design and software features focused on reporting the information. Report writing is the means of producing "hard copy". The reporting entails summarizing, aggregating, formatting, and totaling (Killian, 1976; Walker, 1982).

Finally, design addressed operations. Already noted is data entry, but the organized structure of operations also include transaction processing (data entry from specific source documents), editing (verifying and updating data), and group or batch processing (structuring transaction processing in an orderly and logical sequence) (Claybrook, 1983).

As evidenced by the items outlined in the objectives and design, for the information system to achieve a high level of effectiveness and efficiency the model consisted of "user developed" functions in contrast to computer system functions carried out by the machine. The environment is applications oriented. The emphasis by the senior human resources manager is on the human technology. The "system" followed an evolutionary cycle consisting of:

a. design of the manual operations,

b. design of the human resource system operations,

c. establishment of the operating system at one site,

236

d.   replication of the system at all sites, and

e.   linkage of sites.

THE ORGANIZATION

<u>Company Background</u>

Company Y is a $100 million dollar subsidiary of a multi-billion dollar communications conglomerate. its growth is a brisk 30% annually in revenues and personnel. Acquisitions and internal business diversification accounts for the increases. The company has a strong centralized administration with business units and operating site locations built as a function of organizational design. Though the company is high technology driven, its operations are labor intensive.

As a subsidiary, it was itself an acquisition. the parent left intact the management team with its entrepreneurial president. The company's principal business is financial services to the bank card industry. The growth strategy involves: a) vertical integration of other financial services, and b) horizontal integration of like businesses. Compounding the growth is market expansion.

Within the organization Human Resources is under the direction of a corporate officer, Vice President of Human Resources. Though corporate directs personnel operations, each business unit and operating site (of sufficient size) managers its own personnel administration, benefit and compensation administration, and employee relations. Staffing of the human resource function varies by location.

The Human Resources System conforms to the layout in Figure 3. Each location is responsible for all record transaction processing, administration of H.R. programs (as assigned from corporate), and system maintenance. Each week all locations forward their employee file updates via magnetic media to corporate. The corporate H.R. merges the files for consolidated reporting. At corporate, Human Resources manages the program design, policy and proce-dures development of: benefits, compensation, manpower planning, government compliance, and human resources performance measurement.

Each site has a comparable system configuration. The system is secured in its own space, and a key operator controls it. The H.R. vice president directs system implementation and management. He divines policies governing human resources and organizational development.

Corporate sets the guidelines concerning the basic software configura-tion and what information to maintain, update, and report. The policy requires uniform records for all locations. Though each site manager has the discretion to administer and uphold policies, he or she shares key issues with corporate for co-joint resolution. This maintains conformity of application of like instances of the same issue at other sites. Each location's personnel manager handles the authorized employment activity work force behavior issues, head count reports, benefit and compensation administration, and performance appraisal process.

All planning, policy or procedures development, and program changes or development are under the direction of corporate human resources. The Vice President of H.R. has a computer system in his office.

<u>System Management</u>

The organization exemplifies the hypothesis about the "micro"

technology's contribution to increasing the involvement of the end-user in
the control of his/her computer applications. In fact, it meant a partial
redefinition of the end user concept. The human resources software at the
company provides the capability to decide on the specific data base
configuration. This includes record structure, data fields, naming
conventions (for files, fields, and records), password security , and system
controls (reindexing files, creating new file and fields, etc.). Of course,
H.R. has control of information and reporting. Consequently, the end-users
are now the people whoreceive reports whether human resources people, line or
executive managers.

Critical issues in the analysis of the appropriate product were:

1. Ease of the system's adaptation to the organization and
    the ability to meet the company's growth and expansion
    requirements.

2. Ease and expediency of implementation at corporate and each
    remote site. Facility to handle data transfer.

3. Ability to handle the consolidation of information for
    the organization, yet allow corporate location reporting as
    needed.

4. Ability to achieve the function of a management support system at
    corporate within limiting time constraints.

5   Avoidance of data processing intervention to support the
    implementation and maintenance of the system.

The microcomputer approach proved the most cost effective and efficient means
of introducing automation and a distributed information system for human
resources.

The company initiated the first installation of its largest site in
September, 1984, with a concurrent install at corporate. By December all
remote sites were active. Human resources considered implementation
accomplished when a site loaded all employee master files. In January,
19854, the H.R. corporate center had access to all current status
information about the organization's employees and three years of history.

With implementation complete the company is focusing on policy issues
relative to system management and human resources program management. The
attention outside corporate is on information gathering and information
evaluation. With new acquisitions on the horizon the department strategy is
to follow the same basic implementation scenario. The distinction will be
that the employee information gathered initially will help human resources
to manage the integration and fit of the acquired organization's employees
into the organizational structure.

From the outset the objective of the DIS was to monitor each operating
unit to assure conformity to current and newly instituted corporate
policies. Personnel managers spend considerable time on application issues
-- particularly cost containment and cost avoidance. This began with
compensation and benefits.

For the most part the company has a real system orientation (Katzan,
1979). Human Resources translates inferred from the employee data into
reports. They are inquiry/response driven - particularly at remote sites.

The H.R. vice president is moving toward a conceptual system

orientation (Katzan, 1979). In this state, Human Resources uses logical
concepts to model the real system for trend analysis and prediction.

<u>Personnel Staff Roles</u>

As noted earlier, the personnel managers and specialists are not the
typical end users. They are not always at the end of the chain of
information consumers. They are more often the processors and providers of
information (Killian, 1976; Walker, 1982). The dramatic change for these
people is the new skills and knowledge to operate and control the
technology. Though the organization is computer oriented, data processing
expertise was not resident in human resources. The skill and knowledge
requirements for effective system utilization are:

1. Basic systems logic,

2. File and data base management skills,

3. Flow diagramming (mapping information flow) skills,

4. Systems analysis techniques,

5. Report layout techniques,

6. Forms design (particularly transaction and turnover documents)
    skills,

7. Communication systems techniques,

8. Distributed systems management knowledge, and

9. Standards and procedures development skills.

This compendium of systems abilities did not reside with anyone in
human resources at the outset of implementation. Though the initial
installation training and subsequent system use everyone now exhibits some
of the skills. Beyond the on-the-job skill development human resources
acquired new skilled people to complement the staff. Also, the very
excitement of using the system and experiencing the productivity
improvements provides a self-education inducement. A near competitive
situation exists where staff demonstrates to each other new found techniques
and approaches to meeting information management needs. The experience
moved the people from computer illiteracy and fear to computer dependence
and inquisitive enthusiasm in nine months.

<u>Application Issues - Real System and Conceptual System</u>

The first mission of Human Resources is to control, monitor, and
maintain a stable work force. The system applications performed by the
remote sites include:

1. Head counts for government, local and corporate use.

    a. new hires   e. promotion/transfers

    b. terminations   f. EEO-1 reports

    c. work force counts   g. employee listings

    d. management listings

2. Merit planning

    a. budget development   d. merit awards due listing

    b. authorizations   e. plan vs. actual analysis

    c. analysis of increase

3. Worker compensation claim tracking

4. Turnover analysis

5. Seniority listings

6. Education records

7. Performance evaluation

8. Merit vs. performance analysis

9. Benefit enrollment & administration

10. Job posting and bidding

11. Salary administration

12. Job history analysis

Specific Corporate application includes:

1. Comparative analyses by business unit and operating site

    a. benefits   c. compensation

    b. job movement   d. compliance issues

2. Trend analysis for the corporation on issues like heath
care, benefits participation, compensation, and job opportunities.

3. Reports on business units and operating sites

    a. performance issues   d. compliance issues

    b. benefit enrollment   e. insurance premiums/claims

    c. system management   f. policies and practices

In addition, there are forecasts and trend reports to assist with
establishing policies. The concern is for managing the predictable and
preparing for the unknown (like acquisitions). Specific reports include an
organization chart, analyses of pay by various criteria, job movement among
critical jobs, and job experience analysis.

THE IMPLICATIONS AND IMPACT ON HUMAN RESOURCES

Conditions and Trends in the Technology

What the microcomputer wrought for the organization is straightforward. Before 1983 the capital investment to obtain automation in human
resources for this organization was prohibitive. The technology made it
cost effective.

The weekly changes through after-market innovations and manufacturer enhancements suggest that the interim inconveniences of the microcomputer as a DIS are short-lived. The weaknesses are problems in communication which networking and data transfer technologies will solve by early 1986.

They marvel with the facility and ease of the human resource information processing. The total system is managed with the confines of personnel. They save time. Information is more reliable. Reports are more comprehensive and up-to-date. They have time for more productive activity. Yet, the wellspring of technology will bring even greater improvements to system management. The keyboard will give way to the telephone as a data entry device. The voice will solicit information and execute programs. Sophisticated software will reduce the statistical hodgepodge of numbers on green bar paper to elegant color graphics supported with interpretive hard copy reports.

The concept of specific application software anchored to the dedicated computer or computers will give way to office automated systems. Policies, decisions, memoranda, and telephone messages will be transmitted via the same communication linkage now dedicated to transferring employee information.

The amazing dimensions in this picture of the future are that the changes are underway; and that the incremental costs for adopting them are very low.

The implications for this organization's human resources group have been and will be mostly beneficial. The pre-automation environment committed staff to fire-fighting critical events as they occurred. Most reporting was speculative, time-consuming and laborious. The greater the degree of reliability desired, the greater the amount of time consumed and cost incurred. Still, outputs were deficient. They suffered a two to three month information lag. The DIS concept put the responsibility for information gathering and data entry on many H.R. staffers. It facilitated implementation and allowed the human resources management system to evolve without the delay of using a single dedicated microcomputer for data entry. That single convenience shaved six months off the initial installation time table. Today, discrepancies between an employee's record at corporate H.R. and the employee's actual status are related to the policy of weekly updates.

No commercial software product can be expected to do everything. In the case of the package used by the company there are no statistical conventions to use, nor any spreadsheet features beyond simple cross-tabulations. However, one can merge report writer files with such other commercial software. This capability is producing the change to the "conceptual system" orientation.

Networking to permit multiple users at a single site is the most significant next step. The opportunity for each specialist at each site to manage his/her function interactively on the computer will be another improvement in productivity. These people can respond to corporate directives by contributing in-depth analysis from site to site. This will reduce corporate human resource's.'s need to do multiple iterations of a report sorted for the various locations. Again, the technology offers "intelligent workstations" for such networks at much less cost than the standard desk-top computer. Incremental growth of the technology is available for very little money.

These networks are not multi-tasking, but only multi-user. The same files and records can not be shared by the same user at the same time. Both

group processing and the division of the work by personnel function will
eliminate the problems of this limitation.

The Operating Environment

How work gets done changed significantly with automation. The
concerted effort and time commitment to load all employee records with a
three year history proved worthwhile. Within thirty days of implementation
at each site most basic reports were available. By January, 1985, the
concerns over management were reduced to regimenting transaction processing
and data transfer to corporate. Though human resources maintains hard copy
files on employees, the computer is the primary reference source.

Information privacy and security is much better. There is a heightened
sensitivity about information access. The system imposes user restrictions
by menu option. The corporate policy is access on "a need to know" basis.
The division by personnel function services to set the criteria for access.

When the personnel manager discussed key issues with the vice
president, both parties can simultaneously look at reports or records. This
facilitates communications and decision-making. It is not uncommon for the
two parties to write reports while conversing over the telephone. In
several instances this level of communication saved travel expenses for the
organization. It is standard practice to conduct reviews of H.R. issues in
this fashion before meetings and travel are set.

System Management

The personal goal of the H.R. Vice President is to change the function
from staff administration to management support. Ideally, human resources
can perform a decision support role. By identifying costs, predicting
trends, scrutinizing employee and management actions, and analyzing impacts
of changes the department contributes to the bottom line.

A case sample was insurance. The insurer set premium rates based on
prior claims experience and employee/dependent demographics. An analysis of
the present employee population revealed a discrepancy in the insurer's
calculations. The company received a $20,000 refund.

More importantly, the locations are in various states. Some locations
have different benefit and compensation programs, different external
reporting requirements, and different work schedules and holidays. Through
the construction of the DIS and the conformity demanded without sacrificing
the ability of managing the unique circumstances imposed by location.

As the corporate H.R. moves toward the "conceptual system" orientation,
each location takes on more responsibility for the "real system" activity.
The result is more attention on new software to manage the activities, on
improving staff knowledge of the computer and software, and on structuring
system performance objectives. The last point is a methodology designed to
assure the integrity of the system. It employs techniques of basic system
analysis with concepts from performance management. The approach is called
a "performance based H.R. System" (Wilson, 1985). The process breaks the
system into six components: skills, information requirements, policies and
practices, structure, system procedures, and resource management (Wilson,
1985). Human Resources examines each dimension by following a systematic
analysis (Figure 4). The approach reinforces goal development and goal
management.

The vice president expects the impact to be a greater adherence to the
pyramid structure of Figure 2 with clearer definition of staff responsibility
between levels.

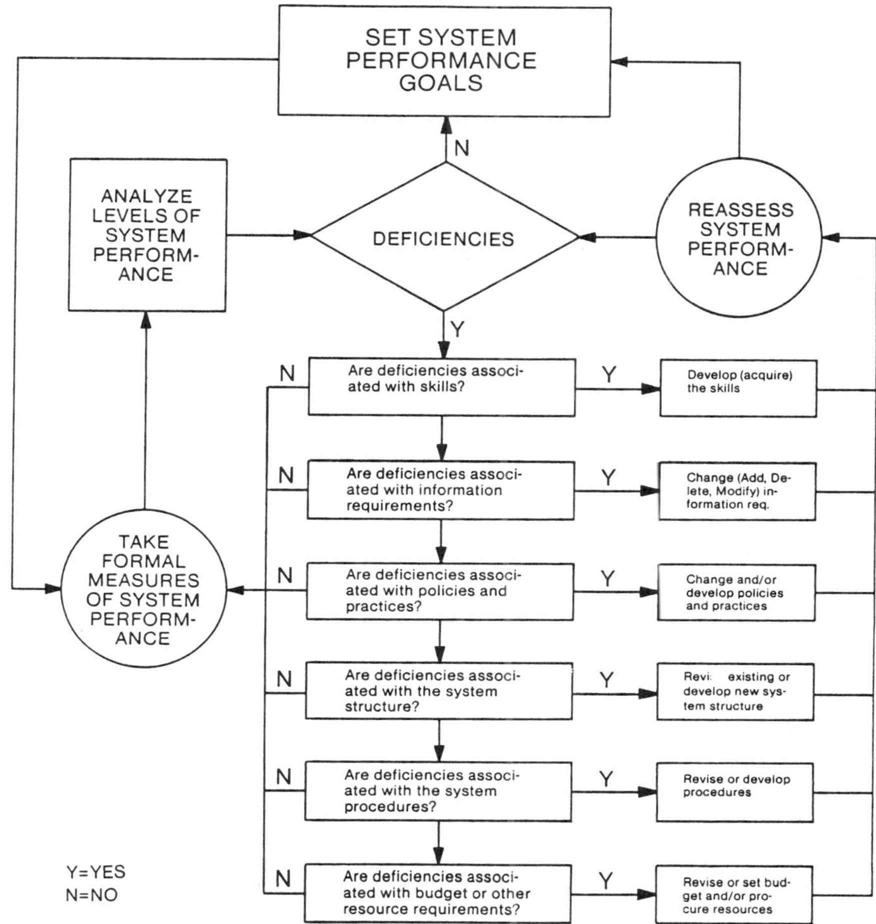

Figure 4: The Performance Based Human Resource System Model

Staff Development

Early in the development of the HRMS in the organization the greatest deficiencies and discrepancies in the implementation and management of the system were among staff who lacked the knowledge and skills.

Experience and structured on-the-job training produced good results. Now, the department anticipates acquiring people with the skills and embarking on a program to further develop proficiencies with the computer and various software. People have a library of topical articles to provide information on human resource system management.

Information Outputs

Consensus reasons for automation invariably include "better and more timely information". At this organization there is certainly a relief and positive endorsement for automation's satisfaction of information output needs. Since the examples are numerous, below are special instances of the

REAL SYSTEM ORIENTATION (RSO)
TIME   TERMINATION ANALYSIS   DATE

Date From: Date To:

Last Name	First Name	Department	Job Title	Emp Status	Termination Reason
Marshall	Nicole	Computer Center	Comp Oper II	Reg FT - N	Job Performance
Smith	Mary	Processing	Clerk Typist	Reg FT - N	Job Performance
Hollis	John	Purchasing	Purch Rep	Reg FT - E	Medical
George	Sherri	Internal Svc	Secretary	Reg FT - N	Other Employment
Williams	Mark	Internal Svc	Admin Asst	Reg FT - E	Other Employment

RSO Report: Listing by termination reason

CONCEPTUAL SYSTEM ORIENTATION (CSO)
TIME   TERMINATION ANALYSIS   DATE

Date From: Date To:

***** TERMINATION REASON ******

Department	EDU	MED	INS	JPR	FAM	QNR	EMP	REL	VOP	TRN	UAS	OTH	TOT
Computer Center	2	1		2	2			2	2			2	12
Processing		1		3	1	4	2	1	1	1	1		15
Purchasing	1				1			2		1			5
Admin Services				4			4						8
Client Services	1		2		1			2				2	8
Data Center	1		1	1		3	3		1				10
									Total Terminations:				58

CSO Report: Department by termination reason, Job title by termination reason, Supervisor by termination reason

Figure 5:   Example 1: Termination Analysis

impact of reports. This is followed with sample reports on successive pages.

Termination Analysis (Example 1) The first design of the report shown in Figure 5, was a general listing of who left the organization in a given period of time. The report was sorted by the reason for termination. It satisfied the "real system" orientation to document the employee terminations.

To provide insight into where and why terminations occurred and to know in what jobs and under whose direction these people worked, the "conceptual system" oriented report, also shown in Figure 5, was developed. By cross-tabulating termination reasons against other criteria new pictures emerged about terminations.

Another enhancement will be a statistical analysis of the information to determine what variables contributed most to which termination reasons. The design for a step-wise regression model is underway. The reports supported changes in hiring practices, the orientation process, and supervision of employees in the areas where the greatest number of terminations occurred.

Budget Status Report (Example 2). The first report, shown in Figure 6, is a listing for the budget planning year of each employee with salary information and proposed changes. The sort is by department. This is an excellent feedback tool which can help in planning. It is again real system oriented.

The next version consolidates the department budgets. It gives the location a different perspective of wage/salary administration; and it gives corporate various views of the issue by location or for the organization. It

REAL SYSTEM ORIENTATION

TIME   **BUDGET STATUS REPORT**   DATE

Plan Year 1985   Department

Last Name / Job Title	First Name	Annual Pay	Budget Amt	%	Actual Amt	%	Variance +1-	New Salary
Norman Personnel Mgr	Mark	30,900	2,130	6.8	2,130	6.8	0	33,030
Mobley Personnel Mgr	Bruce	26,890	1,575	5.8	5,500	20.3	+ 14.5	32,390
Lewis Personnel Spl	Grace	18,600	1,350	7.2	1,800	9.8	+ 2.6	20,400
Total for Dept:		76,390	5,055	6.6	9,430	12.3	+ 5.7	85,820

CONCEPTUAL SYSTEM ORIENTATION

TIME   **BUDGET STATUS REPORT**   DATE

Plan Year 1985

Location: Department	Total Ann. Pay	Budget Amt	%	Actual Amt	%	Variance	New Salary	Avg Inc	Avg Perf Rtg
Computer Center	368,220	19,147	5.20	21,655	5.90	+ 0.7	389,875	1,203	3.5
Processing	621,780	30,467	4.90	26,567	4.30	- 0.6	648,347	857	2.9
Purchasing	210,900	10,545	5.00	12,260	5.80	+ 0.8	223,160	943	3.2
Admin Services	718,400	39,534	5.50	30,658	4.20	- 1.3	749,058	1,460	4.1
Total for Dept:	1,919,300	99,693	5.15	91,140	5.05	- 0.1	2,010,440	1,116	3.4

Figure 6: Example 2: Budget Status Report

adds the average performance rating as an indicator of manager's general performance management actions against compensation management. It provides an indicator of adherence to global salary administration policy. With guidelines on percentage increases given a specific performance rating, a new report will indicate deviations outside the permitted range.

The next generation report will run correlations between pay increases and performance factors. It will indicate standard deviations around the mean salary increase. It will have an option to include other factors like length of service in the organization and department. With these reports human resources and management decided on changes in guidelines governing the process of budgeting labor costs and the authorization and approval process for increases. The more rigid policies saved money, provided more equitable treatment of employees, and gave managers more meaningful controls for administering merit raises.

Wage Schedule Analysis (Example 3). The basic report is a general listing for a pay grade and a job within the grade by name. The objective is to examine dispersion of salaries within the job. This is a real system oriented report.

The new design of the report, shown in Figure 7, carries the analysis to another level by looking at factors on the average for a given job. It removes redundancy and considers other job related information like length of service. Also, all jobs in the same pay grade are examined on the one report with much less paper.

The next level of report analysis will be statistical. The report will generate basic descriptive statistics and run a correlation analysis of pay to job, length of service, and performance.

The reports provide insights into the wage relation to jobs and job

REAL SYSTEM ORIENTATION

REAL SYSTEM ORIENTATION
TIME   **WAGE SCHEDULE ANALYSIS**   **DATE**

Last Name	First Name	Job Title	Annual Pay	Pay Grade	MIN	MID	MAX
Franks	L	Comp Oper	16,380	7	16,380	20,657	24,570
Harris	C	Comp Oper	17,650	7	16,380	20,657	24,570
Morris	R	Comp Oper	21,220	7	16,380	20,657	24,570
Peters	B	Comp Oper	22,580	7	16,380	20,657	24,570
Weber	M	Comp Oper	19,100	7	16,380	20,657	24,570

RSO Report: Listing for Pay Grade for Job title by Name

CONCEPTUAL SYSTEM ORIENTATION
TIME   **WAGE SCHEDULE ANALYSIS**   **DATE**

Pay Grade 7   16,380 - 20,657 - 24,570

Job Title:	Computer Operator	No. of Incumbents = 5	Avg. Sal. = 17,386	
Lowest Salary = 16,380	Highest Salary = 22,580	Avg. Service = 3.7	Avg. Inc. = 1,015	Avg. % = 5.20
Least Service = 0.5	Most Service = 4.2	Group Comp. Ratio = .84		

Job Title:	Processing Assistant II	No. of Incumbents = 7	Avg. Sal. = 20,874	
Lowest Salary = 17,110	Highest Salary = 23,280	Avg. Service = 5.1	Avg. Inc. = 1,235	Avg. % = 5.65
Least Service = 1.2	Most Service = 4.8	Group Comp. Ratio = 1.22		

Figure 7:   Example 3: Wage Schedule Analysis

incumbents. They were helpful during the budgeting process to look at where the organization is relative to pay grades and jobs classified into them.

<u>Job Movement Analysis (Example 4)</u>. To date human resources has only begun exploring the implications of reporting on when and how people move into, through, and out of the organization. There are areas where turnover is a significant factor. The termination analysis report (above) helps through profiling people by reason (age, length of service, education, prior job history, etc.) This helps with the employment selection process. A report, shown in Figure 8, which goes beyond just terminations is the "job movement analysis". The report examines the stock and flow of people in the department for a given period. This is static and non-probabilistic. It is

CONCEPTUAL SYSTEM ORIENTATION
TIME   **JOB MOVEMENT ANALYSIS**   **DATE**

Date From: Date To:

Location:

Department	ST	BV	TI	TO	PR	DE	LA	QT	TE	NH	ET	GL	EV
Computer Center	31	05	01	02					01	06	35	+04	01
Processing	28	01		01							27	-01	02
Authorization	44	06						02	04	12	50	+06	00
Administration	18		02		03			01			16	-02	02
Purchasing	21				02						19	-02	02
Total	142	12	01	03	05			03	05	18	147	+05	07

ST=Starting Total BV=Beginning Vacancies TI=Transfer In TO=Transfer Out PR=Promotion
DE=Demotion LA=Leave of Absence QT=Quit TE=Terminated ET=Ending Total
NH=New Hire GL=Gain Loss EV=Ending Variance

Figure 8:   Example 4: Job Movement Analysis

cross-sectional and, therefore, not dependent on histories, which are
lacking for the two departments on which H.R. focuses. More sophisticated
models are outside the capability of currently available software in the
organization.

These first steps in human resources planning help the organization
decide on resources allocations for employment, training, compensation, and
job changes. It is early to determine the dollar benefits, but expectations
are that they will be significant given the cost of turnovers.

<u>Government Compliance.</u> Not only has the accuracy of reporting increased
EEO-1 reporting and analysis of the Affirmative Action Plan at one location,
but some general system reports on equal pay and worker compensation provide
insights into trouble spots.

The system is a double-edge sword. Without it a discrimination issue
may never be uncovered. With it the organization could be its own worst
witness when such reports become evidence against it.

Human Resource is diligent in its periodic review of sensitive areas.
The preference is to take unilateral and precipitous action to avoid
confrontation. To date the system is very much the ally. It performs the
detective work with minimum intervention and with the greatest objectivity.

There are at least twenty five basic reports and half again that number
customized to address the informational requirements of human resources and
management generally. They cover all the application areas noted above.
This sampling is suggestive of the power and influence the microcomputer
system provides the organization.

GENERAL CONCLUSIONS AND SUMMARY

Conclusions

Some basic observations about the microcomputer HRMS is a distributed
information system environment are:

1. Such a system can be installed and implemented expediently. The
   organizational experience was that each install took about 30 to 45
   days. After that time, reports could be written.

2. The DIS approach permitted data processing controlled by human
   resources in an environment which closely corresponds to the
   decentralized organizational patterns.

3. The system accommodates incremental growth and sustains the total
   system at the corporate office. This provides an economy of scale
   not available with other computer hardware technologies.
   Enhancements or expansion are a function of increased work load per
   site, or organizational expansion (acquisitions, etc.).

4 The system gives the organization a consistently updated data base
   for comprehensive, timely, and accurate reporting.

5. With the software's flexibility operating sites provide the required
   corporate employee information without sacrificing local information
   needs. Each site can add files and fields to its data base and not
   disrupt the operating environment.

6. Human Resources and the organization have a new sensitivity and
responsiveness to easily identifiable or predictable situations or
trends in the work force.

<u>Summary</u>

Since 1969 we have been automating the human resources function. The
popularity of adopting the technology increases by the day. It is not a
panacea to solving the multitude of problems confronting the profession;
but, it is a significant tool to help alleviate many of the administrative
frustrations.

What was an experiment in facilitating information management fifteen
years ago, is now an accepted practice for meeting the challenge of the
risks and costs of decision making in human resources.

The thesis here holds two hypotheses. First, microcomputer technology
adequately suited the particular case's environment. Second, Human
Resources need not leave systems with the technicians. The new products
(hardware and software) and the emergence from computer illiteracy and fear
permit seizing control of the system. Such a move should be done with the
commitment and support of MIS (if available). Such cooperation enhances the
prospect of having good system support and a source for staff education
(Guimaraes, 1984).

The corollary to the first hypothesis is that organizations with very
large populations and a mainframe HRMS will find the microcomputer
advantageous for remote site processing. This means more sophisticated
communications systems and support.

The corollary to the second hypothesis is that choosing to embrace
system management exacts a commitment to skill and knowledge development.
Without it the user will be bound by significant limitations. There will be
limits on exploring the power of the system. There will be limits on the
innovation with information management.

REFERENCES

Claybrook, Bill G., File Management Techniques, (New York, NY: John Wiley &
Sons, Inc., 1983).

Katzan, Harry, Distributed Information Systems, (New York, NY: Petrocelli
Books, Inc., 1979).

Katzan, Harry, Management Support Systems, (New York, NY: Van Nostrand
Reinhold Company, Inc., 1984).

Killian, Ray A., **Managing Human Resources, An ROI Approach**, (New York, NY:
AMACOM, 1976).

Guimaraes, Tor, "The Benefits and Problems of User Computing", Journal of
Information Systems Management, Vol. 1, No. 4 (Fall, 1984), pp. 3-9.

Mazursky, Allan F., "Acquiring and Using Microcomputers", Journal of
Information Systems Management, Vol. 1, No. 1 (Winter, 1984), pp. 47-57.

Moody, H. Gerald, "How to Select the Right Small Computer," Journal of
Information Systems Management, Vol. 1, No. 3 (Summer, 1984), pp. 20-26.

Moss, Clifton, L., "The Information System Plan and the Data Base Plan", Journal of Information Systems Management, Vol. 1, No. 3 (Summer, 1984), pp. 20-26.

Walker, Alfred J., HRIS Development - A Project Team Guide to Building an Effective Personnel Information System, (New York, NY: Van Nostrand Reinhold Company, Inc., 1982).

Wilson, Richard L., "Life After Implementation: Managing the H.R. System", Personnel Journal, (December, 1985).

ABOUT THE EDITOR AND CONTRIBUTORS

RICHARD J. NIEHAUS is Assistant for Human Resources Analysis in the Total
Force Information Resource and Systems Management Division, Office of the
Chief of Naval Operations. He received his B.S.(Physics) from the University
of Santa Clara, M.S.(Industrial Administration) from Carnegie-Mellon University, and D.B.A. from George Washington University. He has organized many
meetings and sessions at national and international conferences on human
resource and manpower planning issues including being Co-Director of two NATO
Conferences in Stresa, Italy and Garmish-Partinkirchen, West Germany respectively. He is author of Computer-Assisted Human Resource Planning and coauthor (with A. Charnes and W.W. Cooper of Studies in Manpower Planning as well
as being author or coauthor of over 60 technical papers. He has been editor
or co-editor of four other volumes. In 1975, he was awarded the NATO Systems
Science Prize for publications on the theory, modeling, data collection, and
management of large-scale manpower and personnel planning systems.

DONALD M. ATWATER, PH.D. is President of DMA Inc. with particular
specialization in mathematical economics as applied to organizational labor
market and regional analysis issues.

EDWARD S. BRES III is a Supervisory Operations Research Analyst as Head,
Civilian Systems Branch, Decision Support Systems Division, U.S. Naval
Military Personnel Command.

RANAE F. BRODERICK, PH.D. is an Assistant Professor of Human Resource
Management/Industrial Relations at the Graduate School of Management,
University of California at Los Angeles.

ROBERT A. BOLDA, PH.D. is Director, Personnel Research, General Motors
Corporation.

DANIEL N. BULLA is Manager of Organizational & Personnel Development at
Houston Lighting and Power Company.

L. S. CECIL is a Management Analyst at the U.S. Navy Office of Civilian
Personnel Management.

BALA CHAKRAVARTHY, PH.D. at the time of this symposium was an Associate
Professor of Management at the Wharton School of the University of
Pennsylvania. He is currently an Associate Professor at the School of
Management, University of Minnesota.

LEE DYER, PH.D. is a Professor of Human Resource Management at the New York
State School of Industrial and Labor Relations, Cornell University.

KAREN N. GAERTNER, PH.D. is an Assistant Professor in the School of Business
Administration at Georgetown University.

WALTER H. GRIGGS, PH.D. is Vice President of Human Resources for Technicare Corporation.

MICHAEL D. HAWKINS, PH.D. is a Lecturer in the Department of Management Science, School of Business Administration, University of Washington and President of Personnel Technology, Inc. which provides consulting assistance in the area of human resource forecasting and modeling.

TERRANCE J. HENSHAW is a Management Systems Analyst in the Human Resource Planning, Systems and Record Department, Lockheed Missiles and Space Company.

IRA T. KAY, PH.D. at the time of this symposium was a Vice President with the Hay Group. Inc. He is currently the Senior Vice President, Director of Compensation at Shearson Lehman Brothers Inc.

LARRY W. LACY, PH.D. is a Senior Labor Economist in the Office of the Assistant Secretary of Defense for Force Management and Personnel.

MARTIN LESHNER, PH.D. is a Vice President with AMEV Holdings, Inc.

VICTOR MACTAGGART is Manager of the Projects Unit in the Human Resource Planning Division in the Canadian Public Service Commission.

SUSAN L. MANRING, PH.D. is President of Griggs-Manring & Associates, Inc. which provides consulting assistance in the areas of the behavioral sciences and human resource planning.

ANTHONY M. PAGANGO, PH.D. is an Associate Professor of Management at the University of Illinois at Chicago.

JAMES D. PORTWOOD, PH.D. is an Associate Professor of Industrial Relations and Organizational Behavior at Temple University.

KARL F. PRICE, PH.D. is a Principal in Philadelphia Consulting Office of Towers, Perrin, Forester, and Crosby

MICHAEL O. QUIGLEY, PH.D. is a Supervisor in the Human Resource Planning Systems and Record Department, Lockheed Missiles and Space Company.

ELISSA ROSASCO is a Senior Personnel Management Analyst in the U.S. Navy Office of Civilian Personnel Management.

PETER M. SCOTT is President of Scott Consulting Group which specializes in general management, manufacturing and human resource management areas.

RICHARD A. SHAFER is National Director of Human Resources, Touche Ross & Co.

FRANCIS J. SHARKEY is Director, Civilian Personnel Programs at the U.S. Naval Sea Systems Command.

JO ANN VERDIN, PH.D. is an Assistant Professor of Management at the University of Illinois at Chicago.

CHARLES L. WEBER is an Operations Research Analyst in the Civilian Systems Branch, Decision Support Systems Division, U.S. Naval Military Personnel Command.

RICHARD L. WILSON is a consultant with Human Resource Systems which specializes in human resource information systems.

INDEX